SECOND EDITION

PROGRAMMING IN PASCAL

▲▼ ADDISON-WESLEY PUBLISHING COMPANY
READING, MASSACHUSETTS / MENLO PARK, CALIFORNIA
LONDON / AMSTERDAM / DON MILLS, ONTARIO / SYDNEY

SECOND EDITION

PROGRAMMING IN PASCAL

PETER GROGONO
CONCORDIA UNIVERSITY

**This book is in the Addison-Wesley Series
in Computer Science**
Consulting Editor: Michael A. Harrison

Sponsoring Editor: James T. DeWolf
Production Manager: Martha K. Morong
Production Editor: William J. Yskamp
Text and Cover Designer: Melinda Grosser
Cover and Chapter-Opening Computer Graphics:
    Melvin L. Prueitt, Los Alamos
    National Laboratory
Art Coordinator: Susanah H. Michener
Manufacturing Supervisor: Hugh J. Crawford

Library of Congress Cataloging in Publication Data

Grogono, Peter.
    Programming in Pascal.

    Includes index.
    1. PASCAL (Computer program language) I. Title.
QA76.73.P2G76   1983   001.64'24   83-8728
ISBN 0-201-12070-4

ABCDEFGHIJ-HA-89876543

PREFACE

In 1976, when I wrote the first draft of this book, Pascal was well known within the academic community but had not achieved the status of a major programming language. The *Pascal User Manual and Report,* by Jensen and Wirth, was the only book available to those who wanted to learn Pascal, and it was a difficult book for the uninitiated. In writing *Programming in Pascal,* my objective was to provide an easier approach to Pascal, moving at a gentler pace than the *User Manual* but nevertheless covering the entire language.

Since 1976, interest in Pascal has increased considerably. Pascal is now taught at most universities, often as a first language. The movement of a generation of students versed in Pascal into the workplace has brought about widespread industrial acceptance of the language and its derivatives. Many books now use Pascal notation in their discussions of problem solving, algorithm design, verification, and other aspects of computer science.

The second edition of this book, like the first, is primarily a language manual for Pascal. It describes the features of the language in a systematic way and presents examples of complete Pascal programs. Top-down development techniques are used in the example programs but are not the central theme of the book. Because programming is a multi-faceted craft, more skills are needed than can be described in a single book. *Problem Solving and Computer Programming* by Sharon H. Nelson and myself (Addison-Wesley, 1982) complements this book by providing background in techniques of problem solving and program development. This background is particularly necessary for those coming to Pascal, or any programming language, without previous knowledge of programming or mathematics.

If you are familiar with the first or revised editions of this book, you will find that I have not altered the basic organization. The changes in this edition are intended to improve the clarity of the text and to fill in details where previous editions required leaps of intuition. I have rewritten the sections in which major programs are discussed to clarify the steps in program development.

Chapters 1 and 10 of this book are devoted to a discussion of the general principles of computer programming. Chapter 10 is naturally more advanced than Chapter 1, but it need not be left until last. Most of it can be understood without an advanced knowledge of Pascal, and it may be studied concurrently with the rest of the book. Chapters 2, 5, 6, 7, and 8 are about the data types of Pascal. Chapters 3 and 4 deal with Pascal statements. This treatment, while systematic, omits some of the more esoteric features of the language. These are tidied up in Chapter 9. If you already know a programming language, you will find that the early chap-

ters are easy reading. Because elementary concepts are defined more precisely in Pascal than in most other languages, you should not omit these chapters altogether.

There are five important supplementary sections at the end of the book. "Remarks, Resources, and References" outlines the history of Pascal and lists the important books and articles that have been written about it. This section also refers to articles about topics related to Pascal. It concludes with a bibliography of Pascal material from 1971 to 1982.

Appendix A, which summarizes the vocabulary of Pascal, and Appendix B, which contains a complete set of syntax diagrams, are for convenient reference. Although there is a Pascal Standard, it is still difficult to write Pascal programs that execute correctly on different systems. Appendix C, which is new to this edition, discusses implementation and portability issues. Finally, Appendix D describes programming conventions that will help you to make your programs readable and easily understood by yourself and others.

Although the programs in this book are for the most part short and simple, they are not just fragments but complete, working programs. You can achieve a superficial understanding of these programs by reading them, but in order to understand them properly, you should attempt to improve them. There are many exercises in the book that indicate ways in which the given examples can be enhanced, and you will learn Pascal rapidly and painlessly by doing these exercises. Most of the other exercises require you to write original programs. The programs specified are not trivial and may require a fair amount of work. It is more instructive to spend a month writing a single, correct program of reasonable size than it is to spend the same time writing half a dozen programs that are unrealistically small or that do not work properly. It is also instructive to learn to program as a member of a team rather than as an individual. Some of the exercises in Chapters 6, 7, 8, and 10 are large enough to warrant solution by a team.

The British Standards Institute (BSI) and the International Standards Organization (ISO) have adopted a Standard for Pascal. It is probable that the American National Standards Institute will adopt a substantially similar standard. I use the term "Standard" in this book to denote the BSI Standard. I have tried to ensure that the language described in this book conforms to this Standard. I have also indicated areas in which many compilers do not conform to the Standard.

ACKNOWLEDGMENTS

I have received much help and encouragement while preparing the various editions of this book. Henry Ledgard and Derek Oppen reviewed the first edition, published in 1978. The Revised Edition of 1980 incorporated suggestions from Barry Cornelius, John McKay, Andy Mickel, David Presberg, David K. Probst, and Samuel E. Rhoads. Many people contributed to the present edition. In particular, I am grateful to Bill Atwood, André Cusson, Paul Eggert, Jiang Kuonan, J. Finley Meehan, Mark Rain, and Eric Regener, and to Sandra Miot who undertook the task of putting the text of the revised edition into machine-readable form.

Appendix B contains a complete set of syntax diagrams for Pascal. The text contains numerous simplified versions of these diagrams. The diagrams are adapted from machine-drawn diagrams prepared by F.E.J. Kruseman Aretz. I am very grateful to Dr. Kruseman Aretz and Philips Research Laboratories, Eindhoven, for permission to use these diagrams.

Finally, Sharon H. Nelson carefully reviewed and revised each of the many drafts of the text.

Montreal   **P. G.**
January 1984

CONTENTS

1

PROGRAMMING CONCEPTS

1.1   PROGRAMS

A *program* is a sequence of instructions. A recipe, a musical score, and a knitting pattern are all programs. Programs in this sense existed long before computers were invented. Before we look more closely at computer programs, we will define some general terms and consider some of the properties that systems of programming have in common.

A program requires an *author* to write it and a *processor* to carry out the instructions. Carrying out the instructions is called *executing,* or *running,* the program, and a running program is called a *process.* A musical score is a set of instructions for performing a piece of music, and the performer is the processor. Executing a recipe is called cooking, and the cook is the processor. All programs share some common features.

- Instructions are executed *sequentially*. Unless explicitly told otherwise, you start at the first instruction and execute each instruction in turn until you have finished. This general pattern may be broken in certain well-defined ways, as, for example, when a musical score indicates that a passage is to be repeated.
- The process has an *effect*. This effect may be a meal or sounds of music. If the program is a computer program, the effect is often in the form of output consisting of printed or displayed symbols.
- The program operates on certain objects. The instruction "grate the nutmeg" assumes that you have some nutmeg to grate. The objects on which a computer operates are called *data*.
- Sometimes the instructions are preceded by a *declaration* of the objects on which they operate. This is true of recipes, which are usually preceded by a list of the necessary ingredients. In many programming languages, the programmer must declare the attributes of the data before writing the instructions to be performed on the data.
- Sometimes the instructions require that a *decision* be made by the processor. "If you are using fresh tomatoes, skin them and add before the onions, but if you are using canned tomatoes, add them last." In this case, the author of the instructions did not know what the processor would do in a particular instance but established a criterion on the basis of which the processor could make a decision.
- It may be necessary to execute an instruction or a group of instructions more than once. This occurs frequently in knitting and crocheting which are inherently repetitive processes. Whenever an instruction is to be repeated, the number of repetitions must be specified. This can be done either directly, by giving the number of repetitions required ("knit ten rows"), or by establishing a criterion which depends on the state of the process ("knit until the end of the row"). Both forms of repetition occur frequently in computer programs. Since modern computers can execute more than a million instructions in a second, a program without repetition would not run for more than a fraction of a second.
- The program itself is a static entity but the process of carrying out the instructions is dynamic. We do not mistake a cook for a recipe or a pianist for a score, and it is equally important that we do not confuse a processor with a program.

These characteristics are shared by all programs, including those written for a computer. We see that a program is essentially a means by which the author of the program communicates with the processor. Communication requires a language, and although natural languages such as English are often used for informal instruction, most programming tasks require a special language. Even recipes use a specialized dialect of natural language, and musicians, choreographers, and knitters have devised entirely original languages in which to communicate their instructions.

1.2 STRUCTURE

The earliest computer programs were no more than lists of the primitive instructions that the computer could execute directly. As time went by, more complicated programs were written and these lists became unmanageable. The reason was that they lacked structure. To a machine, the execution of a list containing a few thousand instructions presents no problems; the machine mechanically performs each instruction without regard to its meaning or consequence. But to the programmer, who is concerned with the meaning of the program, the problem of understanding a list of thousands of undifferentiated instructions becomes insurmountable. The history of programming languages is to a large extent an account of how structure has been added to these primitive lists of instructions.

Structure appeared first in the evaluation of expressions. Suppose that we have to write a computer program to calculate the value of *area*, where

$$area = 3.1415926535 \times 5^2.$$

In the early days, the programmer would write a sequence of instructions something like this

```
enter 3.1415926535
multiply by 5
multiply by 5
store area
```

The programmer would have to be careful to interpret the expression correctly. For example, the expression

$$2 \times 3 + 4$$

corresponds to the program

```
enter 2
multiply by 3
add 4
```

but the expression

$$2 \times (3 + 4)$$

corresponds to the program

```
enter 3
add 4
multiply by 2
```

Programmers realized that the translation from the symbolic expression to a list of machine instructions was a mechanical operation that could be carried out by a machine and, moreover, that the computer was a suitable machine for doing it. Thereafter, programmers wrote expressions in conventional algebraic form.

The next thing that needed structuring was data. The computer has a memory of several thousand *words*. A word may contain a number, a group of characters, or an instruction. The programmer might decide to put a set of one hundred batting averages in words 300 to 399 of the memory and subsequently forget this decision and put something else there. With a language that permits data structuring, we write

$$averages : \textbf{array} \; [1..100] \; \textbf{of} \; integer;$$

and know that this will reserve an area of the memory which will not be used for anything else.

With the problem of structuring data at least partially solved, attention returned to improving the structure of the instructions themselves. It turns out that all computer programs can be expressed in terms of four basic structures.

- the *sequence*
- the *decision*
- the *repetitive structure* or *loop*
- the *procedure*

A *sequence* is a group of instructions executed one after the other. A *decision* is a structure that enables the action of the program to be influenced by the data. Many languages introduce the decision structure with the word "if," and in them we write instructions such as

```
if x ⩾ 0
   then y := x
   else y := −x
```

The *loop* structure is used to execute an instruction or a sequence of instructions several times. Although the instructions are the same each time the loop is executed, the data on which they operate are not. For example, the effect of repeating the instruction

```
add 1 to x
```

one hundred times is to add 100 to x. We must be careful to specify how many times the instructions in the loop are to be executed. If we suppose that initially $x = 0$ and $y \geqslant 0$, then the program

```
repeat
   add 1 to x
until x² > y
```

will give to x the value of the smallest integer whose square exceeds y. This program is safe because we can guarantee that such a value will always be found. The program

```
repeat
   add 1 to x
until x² = y
```

is not safe. If, for instance, $y = 5$, the condition $x^2 = y$ will never be true. In this case, theoretically the program would be stuck in the loop forever. On an actual computer the program would run until x was so large that x^2 could not be represented, and then the program would stop.

The *procedure* enables us to replace a group of instructions with a name that denotes the group. Cookbooks frequently employ procedures. For example, a cookbook might provide a procedure for making cream sauce and then refer to that procedure by name rather than by restating all the details when a recipe called for a sauce of that type. Procedures enable us to give programs a modular structure that makes them easier to write and shorter than they would otherwise be. More importantly, a modular structure enables us to identify the main aspects of a task and to focus on them rather than on the details. Thus the procedure is a mechanism for abstraction. Abstraction is our most powerful tool for managing complexity.

Pascal enables us to use these mechanisms to structure programs. They are incorporated in a simple and elegant fashion that makes Pascal a powerful language that is nonetheless easy to learn and use.

1.3 AN INFORMAL INTRODUCTION TO PASCAL

In this section, we study some very simple Pascal programs in order to see how the structures described in the preceding section are realized in an actual programming language. The three programs in this section are complete, working programs that may be run on a computer. Here is the first.

```
program squarerootofttwo (output);
   begin
     write (sqrt (2))
   end.
```

If this program is executed by a computer, it prints

        1.41421356

which is approximately the value of the square root of 2. The third line,

        write (sqrt (2))

is the heart of Program *squarerootoftwo*. *Write* is a procedure whose effect is to print the value of *sqrt* (2), which is its *argument*. *Sqrt* is one of a number of standard functions of Pascal. The value of *sqrt* (s) is $\sqrt{2}$ within the limits of precision of the computer.

The first line of the program contains the word **program.** This is the first word of all Pascal programs. It is followed by *squarerootoftwo,* which is the *name* of the program. The name of the program is chosen by the programmer and should reflect the function of the program. After the name, we define the relationship between the program and its environment. The word *output* is an indication that the program is going to generate some results. The environment of a program running in a modern computer is usually the *operating system.* The function of the operating system in this instance is to accept the results generated by the program and to transmit them to a printer or a terminal. Finally, note the words **begin** and **end.** As you might expect, these signify the start and finish of the program.

Program *squarerootoftwo* is not very useful. We could have looked up the value of $\sqrt{2}$ in a book if we had really wanted to know it. The following program is an improved version of Program *squarerootoftwo.*

```
program squareroot (input, output);
  var
    x : real;
  begin
    read (x);
    write (sqrt (x))
  end.
```

This program illustrates *sequential structure.* There are two instructions, *read* (x) and *write* (sqrt (x)). These instructions will be executed one after the other in the order in which we have written them. The words **begin** and **end** act as brackets around an instruction sequence. This program contains only one such sequence and hence only one **begin–end** pair. More complicated programs contain many instruction sequences, each bracketed by **begin** and **end.**

Program *squareroot* accepts data from its environment. The first line contains the word *input,* indicating that the program will request data. The procedure *read* actually does the requesting. The effect of the *read* instruction is to obtain a value from the input medium and to give this value to *x*. The nature of the input medium is unknown to the program. We may assume that the value was punched on a card or typed on the keyboard of a terminal.

Program *squareroot* contains a *declaration*:

```
var
  x : real;
```

This declaration introduces a *variable, x,* and attributes the type *real* to it. The type of a variable determines the set of values the variable can assume and the set of operations that can be applied to it. The values of *real* variables are real numbers. The operations we can apply to *real* variables are the conventional operations of arithmetic: addition, subtraction, multiplication, square root, and so on.

Program *squareroot* is still a very poor example of a computer program. *Sqrt* (*x*) will fail if *x* is negative, but there is no way of preventing the user from entering a negative number. Moreover, having calculated one square root, the program stops and has to be restarted before it will calculate another. These defects are remedied in Program *squareroots*.

```
program squareroots (input, output);
  var
    x : real;
  begin
    repeat
      read (x);
      if x ≥ 0
        then write (sqrt (x))
        else write (x,' does not have a real square root.')
    until x = 0
  end.
```

This program incorporates *decision* and *repetition* structures. Having read a value for *x*, the processor has to choose between two courses of action. If the value of *x* is non-negative, the value of $\sqrt{x}$ is printed. If we give it a negative number, such as −3, the program responds

```
−3 does not have a real square root.
```

The **repeat** statement and its matching **until** ensure that the program will continue to run until it has read a zero.

In this program, although the processor executes instructions sequentially, the order in which they are executed is no longer the same as the order in which they are written. After writing a square root, the processor tests the value of *x*. If *x* is nonzero, the processor executes the instruction *read* again. The process terminates only when the expression

$$x = 0$$

is found to be true.

We must distinguish between the static program and the dynamic process of executing the program. When we speak informally, we often blur the distinction by saying "the program does so and so." Remember that this is an abbreviation for "the processor, while executing the program, does so and so." A program is a text; a processor is a machine that executes the instructions contained in the text.

Program *squareroots* is a sound program although it has a rather limited range of usefulness. Its condition for termination, a number with a value of zero, is not very satisfactory. We will encounter more elegant ways of terminating programs later in this book.

1.4   COMPILATION AND EXECUTION

As programming languages became more highly structured, computer programs became more amenable to human composition and analysis. At the same time, the task of translating the programs into the simple instructions executed by the computer became harder. This problem is solved by a program whose function is to translate programs from the programming language into machine instructions. This program is called a *compiler* for the language. The program used to translate Pascal programs into machine instructions is called the *Pascal compiler.*

If we always write correct programs and have access to a good compiler, we can think of the compiler and the computer as a single machine capable of executing programs directly. For practical purposes, we can ignore the translation process altogether. The combination of a compiler and a computer is sometimes called a *virtual machine.* We can think of the combination of a Pascal compiler and a suitable computer as a *Pascal machine.*

Figure 1.1 shows the Pascal machine. In this and subsequent diagrams, circles represent static entities, such as program texts, and rectangles represent processors. The lines represent the flow of data to or from a process, the direction being indicated by an arrowhead. Figure 1.1 shows that the Pascal

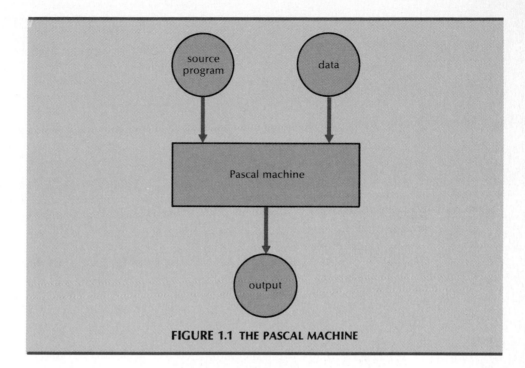

FIGURE 1.1 THE PASCAL MACHINE

machine requires a *source program*, by which is meant any Pascal program, and some *input data*. When the Pascal machine runs, it produces *output data*. Suppose that the source program is Program *squareroots* and the input data is

            2
            3
            4
            0

When we start the Pascal machine, it will run for a little while and then send the results

            1.41421356
            1.73205088
            2.00000000
            0

to the output file.

    As we have seen, the virtual machine consists of a computer and a compiler. These are shown in Fig. 1.2. The processor is now the computer itself and

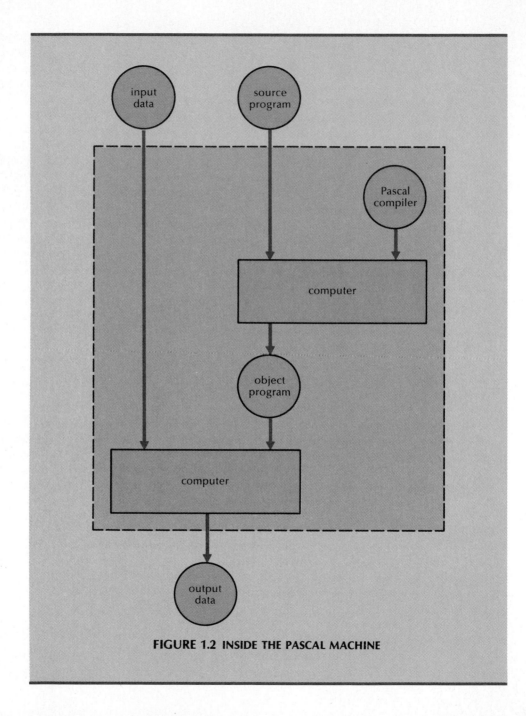

FIGURE 1.2 INSIDE THE PASCAL MACHINE

it is used twice. In the first instance, the program is the Pascal compiler and the input data is the source program. The result is the translation of our source program into machine instructions. These machine instructions constitute the *object program*. The computer is then used again, with the object program as its program and our data as input data. The result is our desired output data.

We would not need to be aware of the internal structure of the Pascal machine were it not for the possibility of errors. There are three important kinds of programming error.

- A *compile-time error* is detected during translation. If, for example, we write **begin** but omit the corresponding **end**, the compiler will detect and report the error.
- A *run-time error* is detected during execution of the object program. If we present Program *squareroot* with an input file containing − 1, the program will fail because *sqrt* does not accept a negative argument.
- There are errors which are not detected by the computer during compilation or execution. If we write

$$sqr\ (x)$$

instead of

$$sqrt\ (x)$$

in Program *squareroots*, the program will run successfully but it will print values of x^2 rather than $\sqrt{x}$.

Figure 1.3 shows the Pascal machine with error detection incorporated. We now obtain three different kinds of output. Errors detected during compilation appear first. If compile-time errors occur, we will obtain diagnostic output and the execution of the object program will be inhibited. If the program compiles successfully, it may fail during execution, and we will get a different kind of diagnostic output. If the program compiles successfully and runs successfully, we will get the output we expect unless the program contains errors of the third kind.

Errors are not necessarily confined to the program; they can also occur in the data. If you were using Program *squareroots* to calculate $\sqrt{5}$ and you inadvertently typed 6, you would get the wrong answer. This is an instance of an *input data error*, and there is no way the Pascal machine can detect an error of this kind.

The designer of a programming language can choose, to a certain extent, whether errors will be detected at compile-time or at run-time. As the amount of redundancy in the language increases, so does the probability of being able to discover an error simply by examining the program text. The philosophy

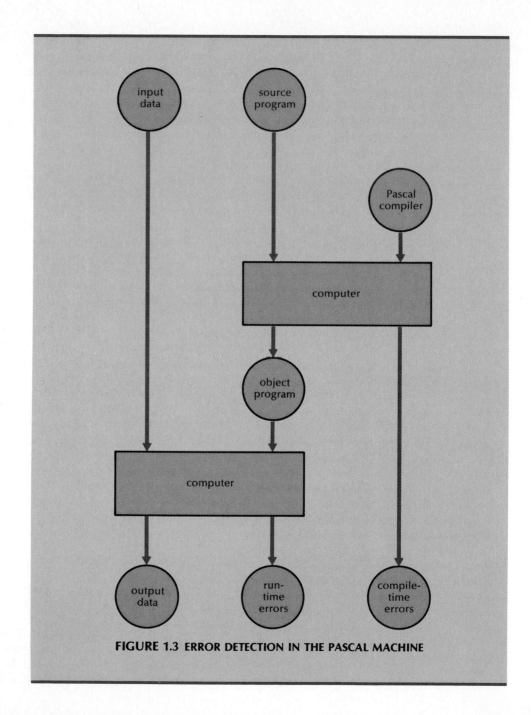

FIGURE 1.3 ERROR DETECTION IN THE PASCAL MACHINE

adopted in Pascal is that as many errors as possible should be recognized at compile-time. Consequently there is a fair amount of redundancy in Pascal. This helps to make Pascal an easier programming language to learn and use than many others.

The compiler can also help us by incorporating *run-time checks* into the compiled program. When you write

```
write (sqrt (x))
```

the effect of the instructions actually generated by the compiler will be

```
if x ⩾ 0
  then write (sqrt (x))
  else halt
```

in which *halt* is a procedure that terminates the program with an appropriate error message. Note that the run-time checks incorporated by the compiler in no way prevent us from including our own checking, as we did in Program *square-roots*.

All this checking inevitably slows down the execution of both the compiler and the running program. In the majority of cases, however, computer time is saved because we arrive at correct programs more rapidly when we are provided with good error diagnostics.

In this book, when we say "this statement is illegal" or "this statement will not be accepted," we mean that the statement will produce an error during compilation. When we say "this will cause a run-time error," we mean that the statement is acceptable to the compiler but that it will not execute correctly.

1.5 REPRESENTATION

To the compiler, a program is merely a string of symbols. The compiler would accept Program *squareroots* if it was written in this form.

```
PROGRAM SQUAREROOTS (INPUT,OUTPUT); VAR X :
REAL; BEGIN REPEAT READ (X); IF X ⩾ 0 THEN
WRITE (SQRT (X)) ELSE WRITE (X,' has no real square root.')
UNTIL X = 0 END.
```

It is for the benefit of human readers that we use a more spacious layout. The layout of a program text should match the structure of the program. A Pascal program is structured in *levels,* and the level of a statement is indicated by how much the statement is indented from the left margin. Program *squareroots* has four levels. The outermost level is defined by **begin** and **end** and the next level by **repeat** and **until.** The **if** statement has two levels, with the **then** and **else** clauses at the inner level. This arrangement allows us to see at a glance which statements are to be repeated. It is much harder to tell which statements are to be repeated in the example above.

There is another way in which we can make programs more readable. Pascal programs use two kinds of words: *reserved words*, such as **begin, end, repeat,** and **until,** have a fixed meaning; *identifiers*, such as *x, real, write*, and *sqrt*, have a meaning that may be redefined. In this book, the reserved words of Pascal programs are written in **lowercase boldface type** and the identifiers are printed in *uppercase* or *lowercase italics*. This, and the use of uppercase and lowercase letters, is only a convention. Most compilers ignore such typographical distinctions.

1.6 APPLICATIONS: SOME SIMPLE PASCAL PROGRAMS

We conclude this chapter with five simple Pascal programs. These programs illustrate some of the concepts introduced in this chapter, including declarations, decisions, sequences, and loops. At this point, you may not understand these programs completely. This brief introduction should enable you to read the programs, and when you have read Chapters 2 and 3 you should be able to understand these programs and write similar programs yourself.

Each program is followed by a typical example of the input data that it would accept and the results it would print when given that data. The results shown here are not always exactly in the form in which the programs would print them. The niceties of presenting results are discussed in Chapter 2.

The first program, *powertable*, prints a table of powers of integers. The line beginning **for** introduces a loop which is executed once for each integral value of *base* from 1 to *tablesize*. The effect of the *assignment operator* ":= " is to calculate the value of the expression on its right and assign this value to the variable whose name is on its left. After executing

$$square := sqr\ (base)$$

we have

$$square = base^2$$

The table gives values of *base*, $base^2$, $base^3$, $base^4$, $1/base$, $1/base^2$, $1/base^3$, and $1/base^4$. Words and messages contained in braces { . . . } are *comments* for the benefit of the human reader; they are ignored altogether by the compiler. The procedure *writeln* is similar to *write*, but after printing the values of its parameters, it starts a new line. The operator "*" is the multiplication operator; most computers do not possess the conventional character "×". Implicit multiplication, as when *ab* is used to represent $a \times b$, is not allowed in most programming languages.

```
{ Print a table of squares, cubes, and fourth powers
  of integers. }
program powertable (input, output);
  var
    tablesize, base, square, cube, quad : integer;
  begin
    read (tablesize);
    for base := 1 to tablesize do
      begin
        square := sqr (base);
        cube := base * square;
        quad := sqr (square);
        writeln (base, square, cube, quad,
                 1/base, 1/square, 1/cube, 1/quad)
      end { for }
  end. { powertable }
```

INPUT				OUTPUT			
5	1	1	1	1	1.000000	1.000000	1.000000	1.000000
	2	4	8	16	0.500000	0.250000	0.125000	0.062500
	3	9	27	81	0.333333	0.111111	0.037037	0.012345
	4	16	64	256	0.250000	0.062500	0.015625	0.003906
	5	25	125	625	0.200000	0.040000	0.008000	0.001600

Program *divisors* reads numbers and calculates their divisors. It terminates when it has read zero or a negative number. The value of

   number **mod** *divisor*

is the remainder when *number* is divided by *divisor*. The value of *divisor* is printed whenever the remainder is zero, and the program prints all the divisors of *number*, not just the prime divisors.

```
{ Read a number and print its divisors including itself but not 1. }
program divisors (input, output);
  var
    number, divisor : integer;
  begin
    repeat
      read (number);
      if number > 0
        then
          begin
            writeln ('The divisors of ', number, ' are :');
            for divisor := 2 to number do
              if number mod divisor = 0
                then writeln (divisor)
          end { then }
    until number ≤ 0
  end. { divisors }
```

INPUT	OUTPUT
20 17 0	The divisors of 20 are:
	2
	4
	5
	10
	20
	The divisors of 17 are:
	17

Program *minimax* reads a string of numbers, counts them, and records the smallest and largest values. *Maxint* is a standard constant denoting the largest integer value that the computer can store. The variable *reading* can have only two values: *true* or *false*. The statements between **begin** and **end** following **while** are executed repetitively as long as *reading* is *true*.

```
{ Read a list of numbers and print the
  largest and smallest values in the list. }
program minimax (input, output);
  var
    reading : boolean;
    number, minimum, maximum, count : integer;
```

```
begin
  reading := true;
  minimum := maxint;
  maximum := - maxint;
  count := 0;
  while reading do
    begin
      read (number);
      if number = 0
        then reading := false
        else
          begin
            count := count + 1;
            if number < minimum
              then minimum := number;
            if number > maximum
              then maximum := number
          end { else }
    end; { while }
  writeln (count, ' numbers read');
  writeln ('The smallest was ', minimum);
  writeln ('The largest was ', maximum)
end. { minimax }
```

INPUT	OUTPUT
-6 3 -15 27 -2 64 1 0	7 numbers read The smallest was -15 The largest was 64

The following two programs, Program *doublechars* and Program *count-chars,* both use variables of type *char.* Values of *char* variables are characters. Both programs read from a file of characters. The function *eof* may return either of the values *true* or *false;* it will return *false* until the end of the input file, at which point it will return *true.* Both programs read from the beginning of the input file and use *eof* to determine when they have reached the end of it. Program *doublechars* detects and reports repeated characters, such as "ee" in "week." Program *countchars* counts each character, blank, comma, and period in the input file. A line-break appears to a Pascal program as a blank, and therefore the number of blanks reported by countchars is 8 rather than 6.

```
{ This program finds and prints the "double characters"
  (e.g., "oo", "ee") in a file. }
program doublechars (input, output);
  const
    blank = ' ';
  var
    oldchar, newchar : char;
  begin
    oldchar := blank;
    while not eof do
      begin
        read (newchar);
        if (newchar ≠ blank) and (oldchar = newchar)
          then writeln (oldchar, newchar);
        oldchar := newchar
      end { while }
  end. { doublechars }
```

INPUT	OUTPUT
Baa, baa, black sheep,	aa
Have you any wool?	aa
	ee
	oo

```
{ This program counts the characters in a text file. }
program countchars (input, output);
  const
    blank = ' ';
    comma = ',';
    period = '.';
  var
    charcount, blankcount, commacount, periodcount : integer;
    character : char;
  begin
    charcount := 0;
    blankcount := 0;
    commacount := 0;
    periodcount := 0;
    while not eof do
```

```
begin
   read (character);
   charcount := charcount + 1;
   if character = blank
      then blankcount := blankcount + 1
   else if character = comma
      then commacount := commacount + 1
   else if character = period
      then periodcount := periodcount + 1
   end; { while }
 writeln (charcount, ' characters');
 writeln (blankcount, ' blanks');
 writeln (commacount, ' commas');
 writeln (periodcount, ' periods')
end. { countchars }
```

INPUT	OUTPUT
Baa, baa, black sheep,	42 characters
Have you any wool?	8 blanks
	3 commas
	0 periods

2

DATA, EXPRESSIONS, AND ASSIGNMENTS

This chapter contains a full discussion of the simple types of Pascal. It is not necessary to master all the details in order to understand the next few chapters of the book, so this chapter may be taken rapidly at a first reading. The fact that the discussion is complete, however, should make this chapter a useful reference source later.

The chapter is divided into two unequal parts. The first part, Sections 2.1 through 2.8, is a discussion of *data*. The second part, Section 2.9, introduces construction of programs.

2.1 SYMBOLS

Pascal programs contain letters, numbers, mathematical symbols, and punctuation marks. The familiarity of these characters can be misleading: we cannot use them as we would in English or in algebra. Pascal programs consist of lexical units called *symbols*, which can be used only in specified ways.

A symbol in a Pascal program belongs to one of the following five classes.

- special symbols
- identifiers
- separators
- numbers
- strings

Pascal provides a number of unalterable symbols. These are called *special symbols*, and their use in a program is determined by the syntax of Pascal. The special symbols include signs, such as

$$+ \quad - \quad := \quad (\quad) \quad ; \quad :$$

and words, such as

begin end if then repeat until

In Pascal programs, we can define entities and give then names. When the name of an entity appears in a Pascal program, it is called an *identifier*. These are identifiers.

integer real write sqrt x count

In this book we distinguish symbol classes by using a variety of type styles. A word which is a special symbol, such as **begin**, is printed in **lowercase bold type**. Identifiers are printed in *uppercase* or *lowercase italic type*.

Separators are used to separate symbols. Each of the following is a separator.

- one or more blanks
- one or more tab characters
- a line break
- a comment

Separators are required between words, whether the words are special symbols or identifiers. The statement

if *ready*
then *doit*

could not be written in the form

ifreadythendoit

On the other hand, separators must not be used inside symbols.

be gin and : =

are not the same as

begin and :=

We also use separators to improve the readability of programs. For example,

apples + oranges

is easier to read than

apples+oranges

2.2   IDENTIFIERS

Some identifiers, called *standard identifiers* in Pascal, are defined by the Pascal processor. We have already encountered the standard identifiers *integer, char, read, sqrt,* and *write.* Every program also contains other identifiers that are defined within the program. We turn first to the rules for constructing valid identifiers.

Identifiers are composed of both letters and digits, but the first character of an identifier must always be a letter. These are valid identifiers.

john
henry8
endofinputdatamarker

These identifiers, on the other hand, are not valid.

first time
next.word
16may77

The first two invalid identifiers contain a character which is not a letter or a digit (blank in the first case, period in the second), and the third begins with a digit.

The rules for constructing identifiers are conveniently summarized in a *syntax diagram*. Figure 2.1 is the syntax diagram for identifiers. A rectangular box in a syntax diagram is a reference to another syntax diagram. Figure 2.1 refers to the syntax diagrams for *letter* (Fig. 2.2) and *digit* (Fig. 2.3). A circle, or box with rounded ends, contains a symbol that must be matched exactly. Using Fig. 2.1, we can construct symbols such as

henry8

but not

$3.00

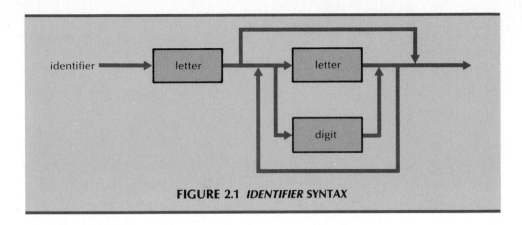

FIGURE 2.1 *IDENTIFIER* SYNTAX

Syntax diagrams may also be used to determine whether or not a given symbol belongs to a syntactic class. Figure 2.1, for example, enables us to determine whether or not a given symbol is an identifier.

Although Fig. 2.1 describes the syntax of an identifier concisely and accurately, it does not tell us how long an identifier can be. An identifier cannot be

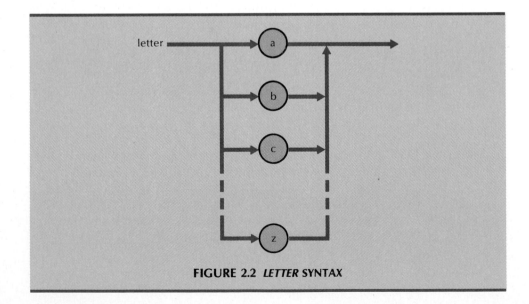

FIGURE 2.2 *LETTER* SYNTAX

split between two lines of a program, and therefore the length of an identifier is limited to 80 characters or so. The original Pascal Report required a Pascal compiler to look at only the first eight characters of an identifier. A compiler using this convention would not distinguish between the identifiers

lengthofbeam

and

lengthofstrut

because the first eight characters, *lengthof,* are the same in each case. Most existing Pascal compilers follow this convention, as does this book. The Standard, however, states that *all* the characters in an identifier are significant: with this convention, *lengthofbeam* and *lengthofstrut* would be distinct identifiers. In practice, it is best to assume that a compiler will look at only the first eight characters. When you want to introduce identifiers with common parts, such as *length,* write the unique parts first, as in

beamlength

and

strutlength

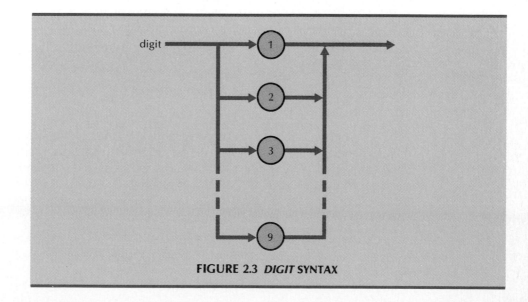

FIGURE 2.3 *DIGIT* SYNTAX

There are two further ways of improving the readability of identifiers. First, we can mix uppercase and lowercase letters, and second, we can introduce a special character to break up long identifiers and improve their readability. This character is called a *break character*. Although the Standard does not suggest a break character, many compilers accept the underscore, "＿". These compilers accept identifiers such as

```
Beam_Length
```

and

```
Strut_Length
```

Choosing identifiers is an important part of good programming. Well-chosen identifiers make programs easier to read and to understand. They also reduce the number of careless errors made in writing, typing, or correcting the program. It is much easier to modify a program written by someone else if the identifiers in it were well chosen. A long identifier is not necessarily better than a short one. If an identifier is to be used only a few times in a short section of the program, a single letter may be used. A single letter is a very poor choice for an identifier that will be used frequently in many different parts of a large program.

There are a few basic rules that should be applied to the choice of identifiers, irrespective of the meaning or the context of the identifier. Avoid using letters or digits that may be ambiguous. Some computer printers do not distinguish between the letter "O" and the digit "0." The tail of the letter "Q" may be indistinct. There is no reason not to use an identifier such as *root*; the context makes it clear that the letter "o" is intended. On the other hand, *to20* is not a good identifier.

2.3   LITERALS AND CONSTANTS

When we are writing a program, we frequently need to use known values. We might know, for instance, that a page contains 60 lines, a particular calculation must be performed exactly 100 times, the value of π is 3.14159, and a file is terminated by the character "$". An entity such as 60, 3.14159, or "$" is called a *literal*. Informally, a literal is anything whose value can be determined by looking at it. We can write literals in a program, as in the following examples.

```
while line < 60 do
  begin
    writeln;                                              (2.1)
    line := line + 1
  end;
```

```
for counter := 1 to 100 do
  calculation;
circumference := 3.14159 * diameter;
repeat
  read (ch)
until ch = '$';
```

In Pascal, we can associate an identifier with a literal value. An identifier that denotes a literal value is called a *constant identifier* or simply a *constant*. The function of the *constant definition section* in a Pascal program is to associate identifiers with literals. Here is an example of a constant definition section:

```
const
  pagesize = 60;
  cyclelimit = 100;                                        (2.2)
  pi = 3.14159;
  endchar = '$';
```

We can rewrite example (2.1) using these definitions in the following way.

```
while line < pagesize do
  begin
    writeln;
    line := line + 1
  end;
for counter := 1 to cyclelimit do
  calculation;
circumference := pi * diameter;
repeat
  read (ch)
until ch = endchar;
```

A precise reading of the first definition in the constant definition section (2.2) is:

Define an object that possesses the two attributes, name and value. The name of the object is the identifier *pagesize*, and the value of the object is the integer 60.

This is a rather pedantic account of a simple concept. We give it here in order to draw attention to the distinction between the name and the value of an object. Loosely, we may make such remarks as "*pagesize* is 60," and in most contexts such a remark is sufficiently precise. Later we will encounter data objects which have one name and several values, as well as data objects with no name at all, and then the reason for this pedantry will become apparent.

There are several good reasons for using constants rather than literals, and well-written programs rarely use literals outside the constant definition section. Suppose that *pagesize* represents the size of the page on which the program will print its results. Suppose also that the program was originally designed to write on sheets of paper which accommodated 60 lines but that it must now be modified to write on sheets of paper that can accommodate only 40

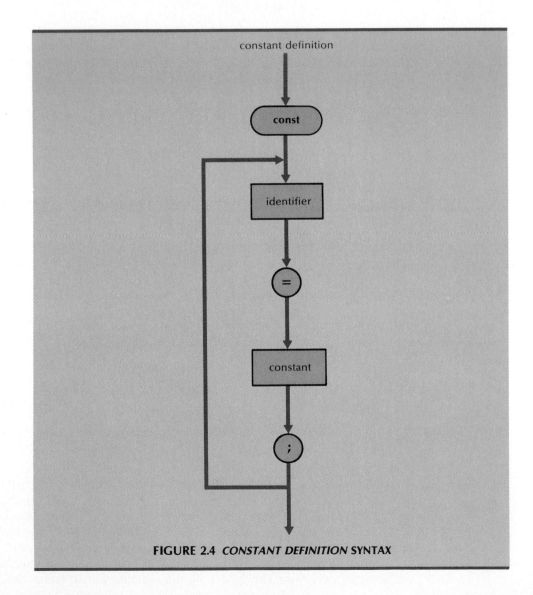

FIGURE 2.4 *CONSTANT DEFINITION* SYNTAX

lines. We need only change the constant definition section of the program. Instead of

$$pagesize = 60;$$

we write

$$pagesize = 40;$$

If the literal 60 had been written throughout the program, the change would have been much harder to make and there would have been two risks of error: a 60 that should be changed might be overlooked or, more insidiously, a 60 that actually referred to something else might be changed to 40. Moreover, the identifier *pagesize* is more meaningful to the reader of the program than the literal 60 (or 40).

CONSTANT DEFINITION SECTION SYNTAX

Figure 2.4 shows the syntax for a *constant definition section,* and Figs. 2.5, 2.6, and 2.7 show various forms of constant. A *constant identifier* is an identifier to

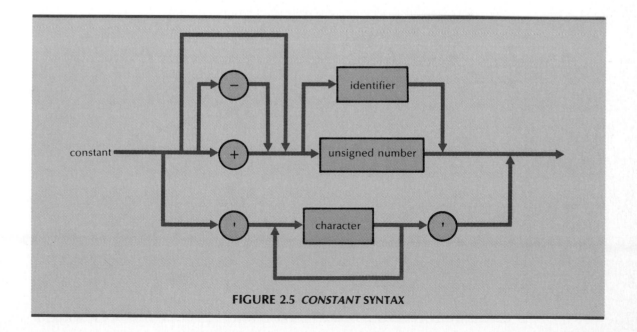

FIGURE 2.5 *CONSTANT* SYNTAX

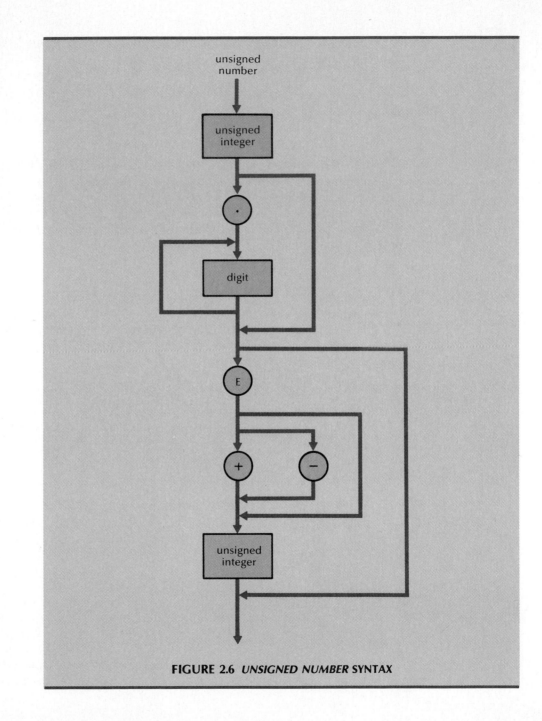

FIGURE 2.6 *UNSIGNED NUMBER* SYNTAX

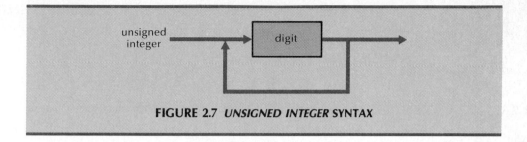

FIGURE 2.7 *UNSIGNED INTEGER* SYNTAX

which a constant value has already been given. For example, we could write

```
const
  biggest = 1000;
  smallest = - biggest;
```

After the first definition, *biggest* is a constant identifier, and so it may be used in the second definition to define *smallest*. The constant definition section may also be used to name characters and character strings, as in this example.

```
const
  blank = ' ';
  date = 'Friday, November 27';
  error = 'Too many cooks';
```

The syntax of Fig. 2.6, for an unsigned number, permits us to write

```
23   1.5   1E5   1.5E-5
```

but we cannot write

```
.5   E3   1.E-2   3.0E
```

Note in particular that an *integer* or *real* literal always starts with a digit.

2.4   DATA

Data in a program play the part of ingredients in a recipe. Each item of data in a program is either a constant or a variable, the difference being that the value of a variable may change during the execution of the program.

Every variable in a program has a *type*. The type determines the values that the variable can assume and the operations that may be performed on it.

The standard types of Pascal are *integer*, *real*, *boolean*, and *char*. The values

$$-100 \quad 0 \quad 9999$$

have the type *integer*. The values

$$-99.9 \quad 0.1 \quad 9999.0$$

have the type *real*. The values

false   true

have the type *boolean* and are in fact the only *boolean* values. Finally,

'1'   'a'   '='

are characters and have the type *char*.

Literals and constants have types, but because their types can be determined by the compiler, we do not have to declare them. When a variable is declared, however, its type must be specified. Figure 2.8 shows the syntax of a *variable declaration section*. Here is an example of a variable declaration section.

```
var
    count, index, numchar : integer;
    firstvalue, lastvalue, middlevalue : real;
    endofdata : boolean;
    ch, endch : char;
```

Expressions may be constructed from constants and variables according to rules very similar to the rules of conventional algebra. After the declaration

```
var
    start, step, count, finish : integer;
```
(2.3)

we can write expressions such as

```
start + count * step
```

in which the symbols "+" and "*" denote the operations of addition and multiplication respectively. An expression has both a type and a value. It is an important feature of Pascal that the type of an expression can always be determined from the text of the program. The expression above uses *integer* operands and *integer* operations and has the type *integer*, whatever the values of *start*, *count*, and *step*. Sections 2.5 through 2.8 show how expressions can be constructed and how their types can be determined.

The value of a variable is altered by the execution of an *assignment statement*. An assignment statement has the general form

```
variable := expression
```

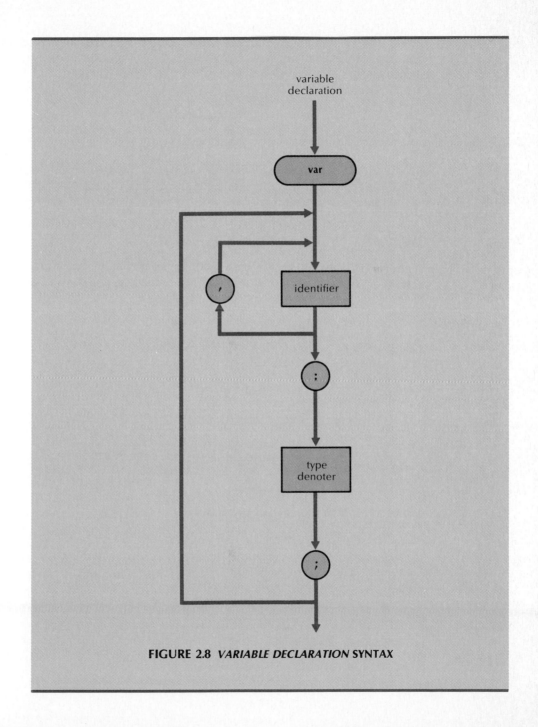

FIGURE 2.8 *VARIABLE DECLARATION* SYNTAX

and its effect is to assign the value of *expression* to *variable*. The operator ": = "
is read "becomes" or, more colloquially, "gets." After the declarations (2.3) we
can write

```
start := 1;
step := 2;
count := 100;
finish := start + count * step;
```

When these statements have been executed, the value of *finish* will be 201.

The types we describe in this chapter are all *ordered types*. This means that
if we take any two distinct values of the same type, one is less than the other. If
tweedledum and *tweedledee* are variables of the same type, the expression

```
tweedledum < tweedledee
```

(read "*tweedledum* is less than *tweedledee*") is meaningful and has one of the
values *true* or *false*. For the type *integer*, for example, the expressions

```
3 < 4
-1 < 1
```

both have the value *true*, and the expressions

```
4 < 3
3 < 3
```

both have the value *false*. Since *true* and *false* are *boolean* values, expressions
like

```
tweedledum < tweedledee
```

are called *boolean expressions*. We discuss them in more detail in Section 2.7.

Associated with each standard type are certain *standard functions*. We
have already encountered the standard function *sqrt*, and you will recall that
the value of *sqrt* (*x*) is $\sqrt{x}$, provided that $x \geqslant 0$. Some functions have the
same type as their arguments. Others, which do not, allow us to convert
values of one type to another type. For example, the function *round* takes a
real argument and returns an *integer* value. A function is defined for a particular set of argument values. This set is called the *domain* of the function.
For example, the domain of the function *ln* (natural logarithm) is the positive
real numbers. The function assumes only certain values. The set of values a
function can assume is called the *range* or *image* of the function. The range
of the function *sin* (trigonometric sine) is the set of real values, *y*, such that
$-1 \leqslant y \leqslant 1$.

2.5   THE TYPE *integer*

Values of type *integer* are whole numbers which may be positive or negative. The numeral 0 is an integer, as are 963 and −25. Numerals such as 1.5 and 2.718281828 are not integers.

A computer can represent only a finite subset of the integers. For any particular computer there is an integer, *maxint*, such that the integer N can be represented only if

$$- maxint \leqslant N \leqslant maxint$$

An attempt to evaluate an expression whose value is outside this range will lead to a run-time error. *Integer* variables are generally used for counters, indices, and so on, and for these purposes the limited range they encompass is adequate.

Some computers can represent the integer $-maxint-1$ correctly. For example, with 16-bit signed arithmetic, the integers are usually −32768, . . . , −1, 0, 1, . . . , 32767. Some versions of Pascal provide an identifier, *minint*, to denote the smallest integer that can be represented. The Standard, however, defines only *maxint*.

The operators

$$+ \quad - \quad * \quad \textbf{div} \quad \textbf{mod}$$

are associated with the type *integer*. They represent the familiar operations of addition, subtraction, multiplication, division, and remaindering. The operators are all infix operators, which means that they are written between their operands, as in conventional algebra. The operator " − " may also be used as a unary operator, as in

-50

Integer variables and constants are combined with these operators to give integer-valued expressions. Following the declarations

```
const
  linesize = 80;
var
  num, count, line : integer;
```

valid *integer* expressions are

```
num + count
num + line div linesize
num − 100
count mod linesize + 1
```

Some examples will show how the values of these expressions are obtained by the computer. For clarity, we use literals in the examples, but integer constants or variables with the same values would give the same results and would be used in an actual program. Multiplication, division, and remaindering are performed before addition and subtraction, so that

$$2 + 3 * 4 = 14.$$

The order of evaluation may be controlled by bracketing, as in conventional algebra.

$$(2 + 3) * 4 = 20.$$

Division always yields an *integer* result, the remainder being ignored.

$$5 \textbf{ div } 2 = 2$$
$$3 \textbf{ div } 4 = 0$$

Programs sometimes produce unexpected results because the programmer has overlooked the fact that the result of an *integer* division is zero whenever the divisor is greater than the dividend. If the remainder is required, it can be found by using the operator **mod**.

$$14 \textbf{ mod } 3 = 2 \tag{2.4}$$

The expression

$$m \textbf{ mod } n$$

is legal only if n is positive and nonzero. The value of m **mod** n is always positive; in fact, it must satisfy two relations. First,

$$0 \leqslant m \textbf{ mod } n < n$$

and second, for some integer k,

$$m \textbf{ mod } n = m - k \times n$$

In (2.4), we chose $k = 4$, so that

$$14 \textbf{ mod } 3 = 14 - 4 \times 3 = 2$$

To evaluate

$$-14 \textbf{ mod } 3 \tag{2.5}$$

we choose $k = -5$, so that

$$-14 \textbf{ mod } 3 = -14 - (-5 \times 3) = 1$$

These are the results specified by the Standard. Not all compilers follow the Standard in this respect. You may find that your computer gives −2 as the value of (2.5).

The operator "/" is used for *real* division. It may be used with *integer* operands, but the results will always be *real*.

```
2 div 3 = 0
2 / 3   = 0.66666667
5 div 1 = 5
5 / 1   = 5.0
```

The value of an integer-valued expression may be *assigned* to an *integer* variable or to a *real* variable. If we have declared

```
var
  velocity, crosssection : integer;
  flowrate : real;
```

then we can write

```
flowrate := velocity * crosssection
```

When this statement is executed, first the *integer* value of the expression on the right side is calculated, and then this value is converted to type *real* so that it can be assigned to *flowrate*. This is called *implicit type conversion* because there is no explicit operator or function indicating that conversion will be performed. Pascal allows implicit *integer* to *real* conversion because on most computers the range of values of a *real* variable includes the range of values of an *integer* variable; consequently, the assignment can never give an indeterminate result and accuracy cannot be lost. We are not allowed, however, to assign a *real* value to an *integer* variable.

If *number* is an *integer* variable, the statement

```
read (number)
```

will read a number from the input medium, convert it to an *integer* value, and assign this value to *number*. The number read from the input medium is in the form of a digit string, such as

```
13564
```

and it is important to realize that the execution of the *read* statement requires an implicit conversion from this form to the internal form of the number used by the computer. The numbers read from the input medium may be preceded by blanks or blank lines. The *read* procedure will skip over them. It will not skip over characters other than blanks, and if such characters are present, the program will fail.

The statement

$$write \ (number : fieldwidth)$$

where *number* is an *integer* variable or *integer* expression, will write the value of *number* on the output medium. Again, a conversion is performed implicitly, this time from the computer's internal form to the decimal string which is printed. The number is right-justified in a field of width *fieldwidth* characters, where *fieldwidth* is another integer expression. For example, if the values of *number* and *fieldwidth* are 173 and 6 respectively, then

$$\square\square\square173$$

would be printed. (Each "$\square$" represents one blank.) If the number contains more than *fieldwidth* characters, it will be correctly printed in a wider field. For example, if the value of *height* is 999, then

$$write \ ('*', \ height:1, \ '*')$$

writes *999* and

$$write \ ('*', \ height:6, \ '*')$$

writes *$\square\square\square$999* where each "$\square$" represents one blank.

The parameter *fieldwidth* may be omitted, in which case a default value is used. If the default value is 10, the statement

$$write \ (number)$$

is equivalent to

$$write \ (number : 10)$$

The functions that may have *integer* arguments and the functions that yield *integer* values are included in Table 2.1. The functions *pred* and *succ* require *integer* arguments and yield *integer* results. The result is the predecessor or the successor of the argument, so we have

$$pred(5) = 4$$
$$succ(5) = 6$$
$$succ(-3) = -2$$

TABLE 2.1					
ARGUMENT VALUE	*integer*	*real*	*boolean*	*char*	*file*
integer	pred succ abs sqr	trunc round	ord	ord	
real	sin cos arctan ln exp sqrt	abs sqr sin cos arctan ln exp sqrt			
boolean	odd		pred succ		eof eoln
char	chr			pred succ	

The functions *abs* and *sqr* yield *integer* results if the type of their arguments is *integer*, or *real* results if the type of their arguments is *real*. *Abs* (*number*) is the absolute value of *number*, conventionally written as |*number*|, and *sqr* (*number*) is the square of *number*. We have

$$abs(10) = 10$$
$$abs(-10) = 10$$
$$abs(0) = 0$$
$$sqr(10) = 100$$
$$sqr(-10) = 100$$
$$sqr(0) = 0$$

The functions *sin*, *cos*, *arctan*, *ln*, *exp*, and *sqrt* may be used with *integer* arguments but their values are *real*, and therefore they are described in the next section.

2.6   THE TYPE *real*

We use variables of type *real* in a program in the same way we use real-valued variables in applied mathematics. The computer can represent only a finite subset of the real numbers. Although this does not usually have a serious effect on the results of a calculation, you must be aware of the possibility that serious inaccuracies can occur in certain cases.

Numbers written in a program in the conventional way are either *integer* or *real* literals. These are examples of *real* literals.

$$12.7 \quad 1.0 \quad 0.00005$$

Scientific calculations often require *real* literals with very large or very small values, and these are not easily represented in decimal notation. For example, the rest mass of the electron is approximately

$$0.000000000000000000000000000910956 \text{ grams}$$

Scientists generally write numbers like these in the more tractable form

$$9.10956 \times 10^{-28}$$

This is possible in Pascal too. The part of the number that is read "times ten to the power of" is abbreviated to "E." The number would be written in a Pascal program as

$$9.10956E-28$$

Most Pascal compilers also accept a lowercase "e." The same number can be written as

$$9.10956e-28$$

Figure 2.6 shows the syntax for unsigned numbers. As we saw above, a literal in a constant declaration may be preceded by a sign. The *E* in a *real* literal can never be mistaken for an identifier because it is always preceded by at least one digit.

The two important characteristics of *real* variables are their *range* and their *precision*. For example, a computer might provide reals with a range of 10^{+75} and a precision of ten places of decimals. This means that a single operation (addition, multiplication, etc.) will be accurate to about ten places of decimals in most circumstances. Certain individual operations may have less accuracy than this, and the final result of a computation involving thousands or even millions of simple operations will almost certainly have less accuracy. Most computers provide real numbers with sufficient range and accuracy for simple calculations in applied mathematics, engineering, or physics, but special programming techniques must be used to maintain precision in the long calculations used in more advanced applications, such as solving sets of simultaneous equations or obtaining numerical solutions to differential equations.

The ordering of *real* variables is the natural one. However, if ξ (xi) and η (eta) are real numbers (in the mathematician's sense), and they are represented in the computer by the *real* variables x and y, then we can safely assume that

$$\xi = \eta \qquad \text{implies} \qquad x = y$$

but it is not always true that

$$\xi < \eta \qquad \text{implies} \qquad x < y$$

because if the values of ξ and η are very close, they will not be distinguishable by the computer. In general we can state only that

$$\xi < \eta \qquad \text{implies} \qquad x \leqslant y.$$

It is roughly true to say that in a computer with a precision of ten places of decimals, two numbers whose values differ only in the eleventh significant digit will have the same representation.

The operators that may be used with *real* operands are

$$+ \quad - \quad \times \quad /$$

which represent addition, subtraction, multiplication, and division respectively. The symbols " $+$ ", " $-$ ", and "$\star$" are used for both *integer* and *real* computations.

Do not expect the results of calculations to be exact. Computer arithmetic is rather like pocket-calculator arithmetic. For example,

$$1000000 + 0.0000001$$

will have the value

$$1000000$$

unless your computer has a precision of fourteen places of decimals or more. The problem is more severe with a computer than with a pocket calculator both because the computer performs many more calculations and because it does not provide any indication that gross errors are accumulating. It is your responsibility to ensure accurate results by using well-designed algorithms and, if necessary, monitoring the values of intermediate results to make sure that all is going well.

Although the convention of performing multiplication and division before addition and subtraction is in accordance with normal algebraic usage, the evaluation of expressions from left to right does not always produce the result we expect. In particular,

```
6 / 3 * 2
```

is evaluated from left to right as

```
(6 / 3) * 2
```

and has the value 4, not 1.

Integer values may be used in *real* expressions. If one operand of any of the operators "+", "−", or "*" is *real*, the other operand is converted automatically to *real* before the operator is applied. Consider the expression

```
(6 + 4) * (1 + 0.1)
```

The subexpressions in parentheses are evaluated first.

$$6 + 4 = 10 \text{ } (integer)$$

In the second subexpression, 0.1 is *real*, and so before the addition is performed, the other operand, 1, is converted to *real*.

$$1 + 0.1 = 1.1 \text{ } (real)$$

The multiplying operator "*" now has an *integer* operand, 10, and a *real* operand, 1.1. The *integer* operand is converted to *real* and we have

$$10.0 * 1.1 = 11.0 \text{ } (real)$$

The type of the result is *real*, even though in this case it happens to have an integer value.

The operator "/" behaves differently. It forces (the technical term is *coerces*) both of its operands to be *real*, and the result is *real*, as we saw in Section 2.5.

Functions that may be used with *real* arguments and functions that yield *real* results are summarized in Table 2.1. The functions *abs* (absolute value) and *sqr* (square) will yield a *real* value when they are used with a *real* argument. The functions *sin* (sine), *cos* (cosine), *arctan* (inverse tangent), *ln* (natural logarithm), *exp* (exponential), and *sqrt* (square root) may have an *integer* or *real* argument, but they always yield a *real* result.

A *real* value cannot be assigned to an *integer* variable. This is because an assignment of this kind would in general result in integer overflow, loss of information, or both. The two remaining functions, *trunc* and *round,* are used to convert *real* values to *integer* values. *Trunc (arg)* is the integer obtained by omitting the fractional part of the real *arg.* Thus

$$trunc\ (3.14159) = 3$$
$$trunc\ (2.71828) = 2$$
$$trunc\ (-4.8) = -4$$

Round (arg) is the integer closest to *arg,* and

$$round\ (3.14159) = 3$$
$$round\ (2.71828) = 3$$
$$round\ (-4.8) = -5$$

If the conversion yields a value too large to be represented as an integer, a run-time error occurs.

If x is a *real* variable, then the statement

$$read\ (x)$$

will read a number from the input medium, convert it to the appropriate internal form, and assign its value to x. The syntax of *real* numbers that may be read is the same as the syntax for unsigned numbers, shown in Fig. 2.6, except that a leading sign (" + " or " – ") is accepted. An error in the syntax of a *real* number will cause a run-time error.

The statement

$$write\ (x : fieldwidth : precision)$$

will write a string of the form

$$\square\square\square dddddd.dddd$$

in which there are *fieldwidth* characters altogether and *precision* digits after the decimal point. Each "d" denotes a digit and each "$\square$" denotes a blank. The parameter *precision* may be omitted, in which case scientific notation will be used:

$$\square\square\square\square 0.ddddddE\pm dd$$

The precision of this result will be determined by the implementation you are using. The parameter *fieldwidth* may also be omitted, and in this case scientific notation with a default width, for example twenty characters, is used.

When you are writing a program that prints *real* values, you should always choose a precision that is suited to both the problem and the computer that you are using. Do not print more digits than are required for the solution or than can be accurately calculated. In particular, never attempt to print more significant digits than your computer is capable of calculating.

You should use consistent output formats throughout a program unless there is a good reason not to do so. Formatting values can be defined in a constant declaration section, as in this example.

```
const
  precision = 6;
  fieldwidth = 16;
var
  result : real;
....
  writeln (result : fieldwidth : precision)
```

If this has been done, it is a simple matter to adapt the program for another computer that has more (or less) accuracy.

The width and precision parameters are not used in most of the examples in this book. This should not be taken to mean that you should not use them. They have been omitted because their actual values are not usually relevant to the points being made and they take up an unreasonable amount of space in short examples. The best values to use will depend to a certain extent on the computer used to run the example programs. You can provide these values yourself. (See Exercise 2.7.)

2.7   THE TYPE *boolean*

Boolean variables may have one of two values which are represented by the standard values *true* and *false*. They are used primarily to control the order in which the statements of a program are executed.

There are three *boolean* operators: **and, or**, and **not**. These operators may also be written $\wedge$ (**and**), $\vee$ (**or**), and $\neg$ (**not**), but in this book we will always use the spelled forms.

If we have made the declarations

```
var
  finished, empty, toobig : boolean;
```

then the following expressions have *boolean* values:

not *empty* **or** *toobig*	(2.6)
finished **and** *empty* **or** *toobig*	(2.7)
toobig **and** (*empty* **or** *finished*)	(2.8)

The operator **not** is always applied first. Expression (2.6) is equivalent to

$$(\textbf{not } empty) \textbf{ or } toobig$$

The operator **and** is always applied before **or.** Expression (2.7) is equivalent to

$$(finished \textbf{ and } empty) \textbf{ or } toobig$$

This order may be altered by bracketing, as expression (2.8) shows.

The values of the simple *boolean* expressions are summarized in Table 2.2. Assume that *left* and *right* are *boolean* variables with the values shown.

In addition to the *boolean* operators, there are *relational,* or *comparison,* operators. These are

<	less than
≤	less than or equal to
=	equal to
≠	not equal to
≥	greater than or equal to
>	greater than

They yield *boolean* values when they are used with expressions of any type on which an ordering has been defined. Thus the value of

$$2 < 3$$

is *true* and the value of

$$3 \leq -5$$

is *false.* Given the declarations

```
var
    count, total : integer;
    length, height : real;
    done : boolean;
```

TABLE 2.2				
left	*right*	**not** *left*	*left* **and** *right*	*left* **or** *right*
true	true	false	true	true
true	false	false	false	true
false	true	true	false	true
false	false	true	false	false

the following expressions yield *boolean* values

```
count < total
(count = total) and (length ≥ height) and done
(count mod total = 0) or (count ≤ 100)
```

Brackets are required when comparative expressions are separated by boolean operators, as in the last two examples.

Mathematicians are accustomed to writing expressions like

$$minimum \leqslant value \leqslant maximum$$

You cannot do this in Pascal. An expression of this kind must always be written out in full.

```
(minimum ≤ value) and (value ≤ maximum)
```

It is best not to test for equality of *real* values because after a series of calculations, numbers that are theoretically equal may be only approximately equal in practice. The comparison

$$a = b$$

in which a and b are *real*, should be replaced by

```
abs (a − b) < epsilon
```

We must choose a suitable value for *epsilon*. If the order of magnitude of a and b is unknown, *epsilon* should be a function of one of them. For example, the expression

```
abs (a − b) < abs (a * 1E–6)
```

will be *true* if a does not differ from b by more than one part in a million.

The value of a *boolean* expression may be assigned to a *boolean* variable. For example, we can declare

```
const
  maximum = 1000;
var
  finished, error : boolean;
  counter : integer;
```

and then write

```
finished := counter > maximum;
error := eof and not finished
```

The functions *eoln* and *eof* have *boolean* values. *Eoln* is *true* at the end of a line of the input file and *false* elsewhere. When *eoln* is *true*, the current character in the input stream is a blank. You can read a file without using *eoln* at all, in which case the file appears to be one long line with occasional extra blanks in it. If the line structure of the file is important, you can use *eoln* to find out where the lines end.

Eof is *true* at the end of the input file. Attempting to read anything from the file after *eof* has become *true* will cause an execution error, so you must always check for end of file before reading:

```
if eof
    then write ('End of file.')
    else read (ch)
```

The *boolean* function *odd* takes an *integer* argument. It returns the value *true* if the argument is odd and *false* if it is even.

If *switch* is a *boolean* variable, then

```
write (switch)
```

will print either "TRUE" or "FALSE" in the output file. The statement

```
write (switch : fieldwidth)
```

will print either "TRUE" preceded by *fieldwidth*–4 blanks or "FALSE" preceded by *fieldwidth*–5 blanks, provided that *fieldwidth* is large enough.

The procedure *read* will not accept a *boolean* argument. It is not difficult, however, to write a program that will interpret "T" as *true* and "F" as *false*.

```
const
    truechar = 'T';
    falsechar = 'F';
var
    ch : char;
    switch : boolean;
....
    read (ch);
    if ch = falsechar
        then switch := false
    else if ch = truechar
        then switch := true
    else write ('Input format error.')
```

2.8   THE TYPE *char*

The value of a variable of type *char* is a character. There is no special character set defined for Pascal because Pascal uses the character set of the computer on which it is running. The Standard, however, does require that the character set have certain properties.

- Each character must have a distinct *ordinal value*. The ordinal value is an integer. For example, the ordinal value of the character *a* is usually 97.
- The ordinal values of the digits 0, 1, 2, . . . , 9 must be ordered and consecutive.
- The ordinal values of the uppercase letters *A*, *B*, . . . , *Z* must be ordered but need not be consecutive.
- The ordinal values of the lowercase letters *a*, *b*, . . . , *z* (if they exist) must be ordered but need not be consecutive.

The two most widely used character sets, ASCII (American Standard Code for Information Interchange) and EBCDIC (Extended Binary Coded Decimal Information Code), both have the required properties.

A *char* literal is a character written between apostrophes.

`'A'` represents the letter A
`'a'` represents the letter a
`' '` represents a blank
`''''` represents the single character ' (apostrophe)

Note that two apostrophes are required to represent one apostrophe.

The function *ord* returns the ordinal value of a character. The first property above states that if *ch1* and *ch2* have the type *char*, and $ch1 \neq ch2$, then

$$ord\ (ch1)\ \neq\ ord\ (ch2)$$

The characters are ordered and the ordering is derived from the ordinal value. The comparison operators

$$<\ \ \leqslant\ \ =\ \ \neq\ \ \geqslant\ \ >$$

are the only operators that may be used with *char* variables, and

$$ch1\ <\ ch2$$

is equivalent to

$$ord\ (ch1)\ <\ ord\ (ch2)$$

The second property says that the sequence

$$ord\ ('0'),\ ord\ ('1'),\ ord\ ('2'),...,\ ord\ ('9')$$

is an increasing sequence of consecutive integers. (In ASCII, this sequence is 48, 49, . . . , 57.) In most character sets

$$ord \; ('0') \neq 0$$

and so *ord* does *not* convert a digit to the corresponding value. To convert a digit *ch* of type *char* to the corresponding numerical value, *num*, you should use a statement of the form

$$num := ord \; (ch) - ord \; ('0')$$

For example, if *ch* is '3', then *ord* (*ch*) is 51 in ASCII and *num* receives the value 51 − 48 = 3.

The third and fourth properties ensure that letters are ordered alphabetically, but not that they will have consecutive ordinal values. In EBCDIC, for example,

$$ord \; ('I') = 201$$

but

$$ord \; ('J') = 209$$

The function *chr* is the inverse of *ord*. It has an *integer* argument and a *char* value and it is only defined over the range of *ord*. If we have declared

var
    charval : integer;

then *chr* (*charval*) is defined only if there exists a character, *ch*, such that *ord* (*ch*) = *charval*. If this is the case, then, as we would expect,

$$chr \; (charval) = ch$$

In particular, if *digit* is an integer and

$$0 \leqslant digit \leqslant 9$$

then the corresponding character will be

$$chr \; (digit + ord \; ('0'))$$

For example,

$$chr \; (3 + ord \; ('0')) = '3'$$

Characters may be read from the input file using the standard procedure *read*. After the declaration

var
    ch : char;

the statement

```
read (ch)
```

will read the next character from the input file. The procedure *read* does not skip over blanks, as it does for *integers* and *reals*, when it is reading characters. If we want to ignore blanks in the input file, we must include explicit statements for this purpose in the program.

```
const
  blank = ' ';
var
  ch : char;
....
  repeat
    read (ch)
  until ch ≠ blank
```

This statement will continue reading until either a non-blank character or the end of the input file is encountered. If the statement terminates successfully, *ch* will contain the next non-blank character.

The statement

```
write (ch)
```

in which *ch* is a character variable or expression, will write the character to the output file. The statement

```
write (ch : fieldwidth)
```

in which *fieldwidth* is an *integer* expression, will write *fieldwidth*−1 blanks and then the character *ch*. A particular use of this is the statement

```
write (' ' : fieldwidth)
```

which will write *fieldwidth* blanks.

2.9   CONSTRUCTION OF PROGRAMS

The rules for constructing entire Pascal programs are just as precise as the rules we have used for constructing program components such as constant and variable declaration sections. In this section we consider the syntax for a sub-language of Pascal, which uses assignment, **while,** compound, *read*, and *write* statements. This simple language is described in a *top-down* fashion. "Top-down" is an important phrase in computer science. It implies a progression from the abstract ("top") to the particular. An architect who starts work by drawing sketches of a proposed building is using a top-down approach, whereas an architect who starts by consulting a brick catalog is using a bottom-up approach. Both techniques have their merits, but for program design the top-down method is usually preferable.

PROGRAMS AND BLOCKS

A *program* consists of a *heading* and a *block,* and it concludes with a period, as Figs. 2.9, 2.10, and 2.11 show. A typical heading looks like this:

program *startrek (input, output);*

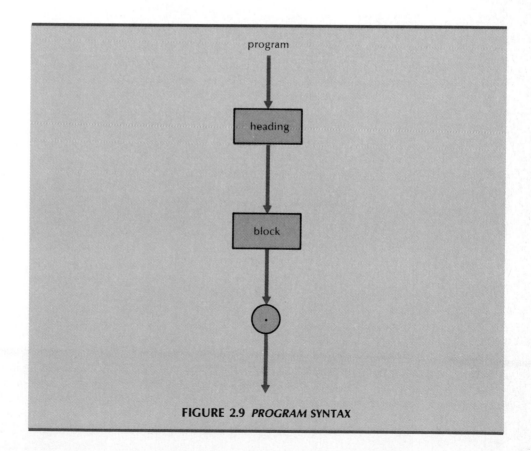

FIGURE 2.9 *PROGRAM* SYNTAX

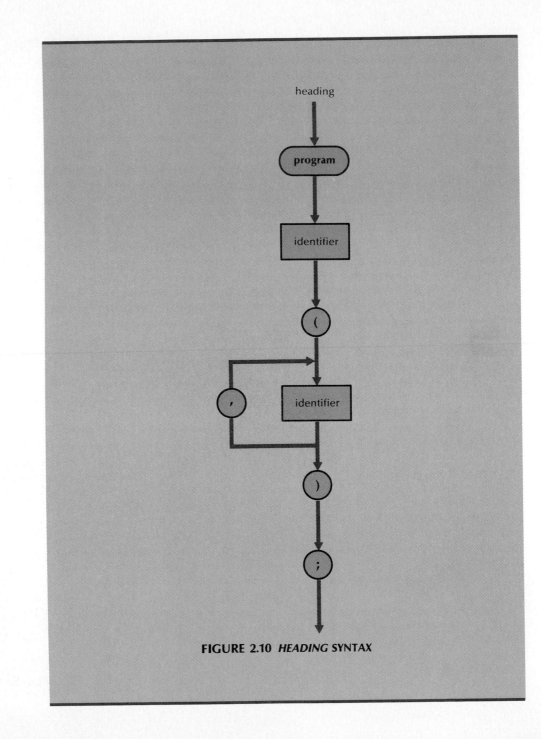

FIGURE 2.10 *HEADING* SYNTAX

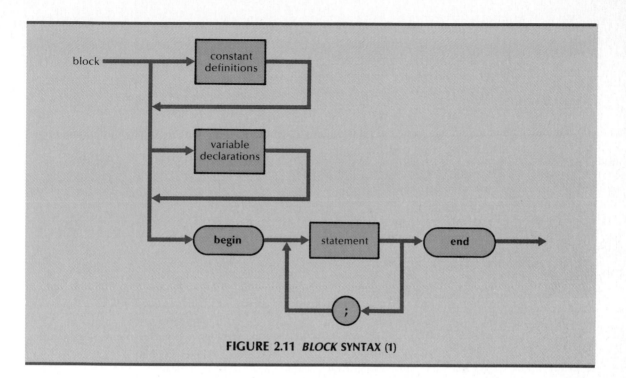

FIGURE 2.11 *BLOCK* SYNTAX (1)

Program is a reserved word and is always the first word of a Pascal program. It is followed by the name of the program and a list of the files that the program uses. We discuss programs that use files other than *input* and *output* in Chapter 7. Some compilers do not require that file names appear in the program heading.

The heading is followed by a *block* (Fig. 2.11). The declarations in the block are optional, but if both are present, constant definitions must precede variable declarations. We have already seen the syntax for constant definitions (Fig. 2.4) and variable declarations (Fig. 2.8).

The annotation "(1)" in the caption of Fig. 2.11 indicates that the syntax diagram is simplified. A subsequent diagram shows the complete form. Appendix B contains complete syntax diagrams for Pascal.

STATEMENTS

A *compound statement* is a sequence of statements introduced by **begin** and terminated by **end**. There must be a semicolon between consecutive statements. The semicolon is *not* part of the statement: it is a statement *separator*. Consequently, a semicolon is not required between the last statement of a compound statement and **end**. Figure 2.12 shows that a *statement* may be a *compound statement*. This is an important construction. At any place in a program where a statement may be written, a compound statement may be written. In Section 3.2, the **while** statement is introduced with the general form

> **while** *condition* **do**
> *statement*

This statement would not be very useful if it were not for the fact that *statement* can be a compound statement, so that we can write

> **while** *condition* **do**
>   **begin**
>   *statement$_1$*;
>   *statement$_2$*;
>   ...
>   *statement$_n$*
>   **end**

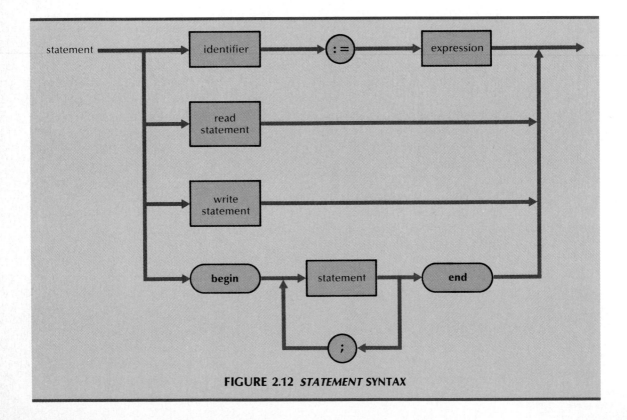

FIGURE 2.12 *STATEMENT* SYNTAX

An *assignment statement* has the form

```
variable := expression
```

The assignment statement is asymmetric. The right side is an expression and it answers the question "what is the value?" The left side is a variable and it answers the question "to what is this value to be assigned?" It is therefore possible to write assignment statements such as

```
firstnumber := 1
circumference := 2 * pi * radius
```

and even

```
nextnumber := nextnumber + 1
```

which has the effect of increasing the value of *nextnumber* by 1. It is not meaningful, however, to write statements like

```
1 := firstnumber
length * width := area
```

because the left sides of these statements are not variables.

We will continue to use *read* and *write* in an informal way until Chapter 7, where they are described in detail. They are indispensable for examples, and their effect is usually obvious. We have seen in the preceding sections of this chapter how *read* and *write* operate with a single argument. They accept multiple arguments as well.

```
read (first);
read (middle);
read (last)
```

may be abbreviated to

```
read (first, middle, last)
```

The procedure *write* also accepts constant and literal strings, so we may write

```
const
  title = 'Small Is Beautiful';
....
  write (title)
```

or simply

```
write ('Small Is Beautiful')
```

The procedure *writeln* starts a new line in the output file.

```
write (top);
write (bottom);
writeln
```

may be abbreviated to

```
writeln (top, bottom)
```

EXPRESSIONS

The syntax of expressions is described in Figs. 2.13 through 2.17. The syntax is designed to reflect the usual precedence relationships of algebraic operators. For example, the *simple expression*

```
a + b * c
```

is the sum of two *terms*, a and b * c, and the second *term* has two *factors*, b and c.

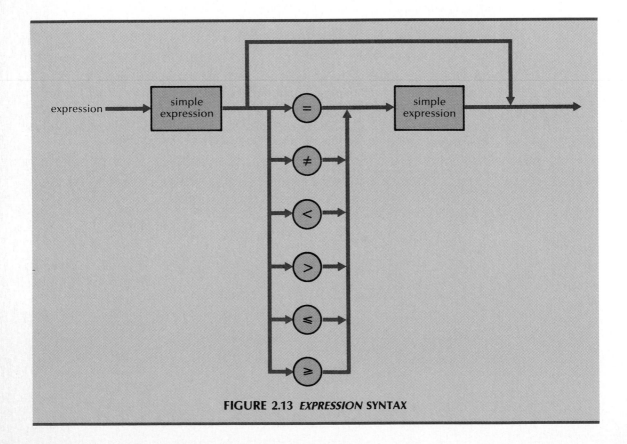

FIGURE 2.13 *EXPRESSION* SYNTAX

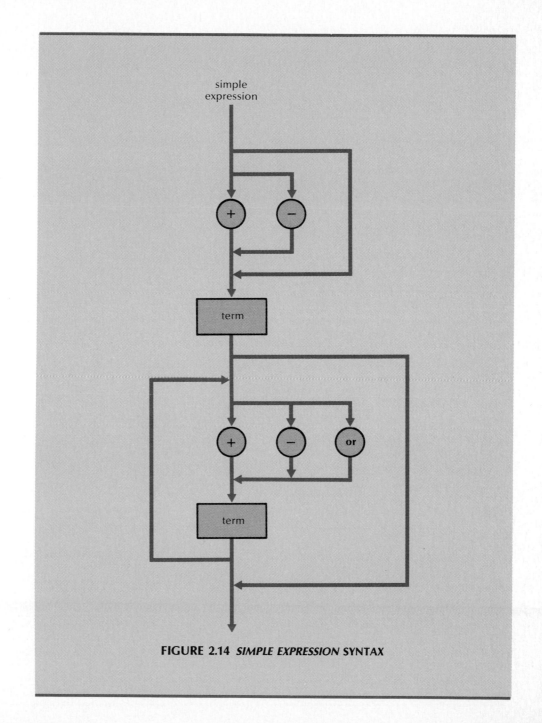

FIGURE 2.14 *SIMPLE EXPRESSION* SYNTAX

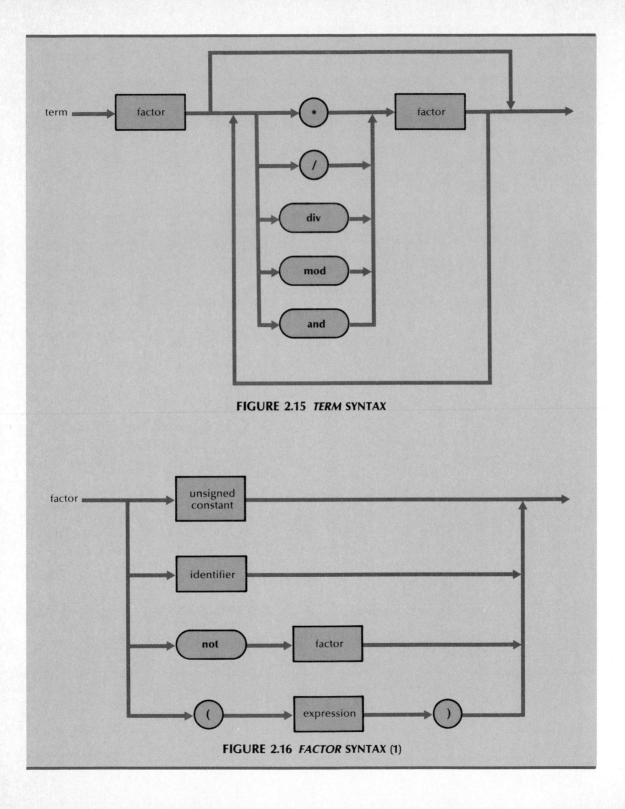

FIGURE 2.15 *TERM* SYNTAX

FIGURE 2.16 *FACTOR* SYNTAX (1)

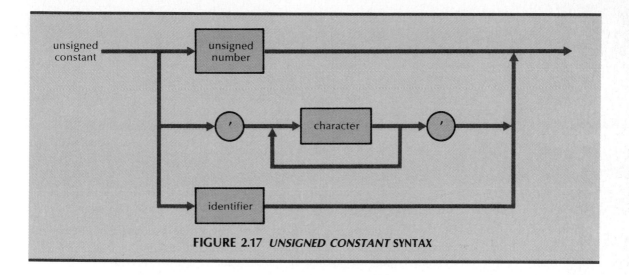

FIGURE 2.17 *UNSIGNED CONSTANT* SYNTAX

Multiplication of factors is performed before terms are added. Note also that **and** is a multiplicative operator, **or** is an additive operator, and **not**, being a part of *factor* syntax, takes precedence over either. From these syntax diagrams you can see why parentheses are necessary in expressions such as

$$(minimum \leq value) \textbf{ and } (value \leq maximum)$$

BLANKS AND COMMENTS

Blanks are not mentioned in the syntax diagrams. Their inclusion in syntax diagrams would produce great confusion because they can occur almost anywhere in the program text. Blanks must not appear inside reserved words, identifiers, or compound symbols. The *compound symbols* are

$$:= \qquad ..$$

In some implementations of Pascal there may be other compound symbols. For example,

$$\leq \qquad \neq \qquad \geq \qquad \{ \qquad \}$$

may be represented by

$$<= \qquad <> \qquad >= \qquad (* \qquad *)$$

and in these cases there must not be a blank between the two characters.

Several blanks are equivalent to one blank. There is an implicit blank between any two lines of a program; therefore a reserved word, identifier, or compound symbol cannot be split between two lines.

A *comment* has the form

```
{ character string }
```

The character string may contain any character except "}". A comment is equivalent to a blank, so comments may be placed wherever blanks are allowed. Comments are inserted into programs as an aid to the reader. The programs in this book do not contain many comments because the surrounding text contains explanations of how the programs work.

USING THE SYNTAX DIAGRAMS

This completes our account of a simple sublanguage of Pascal. You should verify that the following example program can be analyzed using the syntax diagrams that have been presented in this chapter.

```
{ Print the surface area and volume of a sphere,
  given its radius. }
program sphere (input, output);
  const
    pi = 3.1415926535;
    width = 10;
    prec = 4;
  var
    radius, surfacearea, volume : real;
  begin
    read (radius);
    surfacearea := 4 * pi * sqr (radius);
    volume := radius * surfacearea / 3;
    writeln ('Measurements of a Sphere');
    writeln ('Radius      = ', radius : width : prec);
    writeln ('Surface Area = ', surfacearea : width : prec);
    writeln ('Volume      = ', volume : width : prec)
  end. { sphere }
```

INPUT	OUTPUT
10	Measurements of a Sphere
	Radius = 10.0000
	Surface Area = 1256.6372
	Volume = 4188.7906

2.10 EXERCISES

2.1 Draw syntax diagrams for mailing addresses. Give examples of valid and invalid addresses.

2.2 Write constant definition sections from the following program outlines. Choose identifiers carefully.

a) A text formatter prints lines of 70 characters on pages 66 lines long, and paragraphs are indented five columns. A word may be hyphenated only if it is more than ten characters long. The character "&" is to be changed to "and" and the character "%" signals a new page.

b) A program performs elasticity calculations. These values of λ and μ are used.

	STEEL	COPPER	ALUMINUM	
λ	11.2	9.5	2.6	(all $\times$ 10^{11})
μ	8.1	4.5	2.6	(all $\times$ 10^{11})

2.3 The following definitions and declarations have been made.

```
const
    twoblanks = '  ';
var
    m, n : integer;
    a, b : real;
    p, q : boolean;
    c1, c2 : char;
```

State whether or not each of the following statements is valid, giving reasons.

a) $m := trunc\ (b) + a$

b) $p := m + n$

c) $read\ (c1,\ c2,'\ ')$

d) $c1 := twoblanks$

e) $p := q$ **and** $(ord\ (c1) \neq\ 'a')$

f) $m := n$ **mod** a

g) $'c1' := 'c2'$

h) $c2 := chr\ ('a')$

i) $m := m - ord\ ('0')$

j) $writeln\ (a,\ p,\ m,\ n,\ q,\ q,\ b)$

k) $n := a - trunc\ (a)$

l) $b := 2.99 * 10^9$

m) $a := m\ /\ n$

n) $b := ord\ (c1) + ord\ (c2)$

2.4 Give the type and, if it can be ascertained, the value of each of the following expressions. The letters p, q, r, and s are *boolean* variables and k is an *integer* variable.

a) $sqr\ (2)$

b) $sqr\ (2.0)$

c) ord ('z') − ord ('a')
d) $trunc$ (−99.9)
e) − $round$ (99.9)
f) − $round$ (−99.9)
g) **not** (p **and** q) = **not** (**not** p **and** **not** q)
h) 10 **div** 3
i) 10 / 3
j) 126 **div** 3 **mod** 5
k) (p **and** (q **and** **not** q)) **or** **not** (r **or** (s **or** **not** s))
l) ($round$ (−65.3) < $trunc$ (−65.3)) **and** p
m) odd (k) **or** odd (k + 1)

2.5 Write Pascal assignment statements that correspond to the formulas below. Choose appropriate identifiers, assume that all variables are real, and define constants where necessary.

a) The period t of a pendulum of length h is given by

$$t = 2\pi \sqrt{h/g}$$

where g is the local gravitational constant (981 cm/sec^2).

b) The attractive force F between bodies of mass m_1 and m_2 separated by a distance r is

$$F = \frac{Gm_1m_2}{r^2}$$

where $G = 6.673 \times 10^{-8}$cm^3/g sec^2 is the universal gravitational constant.

c) The pressure p and volume v of a confined gas are related by

$$pv^\gamma = C$$

where γ and C are constants. (*Hint:* $v^\gamma = e^{\gamma \ln(v)}$.)

d) The area of a triangle whose sides are of length a, b, and c is

$$A = \sqrt{s(s - a)(s - b)(s - c)}$$

where

$$s = \frac{a + b + c}{2}.$$

e) The perimeter p of an n-sided polygon circumscribing a circle of radius r is

$$p = 2nr \times \tan\left(\frac{\pi}{n}\right).$$

f) The distance s from the point (ξ, η) to the line

$$Ax + By + C = 0$$

is given by

$$s = \frac{A\xi + B\eta + C}{A^2 + B^2}.$$

g) The emissive power E at wavelength λ of a black body radiator at absolute temperature T is

$$E = \frac{2\pi ch\lambda^{-5}}{e^{ch/B\lambda T} - 1}$$

where

$c = 2.997924 \times 10^8$ is the velocity of light,

$h = 6.6252 \times 10^{-34}$ is Planck's constant, and

$B = 5.6687 \times 10^{-8}$ is Boltzmann's constant.

2.6 For what values of x might you be suspicious of the validity or precision of the following expressions?

a) $exp\,(x) - exp\,(-x)$

b) $\dfrac{(x - 1)}{(x + 1)}$

c) $1 - x + \dfrac{x^2}{2!} - \dfrac{x^3}{3!} + \ldots + \dfrac{x^n}{n!}$ where n is large enough to ensure that $\dfrac{x^n}{n!}$ is much

less than 1.

2.7 Find the following values for your computer system:
   a) the largest possible *integer* (*maxint*);
   b) the most negative *integer* (which may not be $-maxint$);
   c) the largest possible *real*;
   d) the approximate precision of *reals*;
   e) the smallest value of $|x|$ distinct from zero, where x is *real*;
   f) the smallest value of δ such that your computer can distinguish 1 and $1 + \delta$;
   g) the characters that can be represented and their ordinal values.

3

DECISION
AND REPETITION

It is often necessary to specify two or more possible courses of action in a program and to allow the processor executing the program to select one of them during the execution. We have already seen an instance of this in Chapter 1: Program *squareroots* prints one message if $x \geqslant 0$ and another if $x < 0$. The **if** statement enables the processor to select one of two actions. The selection is made by evaluating a boolean expression. The **if** statement is often called a *conditional statement*, and in the context of an **if** statement, a boolean expression may be called a *condition* or *predicate*.

It may be necessary to execute a statement or group of statements repeatedly. Although the statements themselves remain the same, the data on which they operate change during the repetition. A group of statements which is executed repeatedly is called a *loop*. One execution of the group of statements in the loop is called an *iteration*. Every loop must terminate after a finite number of iterations, therefore a decision as to whether to carry on or to stop must be made during each iteration. The criterion for this decision is called the *termination condition* of the loop.

3.1   THE if STATEMENT

We use the keyword **if** in Pascal in much the same way we use the word "if" in English. The English sentence

"If it's raining, I'll take the car, otherwise I'll walk."

is similar in structure to the Pascal statement

```
if raining
   then drive
   else walk
```

This statement is a particular **if** statement and it is an instance of the general form

```
if boolean expression
   then statement₁                                              (3.1)
   else statement₂
```

The term *condition* may be used as a synonym for *boolean expression* in this context. If the value of the condition is *true*, the statement following **then** (*statement₁* in (3.1)) is executed, and if the value of the condition is *false*, the statement following **else** (*statement₂* in (3.1)) is executed. In English it is idiomatic to use "otherwise," but **else** has become traditional for programming languages, probably because there is less chance of misspelling it. The following are examples of **if** statements.

```
var
   number, radix : integer;
   side, area : real;
begin
   ....
   if number < radix - 1
     then number := succ (number)
     else number := 0;
   ....
   if area ⩾ 0
     then side := sqrt (area)
     else
       begin
         side := 0;
         write ('The area is negative.')
       end;
   ....
```

if STATEMENT SYNTAX

Figure 3.1 is the syntax diagram for the **if** statement. It reveals that the **else** clause may be omitted. If there is no **else** clause and the condition yields *false*, the **if** statement has no effect. There are no semicolons in an **if** statement and it is wrong to put a semicolon before **then** or before **else**. Each statement may be a compound statement; for example, we may write

```
var
  big, small : real;
....
if big > small
  then
    begin
      big := small;
      small := 0
    end
```

This has quite a different effect from the statements

```
if big > small
  then big := small;
small := 0
```

because in the second case the assignment *small* := 0 is executed, regardless of whether *big* > *small* or not.

The layout of **if** statements is very important. The principle to follow is that the **then** and **else** parts are always indented with respect to the **if**. The normal layout for an **if** statement is

```
if condition
  then statement₁
  else statement₂
```

If the statements are compound, the layout is modified in this way:

```
if condition
  then
    begin
      statements
    end
  else
    begin
      statements
    end
```

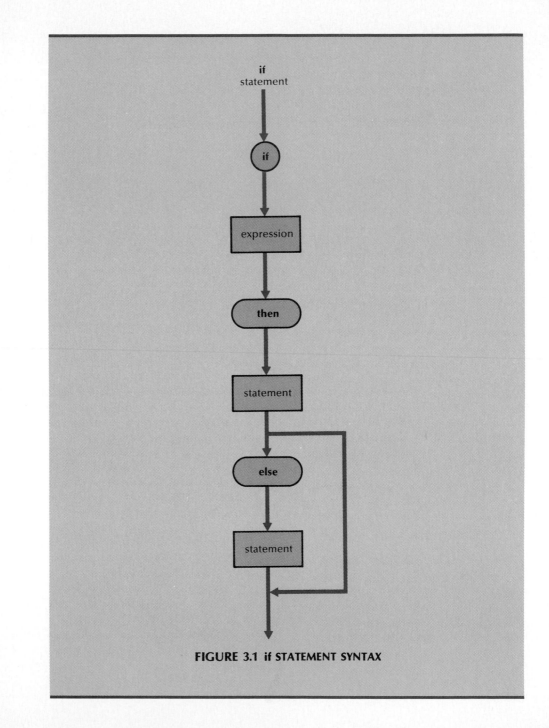

FIGURE 3.1 if STATEMENT SYNTAX

COMPOUND if STATEMENTS

The statements after **then** and **else** may themselves be **if** statements, and in this case the statement is called a *compound* **if** *statement*. The following statement is a compound **if** statement.

```
if charkind = digit
   then readnumber
   else
      if charkind = letter
         then readname
         else reporterror
```

Exactly one of the three actions, *readnumber*, *readname*, or *reporterror* will be executed, whatever the value of *charkind*. In this case, the **else** clause of the **if** statement is an **if** statement. If there are a number of successive tests of this form, the text will eventually drift off the right side of the page. The alternative layout shown below is recommended for deeply nested **if** statements. Note that this layout is still indicative of the action taken by the program.

```
if charkind = digit
   then readnumber
else if charkind = letter
   then readname
else reporterror
```

The other type of compound **if** statement, in which the **then** clause of an **if** statement is itself an **if** statement, looks like this.

```
if shape = circle
   then
      if radius > distance                          (3.2)
         then enclosed := true
         else enclosed := false
   else write ('Wrong shape.')
```

This kind of compound statement is better written in this form.

```
if shape ≠ circle
   then write ('Wrong shape.')
else if radius > distance
   then enclosed := true
else enclosed := false
```

By now, you may have realized that there is an even better way to write this statement.

```
if shape = circle
   then enclosed := radius > distance
   else write ('Wrong shape.')
```

When you cannot avoid writing a compound **if** statement of the form (3.2), use this layout:

```
if condition₁
   then
      if condition₂
         then
            if condition₃                        (3.3)
               then statement₁
               else statement₂
            else statement₃
      else statement₄
```

The following compound **if** statement is potentially ambiguous.

```
if condition₁
   then
      if condition₂
         then statement₁
         else statement₂
```

To which *if* does the **else** clause belong? The ambiguity cannot be resolved from the syntax diagrams. The rule is that the **else** clause belongs to the nearest **if** for which there is no **else** clause. This is what makes the compound **if** statements (3.2) and (3.3) confusing. Removing "**else** *statement₃*" from statement (3.3), for instance, changes the significance of "**else** *statement₄*."

APPLICATION: SOLVING A QUADRATIC EQUATION

As a less trivial example of the use of the **if** statement, we will design a program that attempts to find the roots of the quadratic equation

$$ax^2 + bx + c = 0.$$

The mathematician is in the fortunate position of being able to say that this is a quadratic equation only if $a \neq 0$, because this is how a quadratic equation is defined. The mathematician can then claim that all quadratic equations have exactly two roots, which may in some instances be equal to one another. Programmers are not as fortunate. We cannot assume, just because the user tells us to solve a quadratic equation, that $a \neq 0$. If our program is to be generally useful, it must handle the following cases correctly.

- If $a = 0$ and $b = 0$, the equation is either tautologous ($c = 0$) or contradictory ($c \neq 0$). In this case, we will print a message saying that the equation is degenerate.

■ If $a = 0$ and $b \neq 0$, there is one root with the value $-c/b$.
■ If $a \neq 0$ and $c = 0$, there are two roots, $-b/a$ and 0.
■ If none of these conditions apply, the equation is either

$$ax^2 + bx + c = 0 \qquad \text{(all coefficients nonzero)}$$

or

$$ax^2 + c = 0 \qquad (a \neq 0 \text{ and } c \neq 0).$$

In either of these cases we use the formula

$$\text{roots} = \frac{-b \pm \sqrt{b^2 - 4ac}}{2a}.$$

The quantity $b^2 - 4ac$ is called the *discriminant* of the equation. If *discriminant* > 0, there are two real roots; if *discriminant* $= 0$, there are two equal real roots; and if *discriminant* < 0, there are two complex roots. These considerations lead to the following program.

```pascal
{ Find the roots of a quadratic equation with given coefficients. }
program quadratic (input, output);
  var
    a, b, c, discriminant, re, im : real;
  begin
    read (a, b, c);
    if (a = 0) and (b = 0)
      then writeln ('The equation is degenerate.')
    else if a = 0
      then writeln ('The only root is ', -c / b)
    else if c = 0
      then writeln ('The roots are ', -b / a, ' and ', 0)
    else
      begin
        re := -b / (2 * a);
        discriminant := sqr (b) - 4 * a * c;
        im := sqrt (abs (discriminant)) / (2 * a);
        if discriminant ⩾ 0
          then writeln ('The roots are ', re + im,
                                      ' and ', re - im)
          else writeln ('The roots are complex: ',
                                re, '+I*', im,
                        ' and ', re, '-I*', im)
      end { else }
  end. { quadratic }
```

INPUT			OUTPUT
0	0	7	The equation is degenerate.
0	10	2	The only root is −0.200000
2	3	0	The roots are −1.500000 and 0
1	5	6	The roots are −2.000000 and −3.000000
1	1	1	The roots are complex: −5.000000 +I* 0.866025 and −5.000000 −I* 0.866025

There is one circumstance in which this program might give unreliable results. If b^2 is much larger than $4ac$, then

$$discriminant \simeq b^2$$

and one of the roots will be very small. The calculation of the small root involves the subtraction of two numbers that are almost equal. This may lead to a loss of precision. In this case, it would be better to calculate the value of the larger root first and then to find the smaller root from the relation

$$smallroot = c \,/\, (a \times largeroot)$$

3.2   THE while STATEMENT

We can specify a loop in a Pascal program by means of a **while**, **repeat**, or **for** statement. The form of the **while** statement is

while *condition* **do**
  statement

Statement is called the *body* of the **while** loop. The **while** statement is executed in the following way. First the processor evaluates *condition*. If the result is *false*, execution of the **while** statement is complete. If the result is *true*, *statement* is executed once, *condition* is tested again, and so on. After the **while** statement has been executed, we know that *condition* is *false*. For example, if we want to eliminate factors of 2 from the value of *product*, we can write

while not *odd* (*product*) **do**
  product := *product* **div** 2   (3.4)

If *product* is initially 60, the body of (3.4) will be executed twice and the final value of *product* will be 15. If *product* is an odd number on entry to (3.4) then the body will not be executed at all. This is an important and useful feature of the **while** statement; we will see many situations in which we may want to execute a loop zero times.

It is essential that the statement within the loop should eventually change the value of the condition because otherwise the loop will continue executing indefinitely. In the case of the **while** statement, there is the further requirement that the condition should have a well-defined value on entry to the statement.

In (3.4), the condition has a well-defined value on entry to the loop provided that the value of *product* is well defined. In order for the statement to terminate, the assignment must change the value of *product*, which it does unless

$$product = 0.$$

Statement (3.4) will loop indefinitely if it is executed with *product* = 0. We can prevent this by "guarding" it with an **if** statement.

(3.5)

```
if product ≠ 0
   then
      while not odd (product) do
         product := product div 2
```

The statement controlled by **while** can be a compound statement. In order to discover how many times the assignment in (3.5) is executed, we can insert a counter:

```
counter := 0;
if product ≠ 0
   then
      while not odd (product) do
         begin
           product := product div 2;
           counter := succ (counter)
         end
```

The next example is intended to clarify a common misconception about the **while** statement. What will the following program print?

```
{ Demonstrate operation of the while statement. }
program puzzle (output);
  var
    number : integer;
  begin
    number := 0;
    while number ≤ 10 do
      begin
        number := number + 1;
        write (number)
      end { while }
  end. { puzzle }
```

This program prints

$$1 \ 2 \ 3 \ 4 \ 5 \ 6 \ 7 \ 8 \ 9 \ 10 \ 11$$

At the beginning of the last iteration, *number* has the value 10 and the condition is *true*. During the last iteration, the statement

$$number := number + 1$$

assigns the value 11 to *number*, and this value is printed. It is sometimes assumed that the **while** statement watches the changing value of *number* in some mysterious way and terminates the loop as soon as *number* = 10, but this is not so. Remember, the condition is evaluated only at the beginning of each iteration.

Figure 3.2 shows the syntax of the **while** statement. The loop consists of a single statement. In most **while** statements, this will be a compound statement.

APPLICATION: NUMBER CONVERSION

As an example of the use of the **while** statement, we will design a program for number conversion. The standard procedure *read* is used to read from the input file. It converts a number from its representation as a string of decimal digits to its representation in the computer's internal form. *Read* cannot be used to perform this automatic conversion if there are non-numeric characters in the input file. For example, it could not be used if the input file contained messages such as

```
The values are 100 and 504.75
10 * (14.75 - 8.60)
```

Program *convert* is a program that will read from the input medium until it finds a digit, read more digits until it reaches the end of the number, and perform the conversion to internal form. Figure 3.3 is a syntax diagram of the numbers that Program *convert* can read. A number may contain a decimal point and, if it does, any digits after the decimal point will be read and interpreted correctly. The program will read these numbers correctly.

$$5 \qquad 7. \qquad 19.5 \qquad 0.732$$

It will ignore the decimal point in

$$.732$$

and read it as 732 because it recognizes a number by its first digit. Numbers with a fractional part are first read and converted as if they were integers; the program then counts the number of digits after the decimal point and uses this count as a scaling factor when all the digits have been read. For example, after reading

$$1234.5678$$

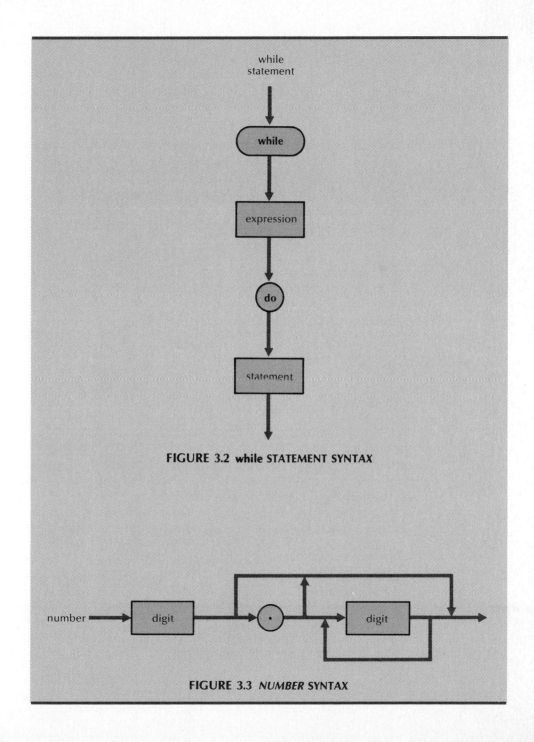

FIGURE 3.2 while STATEMENT SYNTAX

FIGURE 3.3 *NUMBER* SYNTAX

we have

$$value = 12345678$$
$$scale = 4$$

The conversion is completed by dividing *value* by 10^{scale} and in this case we have

$$12345678 / 10^4 = 1234.5678$$

as required. Rather than calculating the scale directly, the program repeatedly divides by 10. This is excusable in this instance because the program is clearly not intended to read very small numbers (smaller than 10^{-10}, say). A more efficient scaling algorithm would be used in a program intended to read numbers in scientific notation.

When Program *convert* has read a number, it will have read one character after the last digit of the number. This is inevitable because the only way the program can determine that the end of a number has been reached is to read a character that is not a digit.

The program has the following structure.

```
look for a digit;
read integer part of number;
if there is a decimal point
  then
     read the digits following the decimal point;
     scale the number;
write the result.
```

This kind of outline for a program, in which we use informal English to describe the actions and omit low-level coding details while defining the overall structure of the program, is often called *pseudo-code*. By writing pseudo-code, we can ease the transition from specification to final program. Pseudo-code is one of several ways of implementing the top-down strategy of programming mentioned at the end of Chapter 2. If we concentrate on getting the structure correct at an early stage, we can pay attention to the details later.

The pseudo-code statements "look for a digit," "read integer part of number," and "read the digits following the decimal point" all become **while** statements in the Pascal program. In each case we are interested only in whether or not the character is a digit. If we use *ch* to denote the last character read,

$$('0' \leqslant ch) \textbf{ and } (ch \leqslant '9')$$

is a suitable termination condition for the loop. In "look for a digit," we want to skip over characters other than digits, so we use the negated form of the expression:

$$\textbf{not } (('0' \leqslant ch) \textbf{ and } (ch \leqslant '9'))$$

We must also ensure that *ch* is defined on entry to the first loop. This is the purpose of the assignment statement *ch := blank*.

```
{ Convert an appropriately formed character string to a real number. }
program convert (input, output);
  const
    blank = ' ';
    point = '.';
    radix = 10;
  var
    result : real;
    scale : integer;
    ch : char;
  begin
    ch := blank;
    while not (('0' ≤ ch) and (ch < chr (ord ('0') + radix)) do
      read (ch);
    result := 0;
    while ('0' ≤ ch) and (ch < chr (ord ('0') + radix)) do
      begin
        result := radix * result + ord (ch) - ord ('0');
        read (ch)
      end; { while }
    if ch = point
      then
        begin
          scale := 0;
          read (ch);
          while ('0' ≤ ch) and (ch < chr (ord ('0') + radix)) do
            begin
              result := radix * result + ord (ch) - ord ('0');
              read (ch);
              scale := scale + 1
            end; { while }
          while scale > 0 do
            begin
              result := result / radix;
              scale := scale - 1
            end { while }
        end; { then }
    writeln (result)
  end. { convert }
```

INPUT	OUTPUT
1234.5678	1234.567800
.124	124.000000
0.999999999999999	1.000000

READING NUMBERS

The procedure *read* can be used with *integer* and *real* arguments, as we saw in Sections 2.4 and 2.5. Some problems arise, however, when we have to read a stream of numbers from the input file. Consider the problem of finding the mean of a set of real numbers. This requires counting the numbers and finding their sum. The following program appears to be a plausible solution.

```
{ Read a list of numbers and print their mean. }
program mean (input, output);
  var
    value, sum : real;
    count : integer;
begin
  sum := 0;
  count := 0;
  while not eof do
    begin
      read (value);
      sum := sum + value;
      count := count + 1
    end; { while }
  writeln ('Mean = ', sum / count)
end. { mean }
```

Unfortunately this program does not work. Suppose that the input file contains a single number, 4.7. This number will be read during the first iteration of the **while** loop, and at the end of this iteration

$$value = 4.7$$
$$sum = 4.7$$
$$count = 1$$

The problem arises because the number, 4.7, may be followed by blanks. If the input file is on cards, there will be blanks on the card. If you type 4.7 at a terminal, the carriage-return will appear to the program as a blank. Consequently, *eof* will not be true at the end of the first **while** cycle and the body of the **while** statement will be executed again. While looking for the next number, *read* will run off the end of the file and you will see an error message such as "Attempted to read past end of file."

There is no easy way to solve this problem. In simple programs we can specify that the file ends with a special value, say zero or a negative number, that acts as a *terminator*. This is an unsatisfactory solution for programs that will be used often, however, because if someone forgets the terminator, the program will abort. A better solution is to read the input character-by-character and perform the conversions explicitly as we did in Program *convert*.

3.3 THE repeat STATEMENT

We have already used the **repeat** statement informally in Program *squareroots* of Chapter 1 and in several other examples in the text. The **repeat** statement has two parts: the *body* and the *termination condition*. The general form of the **repeat** statement is

```
repeat
  statement₁;
  statement₂;
  ....
  statementₙ
until condition
```

The effect of the **repeat** statement is that the statement sequence is executed once and then *condition* is evaluated. If *condition* is *true*, the statement is complete; otherwise the statement sequence is executed again, *condition* is evaluated again, and so on. Unlike the **while** statement, in which the body consists of a single statement, the body of the **repeat** statement consists of a sequence of statements.

Like the **while** statement, the **repeat** statement is used when we do not know at the time of writing the program how many repetitions will be necessary. For example, if we want to know how many terms of the harmonic series are needed to satisfy the inequality

$$1 + \frac{1}{2} + \frac{1}{3} + \ldots + \frac{1}{n} > limit,$$

we can use a **repeat** statement, as in Program *series*.

```
{ Compute partial sums of the harmonic
  series until a given value is achieved. }
program series (input, output);
  var
    termcount : integer;
    sum, limit : real;
  begin
    termcount := 0;
    sum := 0;
    read (limit);
    repeat
      termcount := termcount + 1;
      sum := sum + 1 / termcount
    until sum > limit;
    write (termcount)
  end. { series }
```

INPUT	OUTPUT
5	83
10	12367

CODING LOOPS

There are five things to consider when you are writing a loop.

- The initial conditions must be correct.
- The statements within a loop must be sequenced correctly and there must be at least one statement that has an effect on the terminating condition.
- The termination condition must eventually be satisfied, otherwise the loop would continue forever.
- The control structure should be appropriate to the task performed by the loop. If there are circumstances in which the body of the loop should not be executed at all, a **while** statement is appropriate. If the body of the loop must always be executed at least once, a **repeat** statement may be appropriate.
- The *first* and *last* iterations must be correct.

In well-written Pascal programs, the **while** statement appears more often than the **repeat** statement. This is because a program must always perform correctly in extreme situations. For example, a program that processes a list of items should be able to process a list that contains no items at all. If you are in doubt as to whether **repeat** or **while** is the better construction, try **while** first.

Careless coding of loops often leads to "off-by-one" errors. The program

```
n := 1;
repeat
    write (n);
    n := succ (n)
until n = 10
```
(3.6)

prints

1 2 3 4 5 6 7 8 9

Suppose that this program was intended to print numbers up to 10. It is easy to make a hasty correction such as

```
n := 1;
repeat
    n := succ (n);
    write (n)
until n = 10
```
(3.7)

This program, however, prints

2 3 4 5 6 7 8 9 10

The correct solution is to change one of the boundary conditions: either change the termination condition of (3.6) to n = 11, or change the first assignment statement of (3.7) to n: = 0. Note that in either case the range of values assumed by n is one greater than the range of values printed.

The first two **while** statements of Program *convert* in Section 3.2 can be written as **repeat** statements. The first loop, which looks for a digit, must always examine at least one character, and can be written

```
repeat
    read (ch)
until ('0' ≤ ch) and (ch ≤ '9')
```

On entry to the second loop, we know that *ch* is a digit, and consequently the body of this loop must be executed at least once. We can write the loop in this form:

```
repeat
    result := radix * result + ord (ch) − ord ('0');
    read (ch)
until not (('0' ≤ ch) and (ch ≤ '9'))
```

The termination condition of the repeat statement is clearer if it is written without negation.

$$(ch < '0') \textbf{ or } (ch > '9')$$

The body of the third loop, however, may not be executed at all if there are no digits after the decimal point, and therefore the **while** statement is appropriate.

repeat STATEMENT SYNTAX

Figure 3.4 is the syntax diagram for the **repeat** statement. The reserved words, **repeat** and **until,** act as statement brackets in the same way as **begin** and **end.** Consequently, several statements separated by semicolons may appear between **repeat** and **until.** The layout convention for the **repeat** statement is that the **until** is placed directly underneath the **repeat** to which it corresponds and the statements between **repeat** and **until** are indented.

APPLICATION: CALCULATION OF A SQUARE ROOT

We will use the **repeat** statement to design a more elaborate version of Program *squareroots* (Section 1.3), in which the square root is calculated by the program itself rather than by the standard function *sqrt.* As in Program *squareroots,* we read a number and reject it if its value is negative. If the value is zero, we can print the result immediately. If the value is not zero, we use Newton's method for calculating a square root.

If *app* is an approximation to $\sqrt{number}$

then (*number* / *app* + *app*) / 2 is a better one.

The program uses 1 as a first approximation and then iterates until a sufficiently accurate value of $\sqrt{number}$ is obtained. The problem in writing this program is to select a suitable criterion for ending the iteration. It is not satisfactory to use a condition such as

$$|number - app^2| < 10^{-6}$$

because if $number > 10^{10}$, we are asking for more accuracy than we can reasonably expect, and if $number < 10^{-10}$, we can expect extremely inaccurate

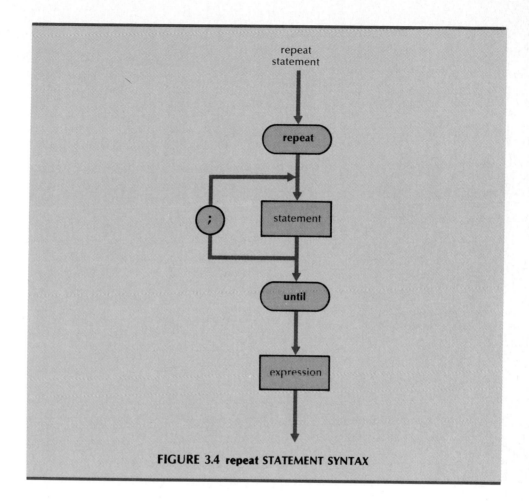

FIGURE 3.4 repeat STATEMENT SYNTAX

results. It is therefore necessary to use a ratio criterion as the termination condition, and we choose

$$|number\ /\ app^2 - 1| < 10^{-6}.$$

This ensures that our result will be accurate to within a few parts per million whatever the value of *number*.

Program *findsquareroots* uses two nested **repeat** statements. The outer loop reads numbers and prints their square roots, terminating when it has read a zero. The inner loop applies Newton's formula until the required precision has been attained.

```
{ Read numbers and print their square roots.
  The program terminates when it reads 0. }
program findsquareroots (input, output);
  const
    epsilon = 1E-6;
  var
    number, root : real;
  begin
    repeat
      read (number);
      if number < 0
        then writeln (number,' does not have a real square root.')
      else if number = 0
        then writeln (0)
      else { number > 0 }
        begin
          root := 1;
          repeat
            root := (number / root + root) / 2
          until abs (number / sqr (root) - 1) < epsilon;
          writeln (root)
        end { else }
    until number = 0
  end. { findsquareroots }
```

INPUT							OUTPUT
1	2	3	4	5	−1	0	1.000000
							1.414214
							1.732051
							2.000000
							2.236067
							−1 does not have a real square root
							0

3.4   THE for STATEMENT

When we wish to execute a statement repetitively and the number of repetitions does not depend on the effect of statements within the loop, the appropriate construction is the **for** loop. At the beginning of Section 3.3, we used the **repeat** statement to find how many terms of the harmonic series are required for their sum to exceed a given limit. The converse problem, finding the sum given the number of terms, is most appropriately expressed with a **for** statement.

```
{ Write the sum of a given number
  of terms of the harmonic series. }
program harmonicseries (input, output);
  var
    term, numberofterms : integer;
    sum : real;
  begin
    read (numberofterms);
    sum := 0.0;
    for term := 1 to numberofterms do
      sum := sum + 1 / term;
    writeln (sum)
  end. { harmonicseries }
```

The effect of the **for** statement in this program is to execute the assignment

```
sum := sum + 1 / term
```

for each integral value of term from 1 to numberofterms. If

```
numberofterms = 1
```

the assignment is executed only once and the program will print 1. If

```
numberofterms < 1
```

the assignment will not be executed at all and the program will print 0.

The general form of the **for** statement is

```
for cv := expression₁ to expression₂ do
  S
```

and it is equivalent to the following compound statement.

```
begin
  temp₁ := expression₁;
  temp₂ := expression₂
  if  temp₁ ≤ temp₂
    then
      begin
        cv := temp₁;
        S;
        while cv ≠ temp₂ do
          begin
            cv := succ (cv);
            S
          end
      end
end
```

The identifier *cv* is called the *control variable* of the **for** statement. The statement *S* is the *body* of the **for** loop. *S* must not contain assignments to *cv*. The variables $temp_1$ and $temp_2$ have the same type as *cv*. They are created by the compiler and cannot be accessed by the program. The point of introducing them is to show that $expression_1$ and $expression_2$ are evaluated only once, before the loop is entered. It follows that the limits of a **for** loop cannot be changed by statements within the loop.

The types of *cv*, $expression_1$, and $expression_2$ must all be the same, and this type must be one for which *succ* is defined. This precludes the use of a control variable of type *real* in a **for** statement. The **for** statement will have no effect if

$$expression_1 > expression_2.$$

When the **for** statement terminates, the value of the control variable is undefined.

The **for** statement is redundant because any **for** statement can be written as a **while** statement. Nevertheless, there are good reasons for using the **for** statement wherever possible. The **for** statement conveys more information to someone reading the program. The values that will be assigned to the control variable and the number of times that the loop will be executed are both immediately apparent. The same information is also useful to the compiler, which may be able to generate more efficient code from a **for** statement than from an equivalent **while** statement.

for STATEMENT SYNTAX

Figure 3.5 is a syntax diagram for the **for** statement. The keyword **to** in the **for** statement may be replaced by **downto**. The **for** statement becomes

$$\textbf{for } cv := expression_1 \textbf{ downto } expression_2 \textbf{ do}$$
$$S$$

In this case the control variable is decremented, rather than incremented, in each iteration. This form of the **for** statement will have no effect if

$$expression_1 < expression_2.$$

APPLICATION: MUSICAL PITCHES

The ratio of two musical notes a semitone apart in the equitempered scale is

$$\sqrt[12]{2} \simeq 1.059463094$$

and the standard concert pitch is usually obtained by tuning middle A to 440 cycles per second. The lowest note on a piano is four octaves below this A and

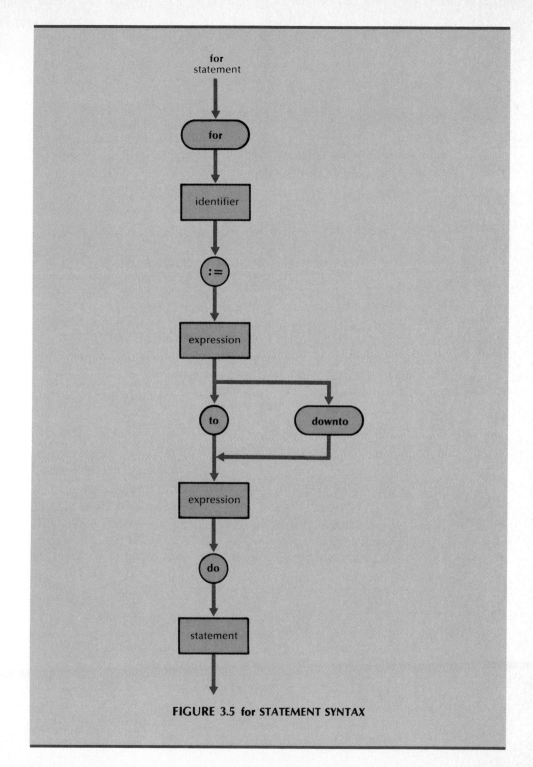

FIGURE 3.5 for STATEMENT SYNTAX

therefore should be tuned to

$$\frac{440}{2^4} = 27.5 \text{ cycles per second.}$$

The following program could be used to calculate the theoretical frequencies of the other notes of the piano.

```
{ Calculate and print the frequency of each piano note. }
program frequencies (output);
  const
    lowestnote = 27.5;            { c/s : frequency of low A }
    keyboardlength = 88;          { Number of keys }
    semitone = 1.05946;           { Frequency ratio of adjacent notes }
  var
    frequency : real;
    note : integer;
  begin
    frequency := lowestnote;
    for note := 1 to keyboardlength do
      begin
        writeln (frequency);
        frequency := frequency * semitone
      end { for }
  end. { frequencies }
```

This program will not give accurate results for the higher notes because multiplication errors will accumulate. When this program is run on a computer that provides seven decimal digits of precision, it gives 4185.952 c/s as the frequency of the highest note. This is about 0.057 c/s lower than the correct frequency, which is 4186.009 c/s to seven significant figures. It is better to calculate each value independently in loops of this kind than to derive each new value from the preceding value, even though the program may execute more slowly as a result. In this case we can use the fact that *frequency* is related to *note* by

$$frequency = lowestnote \times 2^{(note/12)}.$$

The exponent can be calculated from the algebraic identity

$$a^x = e^{x \ln(a)}$$

and in Pascal notation we have

```
frequency := lowestnote * exp (note * ln (2) / 12)
```

The lowest note now corresponds to the value *note* = 0 because *exp* (0) = 1. Accordingly, we change the bounds of the **for** loop to 0 and *keyboardlength*−1.

```
{ Calculate and print the frequency of each note of a piano. }
program frequencies (output);
  const
    lowestnote = 27.5;          { c/s : frequency of low A }
    keyboardlength = 88;        { Number of notes }
  var
    frequency : real;
    note : integer;
  begin
    for note := 0 to keyboardlength - 1 do
      begin
        frequency := lowestnote * exp (note * ln (2) / 12);
        writeln (frequency)
      end { for }
  end. { frequencies }
```

The program will now give accurate results, but it evaluates ln (2)/12 during each iteration: 88 times altogether. We can eliminate this inefficiency by introducing *ratio*, a *real* variable initialized by the assignment

```
ratio := ln (2) / 12
```

Here is the final version of Program *frequencies*.

```
{ Calculate the frequency of each note of a piano. }
program frequencies (output);
  const
    lowestnote = 27.5;          { c/s : frequency of low A }
    keyboardlength = 88;        { Number of notes }
  var
    frequency, ratio : real;
    note : integer;
  begin
    ratio := ln (2) / 12;
    for note := 0 to keyboardlength - 1 do
      begin
        frequency := lowestnote * exp (ratio * note);
        writeln (frequency)
      end { for }
  end. { frequencies }
```

OUTPUT
27.50000
29.13522
30.86769
32.70319
34.64781
36.70808

. . .

4186.003

When this program is run on a computer with a *real* precision of seven decimal digits, the highest frequency calculated is only 0.006 c/s below the correct frequency. Although all three programs produce quite accurate results, the error in the highest frequency calculated by the first version is ten times larger than the corresponding error in the third version.

3.5 EXERCISES

3.1 Write a program that calculates cube roots, using the fact that if α is an approximation for $\sqrt[3]{x}$, a better one is

$$\beta = \frac{2\alpha + x/\alpha^2}{3}.$$

3.2 Modify Program *frequencies* so that it prints two blank lines after each octave. (An octave contains 12 semitones.)

3.3 Show that
   a) any **repeat** statement can be rewritten using **if** and **while**;
   b) any **while** statement can be rewritten using **if** and **repeat**.

3.4 The following statement was found in a badly written Pascal program.

```
if a < b then if c < d then        x := 1
else if a < c then if b < d then x := 2
                                else x := 3
else if a < d then if b < c then x := 4
                                else x := 5
                           else x := 6
                      else x := 7
```

a) Rewrite this statement using a better layout.
b) Are there any redundant or contradictory conditions?
c) Write a statement that has the same effect and is simpler.

3.5 The formula of Newton and Raphson may be used to solve the equation

$$x \times \sin(x) = 1$$

by successive approximation. The recurrence relation is

$$x_{n+1} = \frac{1 + x_n^2 \cos(x_n)}{\sin(x_n) + x_n \cos(x_n)}.$$

Write a program that tabulates the positive roots of this equation.

3.6 Write a program that will make change for any sum of money up to 99 cents using the coins of denomination 1 cent, 5 cents, 10 cents, and 25 cents.

3.7 Extend Program *mean* (Section 3.2) so that it prints the standard deviation, σ, of the numbers read, as well as μ. The value of σ may be calculated from the formula

$$\sigma^2 = \sum_i \frac{(x_i - \mu)^2}{n - 1}.$$

3.8 In the inequality (3.8), n is a positive integer. Write a program to test the truth of this inequality.

$$\frac{1}{n + 1} < \ln\left(\frac{n + 1}{n}\right) < \frac{1}{n} \tag{3.8}$$

3.9 Modify Program *convert* so that it will read and correctly interpret
a) negative numbers;
b) octal (base eight) numbers.

3.10 Write a program that reads and evaluates expressions such as

$$+20 - 4 - 3 + 169;$$

The numbers are integers. Each is preceded by a sign, and the expression is terminated by a semicolon.

3.11 Improve Program *quadratic* so that if

$$4ac < epsilon \times b^2$$

the root with the larger absolute value is calculated first, and the smaller one is calculated from

$$smallroot = \frac{c}{a \times largeroot}.$$

3.12 Write a program that sums the series

$$1 + x + \frac{x^2}{2!} + \frac{x^3}{3!} + \ldots + \frac{x^n}{n!}$$

forwards and backwards and compares the results. Why is this series unreliable as a means of evaluating e^x for some values of x? (Use *real* variables to calculate the factorials, or you may encounter integer overflow.)

3.13 A *trial* consists of tossing a coin until heads appears. The average number of tosses in a trial is

$$\lim_{n \to \infty} \sum_{i=1}^{i=n} \frac{i}{2^i}$$

Find an approximate value for this limit.

4

PROCEDURES AND FUNCTIONS

The control structures described in the previous chapter are the basic building blocks of Pascal programs. It is easy to see, however, that a long program consisting only of variable declarations and statements would be difficult to write and impossible to understand. In this chapter we introduce the principal device for controlling the complexity of large computer programs—the procedure.

In a top-down approach to programming, our starting point is a problem statement. We attempt to divide the problem into subproblems that are easier to solve than the original problem. We continue to divide the subproblems until they correspond to simple programs that consist of a few Pascal statements. For example, many programming problems can be divided immediately into three subproblems: read data, perform calculations, and print results. These subproblems can be treated as individual modules when we write the program.

The final program will consist of a collection of modules, and each module will correspond to a subproblem. In many cases the organization of these modules will be hierarchical. The module that represents the original, undivided problem appears at the "top" of the hierarchy and makes demands on modules "lower" in the hierarchy.

If we are to write programs as collections of modules, we must be able to group statements together to form a module and we must be able to refer to these modules as logical entities. A Pascal procedure is simply a program module that may be referenced by its name.

4.1   PROCEDURES

Suppose we want to write a program that reads text from a file and ignores blanks in the text. For a top-down design, we will need a statement or group of statements to skip over blanks. We may decide to give this task a name such as *skipblanks*. In the final stages of coding, *skipblanks* will assume a concrete form, such as

$$
\begin{array}{ll}
\textbf{repeat} & \\
\quad read\ (ch) & \hspace{3cm}(4.1)\\
\textbf{until}\ ch \neq blank &
\end{array}
$$

The name *skipblanks* was useful in the design because it captured the function of the task (*what* is the task, or what does the module do) without specifying the implementation of the task (*how* the task is performed). *Skipblanks* is an *abstraction* of the concrete statement (4.1). We can retain the separation between abstract and concrete in the program by declaring *skipblanks* as a Pascal procedure. This is done in the following way.

```
procedure skipblanks;
  begin
    repeat
      read (ch)
    until ch ≠ blank
  end;
```

Once we have written this declaration, the statement

```
skipblanks
```

will have precisely the same effect as the original **repeat** statement. The statement *skipblanks* is a *procedure call,* and we say that it *invokes,* or *calls*, the procedure *skipblanks*.

We will use the procedures to develop a program that computes partial sums of the harmonic series. The program will evaluate $H(n)$ for various values of n, where

$$H(n) = 1 + \frac{1}{2} + \frac{1}{3} + \cdots + \frac{1}{n}.$$

The result of the calculation is to be expressed in the form of a rational number, that is, a number of the form

$$\frac{numerator}{denominator}$$

where *numerator* and *denominator* are integers. We represent a rational number in Pascal by two integer variables.

We will need a procedure to remove common factors from the numerator and denominator. The best way to do this is to divide the numerator and the denominator by their greatest common divisor. We use a version of Euclid's algorithm to calculate the greatest common divisor.

```
procedure lowterm;
  begin
    numcopy := numerator;
    dencopy := denominator;
    while dencopy ≠ 0 do
      begin
        remainder := numcopy mod dencopy;
        numcopy := dencopy;
        dencopy := remainder
      end; { while }
    if numcopy > 1
      then
        begin
          numerator := numerator div numcopy;
          denominator := denominator div numcopy
        end
  end; { lowterm }
```

Program *cancelfactors* is a complete program that declares and uses the procedure *lowterm*. Notice the ordering in this program. We have

> program heading
> variable declarations
> procedure declarations
> body of program

When program *cancelfactors* is executed, the first instruction obeyed is

```
read (numerator, denominator)
```

The statements contained in the procedure *lowterm* are not executed until the statement

```
lowterm
```

is executed. This ordering is determined by the Pascal convention that we must define an entity before we use it. The variables are used within the procedure and therefore must be declared before it. The main program makes use of the procedure and therefore must follow it.

The first line of the procedure declaration, in this case

```
procedure lowterm;
```

is called the *procedure head*. The compound statement immediately following it is called the *procedure body*, and it must be terminated with a semicolon. We have put a blank line before and after the procedure declaration to make the structure of the program apparent. For a listing written by a computer printer, we should use an even more spacious layout. A good convention is to have blank lines between constant and variable declaration sections and two or three blank lines to set off procedures.

```
{ Cancel common factors from a fraction. }
program cancelfactors (input, output);
  var
    numerator, denominator, numcopy,
    dencopy, remainder : integer;

  { Divide numerator and denominator by their GCD. }
  procedure lowterm;
    begin
      numcopy := numerator;
      dencopy := denominator;
      while dencopy ≠ 0 do
        begin
          remainder := numcopy mod dencopy;
          numcopy := dencopy;
          dencopy := remainder;
        end; { while }
      if numcopy > 1
        then
          begin
            numerator := numerator div numcopy;
            denominator := denominator div numcopy
          end { then }
    end; { lowterm }
```

```
begin { cancelfactors }
  read (numerator, denominator);
  lowterm;
  writeln (numerator, denominator)
end. { cancelfactors }
```

We have declared the variables *numcopy*, *dencopy*, and *remainder*, along with *numerator* and *denominator*, in the main program. They are called *global variables* and they may be used anywhere in the procedure *lowterm* or in the main program. It is not desirable to use them in the main program, however, because any call to *lowterm* will alter their values. It is clear that they belong to the procedure and not to the program as a whole. We may indicate this by placing their declarations within the procedure:

```
program cancelfactors (input, output);
  var
    numerator, denominator : integer;
  procedure lowterm;
    var
      numcopy, dencopy, remainder : integer;
    ....
```

The variables *numcopy*, *dencopy*, and *remainder* are now *local variables*. Figure 4.1(a) shows the situation before *lowterm* is called; the variables *numcopy*, *dencopy*, and *remainder* have not yet been allocated. Figure 4.1(b) represents

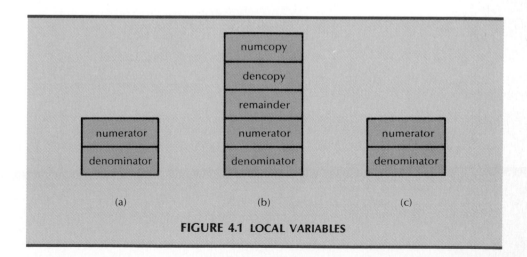

FIGURE 4.1 LOCAL VARIABLES

the situation during the execution of procedure *lowterm: numcopy, dencopy,* and *remainder* have been allocated and are in use. The procedure can still refer to the global variables *numerator* and *denominator.* In Fig. 4.1(c) the procedure has finished executing, and *numcopy, dencopy,* and *remainder* no longer exist. If the procedure is called again, the local variables are reallocated. You must not assume that when a procedure is called for a second time, its local variables still have the values they had during the previous invocation. It is important to distinguish the static situation (the text of the program) from the dynamic situation (the execution of the program). It would be incorrect to use *numcopy* in the main program because *numcopy* is defined only in the procedure *lowterm.*

The section of a program in which a variable can legally be used is called the *scope* of the variable. The scope of a variable begins with its declaration and ends at the end of the block containing the declaration. In the following listing, the outer box indicates the scope of the global variables of program *cancelfactors* and the inner box indicates the scope of its local variables.

```
program cancelfactors (input, output);
   var
      numerator, denominator : integer;
   procedure lowterm;
      var
         numcopy, dencopy, remainder : integer;
      begin
         ....
      end; { lowterm }

   begin
      ....
   end. { cancelfactors }
```

The declaration of the procedure *lowterm* is still restricted. Before we use it, we must make sure that the rational number we want to reduce to its lowest terms is stored in the variables *numerator* and *denominator.* If, for example, it was stored in *top* and *bottom,* we would have to make copies of these variables before calling *lowterm:*

```
numerator := top;
denominator := bottom;
lowterm
```

It would be easier to use *lowterm* if we could give it arguments. We would then be able to reduce *numerator/denominator* to lowest terms by writing

```
lowterm (numerator, denominator)
```

and *top/bottom* to lowest terms by writing

```
lowterm (top, bottom)
```

We can do this quite easily by modifying the declaration of *lowterm* to accommodate the parameters.

```
procedure lowterm (var num, den : integer);
  var
    numcopy, dencopy, remainder : integer;
  begin
    numcopy := num;
    dencopy := den;
    while dencopy ≠ 0 do
      begin
        remainder := numcopy mod dencopy;
        numcopy := dencopy;
        dencopy := remainder
      end; { while }
    if numcopy > 1
      then
        begin
          num := num div numcopy;
          den := den div numcopy;
        end
  end; { lowterm }
```

Num and *den* are now *formal parameters* of *lowterm*. The procedure head is extended by a *parameter list* in which the formal parameters are declared. We invoke the new version of *lowterm* by calling

```
lowterm (numerator, denominator)
```

or

```
lowterm (top, bottom)
```

as above. In these calls, the variables *numerator*, *denominator*, *top*, and *bottom* are *actual parameters*. The version of program *cancelfactors* that follows does the same thing as the previous version, but parameters are used for communication between the main program and procedure *lowterm*. The variables and formal parameters of *lowterm* are all local variables, and the procedure has its own local working space, *numcopy, dencopy,* and *remainder,* and an interface to the rest of the program, *num* and *den*.

```
{ Cancel common factors from a fraction. }
program cancelfactors (input, output);
  var
    numerator, denominator : integer;
  { Divide num and den by their GCD. }
  procedure lowterm (var num, den : integer);
    var
      numcopy, dencopy, remainder : integer;
    begin
      numcopy := num;
      dencopy := den;
      while dencopy ≠ 0 do
        begin
          remainder := numcopy mod dencopy;
          numcopy := dencopy;
          dencopy := remainder
        end; { while }
      if numcopy > 1
        then
          begin
            num := num div numcopy;
            den := den div numcopy
          end { then }
    end; { lowterm }
  begin { cancelfactors }
    read (numerator, denominator);
    lowterm (numerator, denominator);
    writeln (numerator, denominator)
  end. { cancelfactors }
```

INPUT		OUTPUT	
9	24	3	8
1024	128	8	1

The distinction between formal and actual parameters may be clarified by a comparison with the proof of a theorem in elementary geometry. Such a proof is written in terms of symbolic angles and lengths. These angles and lengths correspond to the formal parameters of a procedure. The assertion made by the proof is that if we substituted actual angles and lengths, such as 30 degrees and 4 inches, for the angles and lengths in the proof, every statement in the proof would be true. By making this substitution, we would have proved a particular case of the theorem. This process is analogous to providing actual parameters to a procedure in a program. A geometric proof is true for a class of figures, and a procedure represents a class of computations. An invocation of the procedure performs a computation which is a member of this class. Similarly, we can see that any computer program represents a class of computations and that executing a program with a particular set of input data makes the program perform a computation which is a member of this class.

The program to compute partial sums of the harmonic series requires one more procedure. We have to be able to add two rational numbers according to the formula

$$\frac{num}{den} = \frac{num1}{den1} + \frac{num2}{den2} = \frac{num1 * den2 + num2 * den1}{den1 * den2}.$$

We use this formula to declare the procedure *addrationals*.

```
procedure addrationals (var num, den : integer;
                        num1, den1, num2, den2 : integer);
  begin
    num := num1 * den2 + num2 * den1;
    den := den1 * den2
  end; { addrationals }
```

The parameters *num* and *den* are preceded by the reserved word **var** and are called *variable parameters*. The parameters *num1*, *den1*, *num2*, and *den2* are not preceded by var and are called *value parameters*. We discuss the distinction between variable and value parameters in Section 4.2.

We can modify the procedure *addrationals* so that it uses only four parameters and implements the "assignment"

$$\frac{num1}{den1} := \frac{num1 * den2 + num2 * den1}{den1 * den2}$$

The new declaration is

```
procedure addrationals (var num1, den1 : integer;
                             num2, den2 : integer);
begin
  num1 := num1 * den2 + num2 * den1;
  den1 := den1 * den2
end; { addrationals }
```

Note that although the order of the two assignment statements was immaterial in the first version of *addrationals*, it is significant in this version.

Program *sumharmonics* is a complete program that uses the two procedures we have declared. The partial sums *H* (*n*) are computed for a specified number of terms and each partial sum is printed.

```
{ Sum terms of the harmonic series,
  using exact rational arithmetic. }
program sumharmonics (input, output);
  const
    firstterm = 2;
  var
    numerator, denominator,
    lastterm, termcount : integer;

  { Divide num and den by their GCD. }
  procedure lowterm (var num, den : integer);
    var
      numcopy, dencopy, remainder : integer;
    begin
      numcopy := num;
      dencopy := den;
      while dencopy ≠ 0 do
        begin
          remainder := numcopy mod dencopy;
          numcopy := dencopy;
          dencopy := remainder
        end; { while }
      if numcopy > 1
        then
          begin
            num := num div numcopy;
            den := den div numcopy
          end { then }
    end; { lowterm }
```

```
                { Calculate the exact sum of two rational numbers. }
                procedure addrationals (var num1, den1 : integer;
                                            num2, den2 : integer);
                  begin
                    num1 := num1 * den2 + num2 * den1;
                    den1 := den1 * den2
                  end; { addrationals }
                begin { sumharmonics }
                  numerator := 1;
                  denominator := 1;
                  read (lastterm);
                  for termcount := firstterm to lastterm do
                    begin
                      addrationals (numerator, denominator, 1, termcount);
                      lowterm (numerator, denominator);
                      writeln (numerator : 1, '/', denominator : 1)
                    end { for }
                end. { sumharmonics }
```

INPUT	OUTPUT
10	3/2
	11/6
	25/12
	137/60
	49/20
	363/140
	761/280
	7129/2520
	7381/2520

4.2   VARIABLES AND PARAMETERS

It is now time to look more closely at the distinction between local and global variables and at the two parameter-passing mechanisms that Pascal provides. We will examine these distinctions in the light of a simple example that uses only one procedure.

```
{ Local and global variables (1) }
program simple (output);
  var
    x : integer;
  procedure change;
    begin
      x := 1
    end; { change }
  begin
    x := 0;
    change;
    write (x)
  end. { simple }
```

This program has one variable, x, and it is a global variable. The value of x is initially set to zero by the main program. The program calls the procedure change, which changes the value of x to 1, and this value is printed by the last statement in the program, write (x). Now consider a program that is almost the same but in which the procedure has a local variable declaration.

```
{ Local and global variables (2) }
program simple (output);
  var
    x : integer;
  procedure change;
    var
      x : integer;
    begin
      x := 1
    end; { change }
  begin
    x := 0;
    change;
    write (x)
  end. { simple }
```

This version of the program has two variables, both called x. One of them is a global variable and the other, declared in the procedure, is local to the procedure. The assignment x := 1 in the procedure sets the value of the local x to 1. The declaration of the local variable x overrides the global declaration of x within the body of the procedure. In fact, declaring the local variable x to have the same name as the global variable *x* prevents the procedure from accessing the global variable *x* at all. Accordingly, the statement $x := 1$ inside the procedure *change* has no effect on the global variable *x*, which remains zero, and this is what the program prints.

In the next version of Program *simple*, we give the procedure *change* a parameter.

```
{ Local and global variables (3) }
program simple (output);
  var
    x : integer;
  procedure change (var y : integer);
    begin
      y := 1
    end; { change }
  begin
    x := 0;
    change (x);
    write (x)
  end. { simple }
```

This program has a global variable called *x* and a procedure, *change*, with a formal parameter. We have called the formal parameter *y* to avoid confusion, but in fact the program would work in just the same way if we wrote *x* where *y* occurs. The declaration of *y* in the procedure head is preceded by **var**. This defines *y* as a variable parameter, which in turn means that *y* can be regarded as a *synonym* for the actual parameter *x* during the execution of the procedure: whatever happens to *y* will also happen to *x*. Accordingly, the assignment $y := 1$ will change the value of the actual parameter *x* to 1, and the program prints 1. When the formal parameter is a variable parameter, denoted by **var**, the corresponding actual parameter must be a variable: it cannot be an expression. The calls

> change (2 * x)

and

> change (2)

are not allowed with this declaration of *change* because 2 * x and 2 are expressions, not variables.

The other kind of formal parameter is called a *value parameter* and it is written without the preceding **var**.

```
{ Local and global variables (4) }
program simple (output);
  var
    x : integer;
  procedure change (y : integer);
    begin
      y := 1
    end; { change }
  begin
    x := 0;
    change (x);
    write (x)
  end. { simple }
```

Once again we have a global variable, *x*, and a formal parameter, *y*. The procedure call

$$change \ (x)$$

implicitly executes the assignment statement

$$y := x$$

before executing the first statement of the procedure body. After entry to the procedure body there is no further relationship between *x* and *y*, and the assignment

$$y := 1$$

has no effect on the value of *x*. The program will therefore print zero, the value *x* had on entry to the procedure. When a formal parameter is a value parameter, the corresponding actual parameter may be an expression. With the procedure *change* as it is declared in this example, we could write the calling statements

$$change \ (2 * x)$$

or

$$change \ (2)$$

In the first case, there would be an implicit assignment

$$y := 2 * x$$

and in the second case

$$y := 2$$

before the procedure was executed.

You may find it helpful to remember the distinction between value and variable parameters in the following way. The actual parameter corresponding to a value formal parameter must be an entity that could appear only on the right side of an assignment statement. The actual parameter corresponding to a variable formal parameter must be an entity that could appear on the left side of an assignment statement.

Sometimes an object that may appear on the left side of an assignment statement is called an *L-value* and an object that may appear on the right side of an assignment statement is called an *R-value*. Using this terminology, we can say that an actual variable parameter must be an L-value and an actual value parameter must be an R-value.

The expression corresponding to a value parameter must have the same type as the parameter. As we saw in Chapter 2, however, it is a general rule in Pascal that an *integer* expression may be used wherever a *real* expression is expected, and so we may use an *integer* expression as the actual parameter corresponding to a *real* formal parameter.

The following rules will help you to decide whether to use value or variable parameters.

- If the purpose of the procedure is to change the parameter, use **var**.
- If it is reasonable to pass an expression to the procedure, do not use **var**.
- If neither of these conditions applies, it is usually best to omit **var**. (We discuss the circumstances in which **var** should be included in Section 6.1.)

PROCEDURE SYNTAX

Figure 4.2 is the syntax diagram for a *parameter list*. The parameter list may be omitted altogether, in which case the procedure must refer to nonlocal variables if it is to have any effect on the program. Figure 4.3 shows the syntax diagram for a *procedure declaration*. The *procedure head* comprises the keyword **procedure**, the procedure identifier, and the parameter list. The *procedure body*, a *block*, is the syntactic structure introduced in Fig. 2.11. We can now extend the definition of block to include the declarations of procedures and functions, as shown in Fig. 4.4. We discuss the circumstances in which we use the directive *forward* on page 117.

The syntax diagram for a Pascal program is shown in Fig. 4.5, which is a reproduction of Fig. 2.9. Comparing Figs. 4.3 and 4.5, we see that a program is in fact a procedure with an abnormal head and the special terminator, ".". The standard types, constants, and functions are nonlocal identifiers for this "procedure." This implies that we are allowed to define a new "local" value for any of the standard identifiers in a program. For example, we could redefine *integer* or *sqrt*. Such redefinitions are extremely confusing to anyone who has to read the program and therefore should be avoided.

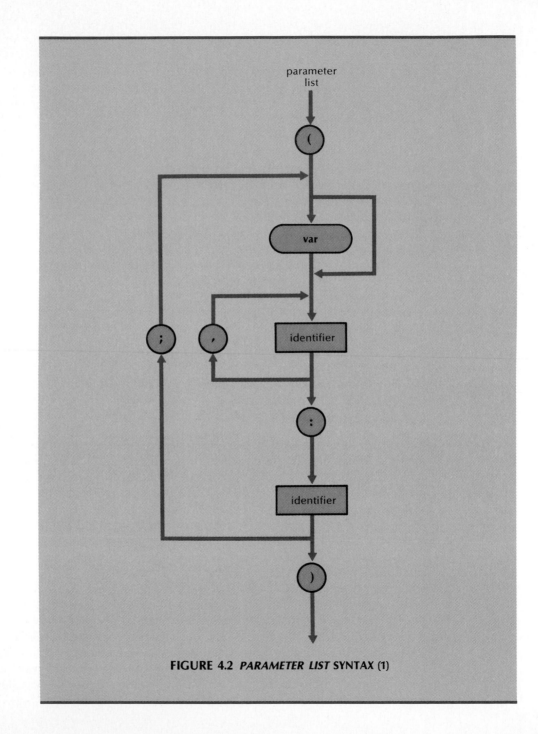

FIGURE 4.2 *PARAMETER LIST* SYNTAX (1)

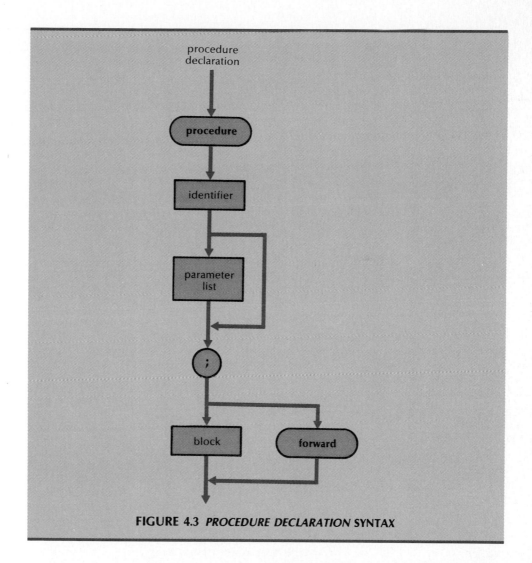

FIGURE 4.3 *PROCEDURE DECLARATION* SYNTAX

We can regard the program as a procedure of the operating system. With this interpretation we can also see that the files *input* and *output* are formal parameters whose corresponding actual parameters are the files given to the program by the operating system when the program is executed.

The syntax diagrams for a procedure declaration (Fig. 4.3) and for a block (Fig. 4.4) are mutually recursive. This implies that procedures can be nested. The skeleton of a program with nested procedures is given below. The procedure bodies are not written out in full and parameters are omitted.

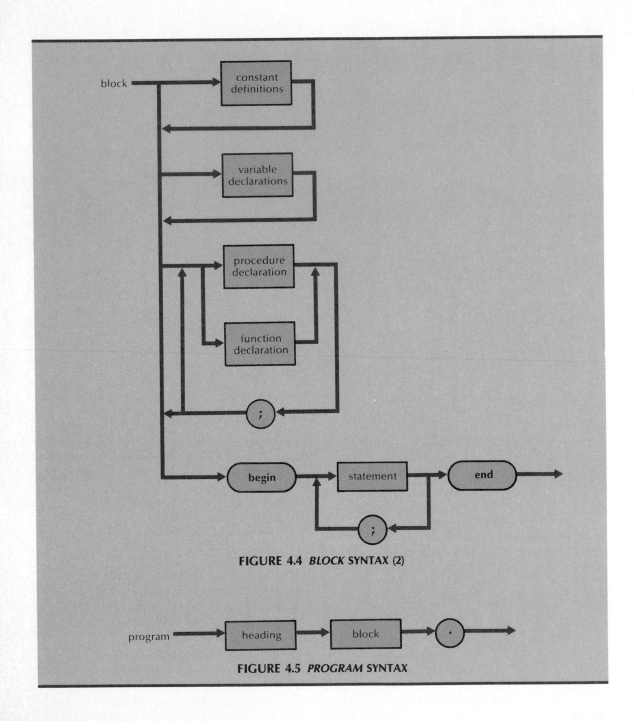

FIGURE 4.4 *BLOCK* SYNTAX (2)

FIGURE 4.5 *PROGRAM* SYNTAX

```
{ Demonstrate nested procedures. }
program nest (input, output);
  var
    a, b : integer;
  procedure outer;
    var
      c, d : integer;
    procedure inner;
      var
        e, f : integer;
      begin { inner }
        { Statements of inner }
        { Accessible variables: a, b, c, d, e, f }
      end; { inner }
    begin { outer }
      { Statements of outer }
      { Accessible variables: a, b, c, d }
    end; { outer }
  begin { nest }
    { Statements of nest }
    { Accessible variables: a, b }
  end. { nest }
```

In this program, the variables *e* and *f* are local to the procedure *inner* and may be used only within the body of *inner*. The variables *c* and *d* are local to the procedure *outer* and may be used within the body of *outer*. Because *inner* is nested within *outer*, the variables *c* and *d* may also be used within *inner*. The variables *a* and *b* are global and may be used anywhere within the program. The procedure *inner* is a local procedure of *outer* and may be called from within the body of *outer* but not by the main program.

Figure 4.6 shows the syntax for a *procedure call*. The actual parameters are written in a list that follows the procedure identifier. For each formal parameter in the procedure declaration, there must be an actual parameter in the calling statement. If the formal parameter is a variable parameter, the actual parameter must be a variable, not an expression. The type of the actual parameter must be the same as the type of the formal parameter, with the single exception that if the formal parameter is a value parameter of type *real*, the actual parameter may be an *integer* expression. This is in accordance with the general rule that an *integer* expression is allowed in any context where a *real* expression is expected.

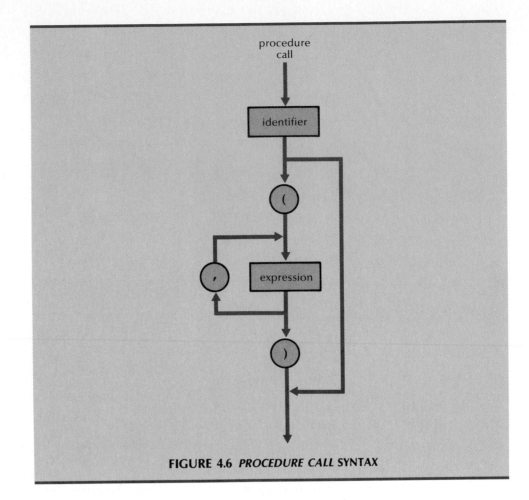

FIGURE 4.6 *PROCEDURE CALL* SYNTAX

4.3   FUNCTIONS

We have already encountered most of the standard functions of Pascal. For example, *sqrt* is a standard function that has a single argument of type *real* or *integer* and yields a value of type *real*. Whereas a procedure has an *effect*, a function has a *value*. Syntactically, a procedure call is a variety of *statement* and a function call is a variety of *factor*. This means that expressions may contain function calls. Using the standard functions *sqrt* and *sqr*, we can write

```
{ Calculate the length of the
  hypotenuse of a right triangle. }
program triangle (input, output);
  var
    opside, adjside, hypotenuse : real;
  begin
    read (opside, adjside);
    hypotenuse := sqrt (sqr (opside) + sqr (adjside));
    write (hypotenuse)
  end. { triangle }
```

This program contains three function calls. *Sqr* is called twice and *sqrt* is called once with the argument

```
sqr (adjside) + sqr (opside)
```

A function declaration is similar to a procedure declaration. There follows a declaration for a function called *squareroot*. This function calculates the square root of its argument using the algorithm we developed for Program *find-squareroots* in Chapter 3.

```
function squareroot (value : real) : real;
  const
    epsilon = 1E-6;
  var
    root : real;
  begin
    if value = 0
      then squareroot := 0
      else
        begin
          root := 1;
          repeat
            root := (value / root + root) / 2
          until abs (value / sqr (root) - 1) < epsilon;
          squareroot := root
        end
  end; { squareroot }
```

The type of the function is written in the *function head* after the parameter list. The type of *squareroot* is *real*, and its parameter, *value*, is also *real*. The value returned by *squareroot* is determined by an assignment statement in which *squareroot* appears on the left. There are two such assignments in this example, *squareroot* := 0, which is executed when *value* = 0, and *squareroot* := root, which is executed if *value* > 0. The function *squareroot* may be used in the same way as the standard function *sqrt*, and so we may write, for example

$$hypotenuse := squareroot\ (sqr\ (opside)\ +\ sqr\ (adjside))$$

There are two important differences between the function *squareroot* that we have declared and the standard function *sqrt*. First, if *sqrt* has a negative argument, the program will halt and an appropriate error message will be printed. If *squareroot* is executed with a negative argument, a misleading error message, such as "dividing by zero," will be printed. It is easy to overcome this defect by testing the value of the argument within the body of the function but it is not so easy to explain the failure to the calling program. Second, basic mathematical functions, such as *sqrt*, are usually written very carefully by a numerical analyst in such a way that the available speed and accuracy of the computer are fully exploited. A function such as *squareroot* will usually be neither as fast nor as accurate as a standard function.

The procedure *lowterm* of Section 4.1 calculates the greatest common divisor of its parameters. We can rewrite it as a function.

```
function gcd (num, den : integer) : integer;
  var
    remainder : integer;
  begin
    while den ≠ 0 do
      begin
        remainder := num mod den;
        num := den;
        den := remainder
      end; { while }
    gcd := num
  end; { gcd }
```

We do not need to make local copies of the parameters within the function. Because *num* and *den* are value parameters, the copying will have been done for us implicitly and nothing we do to *num* and *den* can affect the values of the actual parameters in the calling program. Using the function *gcd*, we can readily declare the procedure *lowterm*.

```
procedure lowterm (var num, den : integer);
  var
    divisor : integer;
  begin
    divisor := gcd (num, den);
    if divisor > 1
      then
        begin
          num := num div divisor;
          den := den div divisor
        end
  end; { lowterm }
```

Consider an alternative declaration of *lowterm*.

```
procedure lowterm (var num, den : integer);
  begin
    num := num div gcd (num, den);
    den := den div gcd (num, den)
  end; { lowterm }
```

Although this declaration is shorter and more readable, it is inferior for several reasons. It wastes time by evaluating the greatest common divisor twice, and it may perform unnecessary divisions when the greatest common divisor is 1. Its important defect, however, is that it does not work; the first assignment may alter the value of *num*, thereby invalidating the second assignment. This kind of trap is easy to fall into if you are programming hastily, and it is more likely to occur if you are programming directly from a mathematical derivation.

FUNCTION SYNTAX

The syntax for a *function declaration* is shown in Fig. 4.7. It differs from the syntax of a procedure declaration in that the keyword **function** replaces the keyword **procedure** and the type of the function follows the parameter list. A function call is a variety of factor. Figure 4.8 is a syntax diagram for *factor* which includes function calls. For each formal parameter in the function declaration, there must be an actual parameter of the same type in the function call.

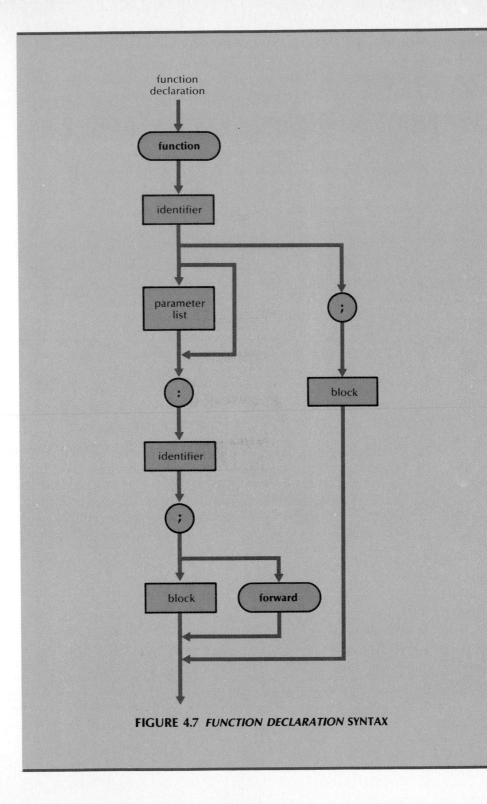

FIGURE 4.7 *FUNCTION DECLARATION* SYNTAX

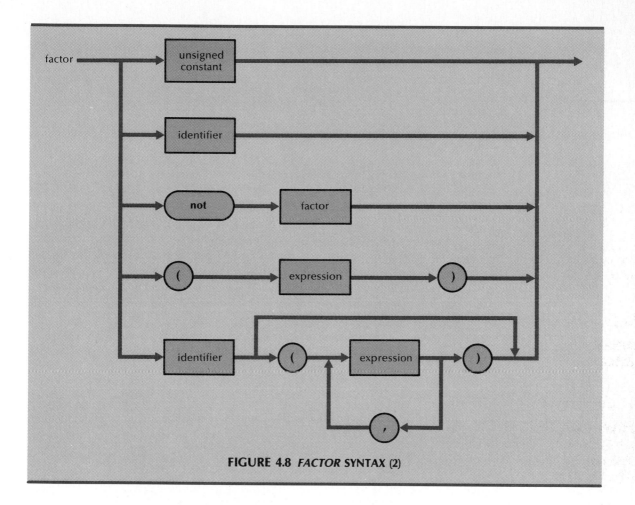

FIGURE 4.8 *FACTOR* SYNTAX (2)

FORWARD REFERENCE

Calls to a procedure or function may precede the declaration of the procedure or function if we provide a *forward reference*, as in this example.

```
procedure excavate (var treasure : real;
                         var found : boolean);
    forward;
    ....
    { invocations of excavate }
    ....
procedure excavate;
    { body of excavate }
```

The formal parameter list is written only once, in the forward reference. It is a good idea, however, to write the formal parameter list as a comment after the second occurrence of the procedure heading.

```
procedure excavate { var treasure : real;
                     var found : boolean } ;
```

The symbol *forward* is called a *directive*. It has a special meaning only in this particular context. Most compilers permit it to be used as an identifier elsewhere in the program.

4.4   RECURSION

Toward the end of the nineteenth century, a game called the Tower of Hanoi appeared in novelty stores in Europe. The popularity of this game was enhanced by accompanying promotional material explaining that priests in the Temple of Brahma were currently playing it and that the end of their game signified the end of the world. The priests' equipment allegedly consisted of a brass platform with three diamond needles on which rested 64 golden disks. The more modest version sold to the public consisted of three wooden posts and eight cardboard disks. The object of the game is to move the tower on the left needle (Fig. 4.9) to the right needle under the conditions that only one disk may be moved at a time and at no stage may a larger disk rest on a smaller disk.

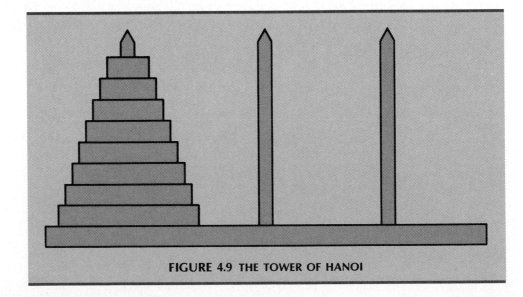

FIGURE 4.9 THE TOWER OF HANOI

We will suppose that the needles are numbered 1, 2, and 3, and that the priests are moving the tower of 64 disks from needle 1 to needle 3. We will denote this task by

movetower (64, 1, 3)

Our problem is to devise an algorithm that will provide the priests with a list of the correct moves to make in order to solve the problem. The insight that leads to a simple solution is that it is more useful to think about the bottom disk on needle 1 than the top one. The task *movetower* (64, 1, 3) is then seen to be equivalent to the following sequence of subtasks.

movetower (63, 1, 2);

move a disk from needle 1 to needle 3;

movetower (63, 2, 3)

This is a small but significant step toward the solution, small because we still have the problem of moving 63 disks twice, significant because we can repeat the analysis as often as necessary. For example, the task

movetower (63, 1, 2)

can be expressed as

movetower (62, 1, 3);

move a disk from needle 1 to needle 2;

movetower (62, 3, 2)

In order to construct a general algorithm, we have to specify which needle is to be used for the temporary tower. We can do this by extending our notation so that

movetower (*n*, *a*, *b*, *c*)

means

move *n* disks from needle *a* to needle *b* using needle *c* for the temporary tower

We can then assert that the task

movetower (*n*, *a*, *b*, *c*)

may be performed in three steps:

movetower (*n* − 1, *a*, *c*, *b*);

move a disk from *a* to *b*;

movetower (*n* − 1, *c*, *b*, *a*)

This algorithm will clearly fail for $n \leqslant 1$, so we add the rule:

do nothing if $n \leqslant 1$

Here is a Pascal procedure that performs these actions.

```
procedure movetower (height, fromneedle,
                          toneedle, usingneedle : integer);
   begin
     if height > 0
       then
         begin
           movetower (height - 1, fromneedle,
                          usingneedle, toneedle);
           movedisk (fromneedle, toneedle);
           movetower (height - 1, usingneedle,
                          toneedle, fromneedle)
         end
   end; { movetower }
```

The question now arises: is a procedure allowed to call itself in this way? Fortunately the answer is yes. Such a call is named a *recursive procedure call*.

Program *hanoi*, which illustrates the use of recursive calls, prints the moves required to transfer a tower of any height from needle 1 to needle 3.

```
{ Print the moves required to solve the "Tower of Hanoi" problem. }
program hanoi (input, output);
   var
      total : integer;        { Number of disks }
   { Move a tower of height disks from fromneedle to toneedle. }
   procedure movetower (height, fromneedle,
                          toneedle, usingneedle : integer);
      { Print a move from takeoff to puton. }
      procedure movedisk (takeoff, puton : integer);
        begin
          writeln (takeoff, '→', puton)
        end; { movedisk }
      begin { movetower }
        if height > 0
          then
            begin
              movetower (height - 1, fromneedle,
                             usingneedle, toneedle);
              movedisk (fromneedle, toneedle);
              movetower (height - 1, usingneedle,
                             toneedle, fromneedle)
            end { then }
      end; { movetower }
```

```
begin { hanoi }
  read (total);
  movetower (total, 1, 3, 2)
end. { hanoi }
```

INPUT	OUTPUT
3	1→3
	1→2
	3→2
	1→3
	2→1
	2→3
	1→3

Recursion is possible in Pascal by virtue of the fact that new local variables are created dynamically when a procedure is called. Suppose that we execute Program *hanoi* with total = 3. The first call to *movetower* is

$$movetower \ (3, \ 1, \ 3, \ 2)$$

On entry to *movetower*,

$$height = 3$$
$$fromneedle = 1$$
$$toneedle = 3$$
$$usingneedle = 2$$

Because *height* > 0, the first action of *movetower* is to call

$$movetower \ (2, \ 1, \ 2, \ 3)$$

This time, when we enter *movetower*,

$$height = 2$$
$$fromneedle = 1$$
$$toneedle = 2$$
$$usingneedle = 3$$

These steps are illustrated in Figs. 4.10(a–c). Variable names are represented by their initial letters in these diagrams. At the second call to *movetower*, new space is allocated for the parameters. The values at the first level are not destroyed but they are not accessible to the program until the second call to *movetower* is completed.

A complete account of the operation of Program *hanoi* for the case *total* = 3 is given in Table 4.1.

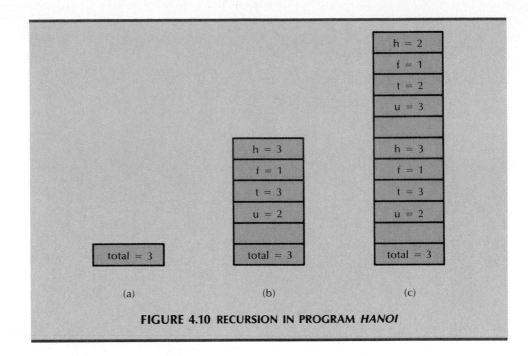

FIGURE 4.10 RECURSION IN PROGRAM *HANOI*

Once again, the names of the variables have been abbreviated to their first letters. A move from needle *a* to needle *b* is written

$$a > b$$

Actions at level 4, on which *height* = 0, are not recorded.

The time required by Program *hanoi* to move a tower of *n* disks is approximately proportional to 2^n. Technically, we may say that the algorithm has *exponential time complexity*. Algorithms of this kind are undesirable because the time required to execute them becomes intolerably large for quite reasonable values of the input data. A very powerful modern computer might calculate, but could not print, one move per microsecond in solving the Tower of Hanoi problem. Even at this rate the computer would require almost a million years to compute the moves required to move a tower of 64 disks.

RECURSION AND ITERATION

A recursive solution to a problem has two steps. The first step of the solution consists of transforming the problem into a new problem that is similar to the original problem but simpler in some way. In the Tower of Hanoi problem this

	TABLE 4.1			
LEVEL 0	**LEVEL 1**	**LEVEL 2**	**LEVEL 3**	**MOVE**
total = 3				
	h = 3			
	f = 1			
	t = 3			
	u = 2			
		h = 2		
		f = 1		
		t = 2		
		u = 3		
			h = 1	
			f = 1	
			t = 3	
			u = 2	
			1 → 3	1 → 3
		1 → 2		1 → 2
			h = 1	
			f = 3	
			t = 2	
			u = 1	
			3 → 2	3 → 2
	1 → 3			1 → 3
		h = 2		
		f = 2		
		t = 3		
		u = 1		
			h = 1	
			f = 2	
			t = 1	
			u = 3	
			2 → 1	2 → 1
		2 → 3		2 → 3
			h = 1	
			f = 1	
			t = 3	
			u = 2	
			1 → 3	1 → 3

step consisted of simplifying the task of moving 64 disks to the task of moving 63 disks. This transformation can be applied repeatedly until the problem becomes trivial. The Tower of Hanoi problem is solved when we have no disks to move.

Many mathematical functions are defined most naturally by recursive equations, and it is often easy to derive Pascal function declarations from such definitions. For example, the following equations define the Fibonacci numbers.

$$\text{Fib}(1) = 1$$
$$\text{Fib}(2) = 1$$
$$\text{Fib}(n) = \text{Fib}(n-1) + \text{Fib}(n-2) \text{ if } n > 2$$

The Pascal function *fib* follows immediately from these equations.

```
function fib (n : integer) : integer;
  begin
    if n ≤ 2
      then fib := 1
      else fib := fib (n - 1) + fib (n - 2)
  end; { fib }
```

This function, however, is very inefficient. During the evaluation of *fib* (5), for example, *fib* (3) and *fib* (1) are each evaluated twice and *fib* (2) is evaluated three times. The Fibonacci numbers can be calculated more efficiently by a non-recursive function that uses a loop. In the function *fastfib, first* and *second* denote the two Fibonacci numbers that are added at each step. This function calculates Fib (1), Fib (2), . . . , Fib (n − 1) in order to find the value of Fib (n), but it calculates each exactly once.

```
function fastfib (n : integer) : integer;
  var
    first, second, count, temp : integer;
  begin
    first := 1;
    second := 1;
    for count := 3 to n do
      begin
        { first = fib (count - 2 ), second = fib (count - 1)}
        temp := second;
        second := first + second;
        first := temp
      end; { for }
    fastfib := second
  end; { fastfib }
```

The choice between iteration and recursion is usually determined by the need for temporary storage. In the Tower of Hanoi problem, the position at each stage must be stored and the problem cannot be solved if this storage is not available. While it would be possible to write a nonrecursive solution, the recursive solution is simple and natural. On the other hand, functions that have definitions of the form

$$F_n(x) = \begin{cases} G(x) & \text{if } n = 0 \\ H(F_{n-1}(x)) & \text{if } n > 0 \end{cases}$$

can always be expressed iteratively and so a recursive solution is unnecessary.

These examples, in which a procedure or a function invokes itself, are instances of *simple recursion*. It is also possible for a procedure, *P*, to call a procedure, *Q*, which calls procedure *P*: this is called *indirect recursion*. The following application employs indirect recursion.

4.5 APPLICATION: POCKET CALCULATOR SIMULATION

In this section we consider in detail the construction of a program that simulates the action of a pocket calculator. The description of the programming techniques illustrates the principle of top-down design and the finished program illustrates the relationship between recursive procedures and recursive data structures.

The program reads a *calculation*, the syntax of which is shown in Fig. 4.11. A calculation (Fig. 4.11(a)) might look like this:

```
180 / (2 * 3.14159), 16 * 62.5 * 27, 169 * (5 + 8);
```

The program would evaluate each of these expressions in turn and would reply:

$$28.647913$$
$$27000$$
$$2197$$

An expression (Fig. 4.11(b)) consists of terms and factors. A factor (Fig. 4.11(d)) may contain an expression, and so expressions can be constructed recursively.

The syntax has been designed to facilitate analysis without *backtracking*. This means that the program can read one character at a time from the input medium and choose the correct course of action without ever going wrong and having to retrace its steps. For example, when a factor is expected, the next

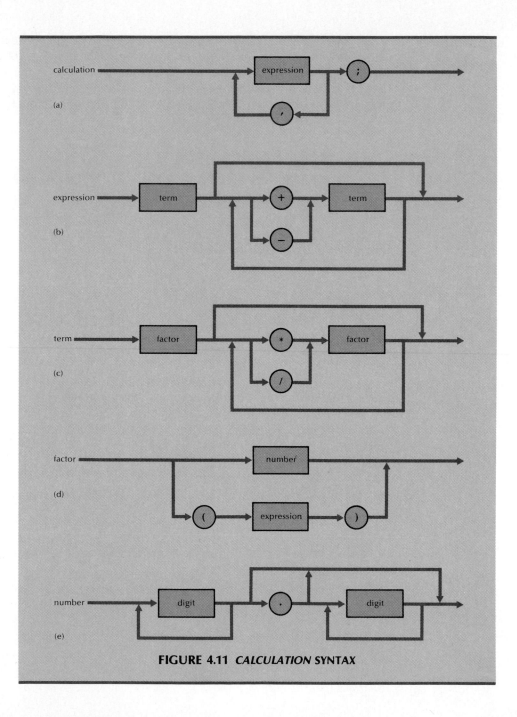

FIGURE 4.11 *CALCULATION* SYNTAX

character must be a digit or a left parenthesis: any other character must be erroneous. Accordingly, we design the program so that the next character is always available for inspection.

We start by writing the main program. This consists of an initialization statement and a **while** loop. The loop corresponds to the loop in Fig. 4.11(a): during each iteration, the program reads one expression.

```
program calculator (input, output);
  const
    terminator = ';';
    separator = ',';
  var
    nextchar : char;
    result : real;
  begin
    readchar (nextchar);
    while nextchar ≠ terminator do
      begin
        readexpression (nextchar, result);
        writeln (result);
        if nextchar = separator
          then readchar (nextchar)
      end { while }
  end. { calculator }
```

The procedure *readchar* reads the next character from the input medium. The procedure *readexpression* continues reading and analyzing until the end of the expression, returning the value of the expression as *result*. If the character following the expression is a semicolon, the program terminates; otherwise it reads another expression. A defect of this version of the program is that it does not check that the separator between expressions is a comma. We remedy this when we describe how the program handles input errors.

We see from the syntax diagram that an expression always starts with a term and that after the first term there may be zero or more terms, each preceded by a sign. The structure of procedure *readexpression* is closely related to the syntax diagram for an expression (Fig. 4.11(b)). The statement

$$readterm \ (exprchar, \ exprvalue)$$

corresponds to the first box, *term*, and the **while** statement corresponds to the loop in the syntax diagram.

```
procedure readexpression (var exprchar : char;
                          var exprvalue : real);
  const
    plus = '+';
    minus = '-';
  var
    addop : char;
    nexttermval : real;
  begin
    readterm (exprchar, exprvalue);
    while (exprchar = plus) or (exprchar = minus) do
      begin
        addop := exprchar;
        readchar (exprchar);
        readterm (exprchar, nexttermval);
        if addop = plus
          then exprvalue := exprvalue + nexttermval
          else exprvalue := exprvalue - nexttermval
      end { while }
  end; { readexpression }
```

We write procedure *readterm* in the same way but we use the multiplicative operators "*" and "/" instead of the additive operators. The procedure *readfactor* is more interesting because there are two cases to consider. A factor begins with either a digit or a left parenthesis (Fig. 4.11(d)). In the first case *readfactor* calls *readnumber* to read the digits and perform the required conversion. In the second case it calls *readexpression* recursively to read the expression between the parentheses.

```
procedure readfactor (var factorchar : char;
                      var factorvalue : real);
  const
    leftparen = '(';
    rightparen = ')';
  begin
    if ('0' <= factorchar) and (factorchar <= '9')
      then readnumber (factorchar, factorvalue)
    else if factorchar = leftparen
      then
        begin
          readchar (factorchar);
          readexpression (factorchar, factorvalue);
          if factorchar = rightparen
            then readchar (factorchar)
```

```
                        else reporterror { ')' expected }
              end
        else reporterror { illegal character }
  end; { readfactor }
```

The procedure *readnumber* is similar to Program *convert* which appeared in Chapter 3. We now consider the procedure *reporterror*.

The program can detect three error conditions: no comma at the end of an expression, no right parenthesis at the end of a bracketed expression, and an illegal character when a factor is expected. Additionally, the procedure *readterm*, which performs multiplications and divisions, should report an error if a divisor is zero. The easy solution is to print one of four messages. This is not very helpful because it does not tell us where the errors are. We make the program more useful by indicating where the errors occur rather than what is wrong. This is quite easy to do if we assign to *readchar* the additional task of reporting the position of the current character in the input line. This implies that *readchar* will have two parameters. The existing procedures will have to be altered accordingly.

In writing *readchar* we include a small refinement that makes the program easier to use: it skips over blanks. The user can now increase the readability of a calculation by embedding blanks in it. We can now write *readchar*.

```
      procedure readchar (var ch : char;
                          var charpos : integer);
        const
          separator = ',';
          blank = ' ';
        begin
          repeat
            if eoln
              then
                begin
                  charpos := 0;
                  ch := blank;
                  readln
                end
              else
                begin
                  charpos := charpos + 1;
                  read (ch)
                end
          until ch ≠ blank
        end; { readchar }
```

The procedure *reporterror* prints a marker underneath the incorrect character. Once an error has been found in an expression, there is no point in analyzing the expression further, and *reporterror* skips through the input file until it finds a comma or a semicolon.

```
procedure reporterror (var errchar : char;
                       var errcharpos : integer);
  const
    marker = '↑';
    separator = ',';
    terminator = ';';
  begin
    writeln (marker : errcharpos);
    while not ((errchar = separator) or (errchar = terminator)) do
      readchar (errchar, errcharpos)
  end; { reporterror }
```

We now give the complete program, incorporating the changes we have described.

```
{ This program calculates the value of expressions. }
program calculator (input, output);
  const
    separator = ',';
    terminator = ';';
  var
    nextchar : char;
    nextpos : integer;
    result : real;
  { Read one nonblank character from the keyboard; return ch, the
    character, and charpos, its position on the line. }
  procedure readchar (var ch : char;
                      var charpos : integer);
    const
      blank = ' ';
    begin
      repeat
        if eoln
          then
```

```
        begin
          charpos := 0;
          ch := blank;
          readln
        end { then }
      else
        begin
          charpos := charpos + 1;
          read (ch)
        end { else }
    until ch ≠ blank
  end; { readchar }
{ Report an error by displaying '↑' under the offending character.
  Skip to the next expression or the end of the input, whichever
  comes first. }
  procedure reporterror (var errchar : char;
                         var errcharpos : integer);

    const
      marker = '↑';
    begin
      writeln (marker : errcharpos);
      while not (errchar - separator) or (errchar = terminator) do
        readchar (errchar, errcharpos)
    end; { reporterror }

  { Read a number. On entry, the current character is a digit.
    Return the value of the number in numvalue. }
  procedure readnumber (var numchar : char;
                        var numpos : integer;
                        var numvalue : real);

    const
      point = '.';
      radix = 10;
    var
      count, scale : integer;
    begin
      numvalue := 0;
      while ('0' ≤ numchar) and (numchar < chr (ord ('0') + radix)) do
        begin
          numvalue := radix * numvalue + ord (numchar)
                                       - ord ('0');
          readchar (numchar, numpos)
        end; { while }
```

```
    if numchar = point
      then
        begin
          readchar (numchar, numpos);
          scale := 0;
          while ('0' ≤ numchar) and (numchar < chr (ord ('0') +
                                              radix)) do
            begin
              numvalue := radix * numvalue + ord (numchar)
                                            - ord ('0');
              readchar (numchar, numpos);
              scale := scale + 1
            end; { while }
          for count := 1 to scale do
            numvalue := numvalue / radix
        end { then }
  end; { readnumber }
{ Read an expression. An expression consists
  of one or more terms separated by '+' or '-'. }
procedure readexpression (var exprchar : char;
                          var exprpos : integer;
                          var exprvalue : real);

  const
    pluschar = '+';
    minuschar = '-';
  var
    addop : char;
    nexttermval : real;

  { Read a term. A term consists of one or
    more factors separated by '*' or '/'. }
  procedure readterm (var termchar : char;
                      var termpos : integer;
                      var termvalue : real);

    const
      multchar = '*';
      divchar = '/';
    var
      mulop : char;
      nextfacval : real;
```

```
{ Read a factor. A factor is either a number
  or an expression enclosed in parentheses. }
procedure readfactor (var factorchar : char;
                      var factorpos : integer;
                      var factorvalue : real);

  const
    radix = 10;
    leftparen = '(';
    rightparen = ')';
  begin { readfactor }
    if ('0' ≤ factorchar) and (factorchar < char (ord ('0') +
                                                   radix))
      then readnumber (factorchar, factorpos, factorvalue)
    else if factorchar = leftparen
      then
        begin
          readchar (factorchar, factorpos);
          readexpression (factorchar, factorpos,
                          factorvalue);
          if factorchar = rightparen
            then readchar (factorchar, factorpos)
            else reporterror (factorchar, factorpos)
        end { then }
    else
      begin
        reporterror (factorchar, factorpos);
        factorvalue := 0
      end { else }
  end; { readfactor }

begin { readterm }
  readfactor (termchar, termpos, termvalue);
  while (termchar = multchar) or (termchar = divchar) do
    begin
      mulop := termchar;
      readchar (termchar, termpos);
      readfactor (termchar, termpos, nextfacval);
      if mulop = multchar
        then termvalue := termvalue * nextfacval
        else if nextfacval ≠ 0
          then termvalue := termvalue / nextfacval
          else reporterror (termchar, termpos)
    end { while }
end; { readterm }
```

```
begin { readexpression }
  readterm (exprchar, exprpos, exprvalue);
  while (exprchar = pluschar) or (exprchar = minuschar) do
    begin
      addop := exprchar;
      readchar (exprchar, exprpos);
      readterm (exprchar, exprpos, nexttermval);
      if addop = pluschar
        then exprvalue := exprvalue + nexttermval
        else exprvalue := exprvalue - nexttermval
    end { while }
end; { readexpression }
begin { calculator }
  nextpos := 0;
  readchar (nextchar, nextpos);
  while nextchar ≠ terminator do
    begin
      readexpression (nextchar, nextpos, result);
      if (nextchar = separator) or (nextchar = terminator)
        then
          begin
            writeln (result);
            if nextchar = separator
              then readchar (nextchar, nextpos)
          end { then }
        else reporterror (nextchar, nextpos)
    end { while }
end. { calculator }
```

4.6   NONLOCAL VARIABLES AND SIDE EFFECTS

We have seen that procedures and functions can access and alter values of
nonlocal variables. A procedure or function that alters the value of a nonlocal
variable is said to have *side effects*. The term "side effect" is familiar from
pharmacology. A drug is supposed to have a specific effect on the body, and any
additional effects are called side effects. The implication is that side effects are
harmful, or at least undesirable. In programming we have complete control
over side effects. Moreover, side effects may do no harm to the program. The
objection to them is that they obscure the program structure and thereby make
the program harder to understand.

The procedures in Program *calculator* do not refer to nonlocal identifiers and they do not have side effects. Each procedure may be read as a complete entity because it refers only to its own constants, variables, and parameters. The overall structure of the program is in some ways obscured by this approach. At any one time, exactly one character is being used, but this character may have any of the names *ch, errorchar, numchar, factorchar, termchar, exprchar,* or *nextchar,* depending on where we look. In Chapter 5 we present another version of *calculator* in which procedures do have side effects. You will be able to compare the two programs.

When you write procedures, carefully weigh the merits of using or not using nonlocal variables. A procedure should access or alter the value of a nonlocal variable only if there is good reason for it to do so. Use the criteria of clarity and security.

When you write functions, do not use or alter the values of nonlocal variables. Think of the word "function" in its mathematical sense and write functions whose values are dependent only on their arguments.

Be alert to *accidental* side effects. Suppose that you use a variable, x, within a procedure but forget to declare it. The compiler will often report this as an error. If you declare x as a variable in an outer procedure or in the main program, however, the compiler cannot detect the error. This can lead to very mysterious behavior by the program. The moral is threefold. Don't use the same variable name at different levels. Don't forget to write declarations: whenever you introduce a new variable, write a declaration for it immediately. Don't use variable names like x.

4.7 PSEUDO-RANDOM NUMBERS

Suppose that we have a means of selecting an integer, r, at random from the set of integers, 1, 2, . . . , N. Simple mechanisms exist for performing this selection for certain small values of N. For $N = 2$ we can toss a coin, for $N = 6$ we can roll a die, and for $N = 36$ we can use a roulette wheel. A sequence

$$r_1, r_2, \ldots$$

of such integers is called a *random sequence.* An algorithm that generates a random or apparently random sequence is called a *random-number generator.* Several examples in this book require a random-number generator, so in this section we digress briefly to look at how random numbers can be generated.

The method most commonly used to generate random numbers is the *linear congruential method.* Each number, r_n, in the sequence is calculated from its predecessor, r_{n-1}, using this formula.

$$r_n = (multiplier \star r_{n-1} + increment) \textbf{ mod } modulus.$$

The numbers generated by repeated use of this formula are not truly random in the sense that tosses of a coin or throws of a die are random; we can always predict the value of r_n given the value of r_{n-1}. The sequence generated by this formula is therefore more correctly called a *pseudo-random sequence*, and its members are called *pseudo-random numbers*. There are many applications of random numbers in computer science, and for most of these, pseudo-random numbers are just as useful, provided some elementary precautions are taken.

Most computer installations have a standard pseudo-random number generator of the linear congruential type, for which the values of *multiplier*, *increment*, and *modulus* have been carefully chosen. If your installation has such a generator and it is accessible to Pascal programs, you should use it. If you do not have access to a good generator, you may use the following algorithm. It will work on most computers, generates 65536 random numbers before repeating itself, and is adequate for the examples given in this book. We use

$$\begin{aligned}
modulus &= 2^{16} = 65536 \\
multiplier &= 25173 \\
increment &= 13849
\end{aligned}$$

and so we have

$$r_n = (25173 * r_{n-1} + 13849) \textbf{ mod } 65536.$$

The pseudo-random number generator is written as a Pascal procedure.

```
procedure random (var randint : integer);
  const
    multiplier = 25173;
    increment = 13849;
    modulus = 65536;
  begin
    random := randint;
    randint := (multiplier * randint + increment) mod modulus
  end;
```

When we use *random* in examples, we will use literals rather than constants for *multiplier*, *increment*, and *modulus*. The procedure generates a permutation of the integers

$$0, 1, 2, \ldots, 65535$$

and then repeats itself. The first number generated is the initial value of *seed*.

For most applications, these numbers should be scaled in some way. For example, if the program is simulating throws of a die, we could write

```
var
  throw, randint : integer;
begin
  ....
  random (randint);
  throw := randint div 10922 + 1
```

The number 10922 is 65536 **div** 6. The assignment

```
  throw := randint mod 6 + 1
```

indicates clearly what we are doing, but it does not yield random throws. The most significant digits of a number generated by the linear congruential method are more random than the least significant digits.

We frequently require a real random value between 0 and 1. For this purpose we can use a modified version of *random*.

```
procedure random (var randint : integer; randval : real);
  begin
    randval := randint / 65536;
    randint := (25173 * randint + 13849) mod 65536
  end;
```

This function will provide random numbers such that after executing *random* (*int*, *val*) we have

$$0.0 \leqslant val < 1.0.$$

APPLICATION: VOLUME CALCULATION

One application of random numbers is the computation of areas and volumes. Suppose that we have an irregular solid, S, that can be enclosed in a cube, C. It is easy to generate random points in C, and it can be shown that the probability that a random point inside C is also inside S is

$$V_S/V_C$$

where V_C is the volume of C and V_S is the volume of S. If there is a simple criterion that enables us to decide whether or not a point is inside S, we can estimate the volume of S by generating random points and counting those points that fall inside S. Program *spherevolume* estimates the volume of a sphere in this way. The cube C is defined by

$$0 \leqslant x \leqslant 1$$
$$0 \leqslant y \leqslant 1$$
$$0 \leqslant z \leqslant 1$$

One-eighth of the sphere

$$x^2 + y^2 + z^2 \leqslant 1$$

fits inside this cube, and if we generate a random point (x, y, z) inside the cube, the probability that it will also lie inside this sector of the sphere is $V_S/8$. This is obviously an absurd way to calculate the volume of a sphere. The method is useful when there is no simple formula for the volume of the solid but a simple inclusion criterion can be defined. (See Exercise 4.14.)

```
{ Use random numbers to estimate the volume of a sphere. }
program spherevolume (input, output);
  var
    try, total, inside, randomseed : integer;
    x, y, z : real;
  { Generate a random real number, r, such that 0 ≤ r < 1.0. }
  procedure random (var randint : integer; var randval : real);
    begin
      randval := randint / 65536;
      randint := (25173 * randint + 13849) mod 65536
    end; { random }
  begin { spherevolume }
    read (total);
    inside := 0;
    randomseed := 10000;    { Initialize the random number generator. }
    for try := 1 to total do
      begin
        random (randomseed, x);
        random (randomseed, y);
        random (randomseed, z);
        if sqr (x) + sqr (y) + sqr (z) ≤ 1.0
          then inside := inside + 1
      end;
    writeln ('Estimated volume = ', 8 * inside / total)
  end. { spherevolume }
```

INPUT	OUTPUT
5000	Estimated volume = 4.16800

4.8 EXERCISES

4.1 What happens when Program *cancelfactors* reads negative numbers? Correct the program so that it gives reasonable results in all cases.

4.2 Predict the output of the programs below and explain your reasoning.

a)
```
program nonsense (output);
  var
    thing : integer;
  procedure cheat (var hee, haw : integer);
    begin
      hee := -1;
      haw := - hee
    end; { cheat }
  begin
    thing := 1;
    cheat (thing, thing);
    writeln (thing)
  end. { nonsense }
```

b)
```
program rubbish (output);
  var
    thing : integer;
  procedure liar (var hee : integer; var haw : integer);
    begin
      hee := 10 * haw
    end; { liar }
  begin
    thing := 10;
    liar (thing, thing);
    writeln (thing)
  end. { rubbish }
```

4.3 Write declarations for the following functions and test your solutions:

a) the inverse trigonometric functions

$$\sin^{-1}(x) = \tan^{-1}(x/\sqrt{(1 - x^2)})$$
$$\cos^{-1}(x) = \tan^{-1}(\sqrt{(1 - x^2)} / x) \qquad (x > 0)$$

b) the hyperbolic functions

$$\sinh(x) = (e^x - e^{-x}) / 2$$
$$\cosh(x) = (e^x + e^{-x}) / 2$$
$$\tanh(x) = \sinh(x) / \cosh(x)$$

c) the inverse hyperbolic functions

$$\sinh^{-1}(x) = \ln(x + \sqrt{(x^2 + 1)})$$
$$\cosh^{-1}(x) = \ln(x + \sqrt{(x^2 - 1)})$$

4.4 Write a function, *digit* (n, k), that returns the value of the kth digit from the right of the number n. For example,

$$digit\ (254693,\ 2) = 9$$
$$digit\ (7622,\ 6) = 0$$

4.5 The function $\theta = \arctan(x)$ returns a value of θ such that $-\pi/2 \leqslant \theta < \pi/2$. Write a function *atan* (x, y) that uses the signs of x and y to calculate a value of θ such that $\tan(\theta) = y/x$ and $-\pi < \theta \leqslant \pi$.

4.6 A jeep can travel 500 miles with a full load of fuel. From an initial cache containing N loads of fuel, the jeep can travel

$$L = 500\left(1 + \frac{1}{3} + \frac{1}{5} + \ldots + \frac{1}{2N-1}\right)$$

miles by establishing caches of fuel *en route*. Write a function that calculates a value of N given L.

4.7 Modify procedure *movetower* of Program *hanoi* so that it does not call itself recursively when there are no disks to be moved. Extend Program *hanoi* so that when it is executed it prints a table similar to Table 4.1.

4.8 Write iterative and recursive functions for calculating values of the *Hermite polynomials* $H_n (x)$ given that

$$H_0(x) = 1$$
$$H_1(x) = 2x$$
$$H_n(x) = 2x\,H_{n-1}(x) - 2(n-1)\,H_{n-2}(x) \qquad \text{for } n > 1$$

Compare the execution times of the two functions.

4.9 Write a recursive function to calculate values of *Ackermann's function*, Ack (m, n), defined for $m \geqslant 0$ and $n \geqslant 0$ by

$$Ack\ (0,\ n) = n + 1$$
$$Ack\ (m,\ 0) = Ack\ (m - 1,\ 1)$$
$$Ack\ (m,\ -n) = Ack\ (m - 1,\ Ack\ (m,\ n - 1)) \qquad \text{for } m > 0 \text{ and } n > 0$$

Include a *write* statement in the function body so that each entry to the function is recorded.

4.10 Program *calculator* will not accept expressions with a leading sign, such as the expressions in this calculation.

$$-16 * 27.5, + 3183 - 2475;$$

Modify first the syntax diagrams and then the program to overcome this deficiency.

4.11 Draw syntax diagrams for expressions that may include the exponential operator "↑", where

$$a \uparrow b = a\ b$$

Exponents are always evaluated before any other operators unless parentheses are used to change the order of evaluation. The expression

$$a \uparrow b \uparrow c$$

is illegal. Write a program that evaluates expressions containing exponents. Use the fact that

$$a^b = \exp(x \star \ln(a)) \qquad \text{for } a > 0.$$

4.12 Draw a syntax diagram suitable for complex constants. Write a procedure to read a complex constant. Use this procedure in a program that evaluates complex expressions.

4.13 How accurate is Program *spherevolume*? Do you think that generating 5,000,000 random points would give better accuracy than generating 50,000 points? Would it be better to generate a rectangular lattice of points instead?

4.14 Use a random technique to estimate the volume enclosed by the lens-shaped surfaces whose equations, in cylindrical polar coordinates (r, θ, z), are

$$|z| \leqslant e^{-r^2}$$
$$r \leqslant 5$$

4.15 A particle performs a *random walk* according to the following rules. At $t = 0$, the particle is at the origin, $x = 0$, $y = 0$. At times $t = 1, 2, 3, \ldots$, the particle makes a random step in one of the four directions given by

$$x := x - 1$$
$$x := x + 1$$
$$y := y - 1$$
$$y := y + 1$$

The walk terminates when $x^2 + y^2 \geqslant R^2$. Determine experimentally the relationship between the time for the walk and the value of R.

4.16 There are many situations in which it is important that random numbers are generated as rapidly as possible. The slowest operator in our random-number generator is likely to be **mod**. In practice, the **mod** operation is usually unnecessary because a computer with k bit words cannot represent a number larger than $2^k - 1$. Write a random-number generator in Pascal that exploits this fact. You may have to suppress range checking within the procedure and you may have problems with the sign bit.

5

VARIABLE TYPES

In Chapter 2 we discussed the standard types of Pascal: *integer, real, boolean,* and *char*. The properties of these types are determined partly by the Pascal Standard and partly by the particular implementation of Pascal that we happen to be using; we have no control over them. In this chapter, and in Chapters 6, 7, and 8, we introduce types for which we can define some of the properties ourselves. The existence of these types contributes to the power of Pascal in several ways. First, we can write programs more clearly and precisely if we use appropriate type definitions than if we restrict ourselves to the standard types. Second, type definitions enable us to give additional information to the compiler. The compiler can use this information to make extensive error checks and to produce efficient programs.

The new types are declared in a *type definition section* that comes between the constant definition and variable declaration sections. Type definitions that appear within the body of a procedure are local to that procedure.

5.1   ENUMERATED TYPES

There are many programming situations in which we know that a variable can assume only a small number of distinct values. We know, for example, that there are seven days in a week. We could use small integers to represent these values in a program: for example, we could define Sunday to be 0, Monday to be 1, and so on. We have already seen the advantages of using names, defined in a constant definition section, rather than the numbers themselves. The *enumerated types* of Pascal provide further advantages by leaving more of the implementation details to the compiler.

An enumerated type is defined by a list of the values that may be assumed by a variable of that type. The definition

```
type
    units = (inches, feet, furlongs, miles);
```

states that a variable of the type *units* may have any one of the four values, *inches, feet, furlongs, miles*, and no other values. The type *units* is used in a variable declaration in the same way as one of the standard types.

```
var
    scale : units;
```

The two declarations may in fact be combined into one:

```
var
    scale : (inches, feet, furlongs, miles);
```

but in most cases it is preferable to keep the type definition and the variable declaration separate. These are other examples of enumerated type definitions.

```
type
    day = (monday, tuesday, wednesday, thursday,
           friday, saturday, sunday);
    relationship = (parent, sibling, offspring, cousin);
    recordtype = (receivable, payable, invoice, creditnote);
    operator = (plus, minus, multiply, divide);
    trigfunction = (sine, cosine, tangent,
                    secant, cosecant, cotangent);
```

In the following variable declaration section we have declared some variables with these types.

```
var
    holiday, workday : day;
    relative : relationship;
    inputrecord, outputrecord : recordtype;
    addingop, multop : operator;
```

A value may not belong to more than one type. The following definitions are incompatible because *tomato* appears in both value lists.

```
type
    fruit = (apple, orange, lemon, pineapple, tomato);
    vegetable = (potato, carrot, tomato, pea, sprout);
```

The names of the values listed in the definition of an enumerated type are constants of that type. Therefore we can write

```
holiday := sunday;
inputrecord := payable;
scale := miles;
addingop := minus;
```

Mixed assignments are not permitted. You may not write

```
holiday := miles
```

or

```
operator := cousin
```

The only operators that can be used with enumerated-type variables are the relational operators. The resulting expressions have a *boolean* value. Enumerated types are ordered by the sequence in which they are listed in the type definition. Consequently, the following expressions are *true*.

```
monday < friday
sibling > parent
multiply < divide
```

The standard type *boolean* is itself an enumerated type, implicitly defined by

```
type
    boolean = (false, true);
```

The functions *pred* and *succ* are defined for enumerated-type arguments. The value returned is of the same type as the argument and is the predecessor or successor of the argument in the definition list. For example,

```
succ (monday) = tuesday
pred (tangent) = cosine
```

The first member of the list has no predecessor and the last member has no successor.

The function *ord* may have an enumerated-type argument. It returns the ordinal number of the identifier in the list that defines the enumerated type. The first value in the list has the ordinal number zero, the second value has the ordinal number one, and so on. Thus we have

```
ord (payable) = 1
ord (plus) = 0
ord (cotangent) = 5
```

Unfortunately, it is not possible in Standard Pascal to read or write the value of an enumerated type directly. If you wrote

```
relative := cousin;
write (relative)
```

you would not see "cousin" in the output. In fact, you would probably not get any output at all because the compiler would have reported an error. You could use

```
write (ord (relative))
```

which would, when executed, print

```
3
```

Several recent Pascal compilers extend the language by allowing values of enumerated types to be read and written.

The **for** statement is often used in conjunction with enumerated-type variables in constructions such as

```
for scale := inches to miles do
    convert
```

Note that in this context, the **for** statement cannot be replaced by a **while** statement. The statements

```
scale := inches;
while scale ≤ miles do
```

```
begin
    convert;
    scale := succ (scale)
end
```

will fail when the expression *succ* (*miles*) is evaluated because *miles* has no successor.

5.2   SUBRANGE TYPES

A *subrange type* is defined by two constants, for example

```
type
    byte = 0..255;
```

A variable of type *byte* is an integer whose range is restricted. The constants in the definition must be distinct and of the same type. The type of the constants may be *integer, char,* or an enumerated type. Subranges of *real* are not allowed. Here are further examples of subrange types.

```
type
    letter = 'a'..'z';
    digit = '0'..'9';
    weekday = monday..friday;
```

The subranges must not have gaps. You may not write definitions such as

```
agereduction = 0..14, 65..100;
```

Weekday is a subrange of the enumerated type *day* that was defined in Section 5.1. The *host type* of a subrange type is the type of the constants used to define it. For example, the host type of *weekday* is *day*. The constants are called the *lower bound* and *upper bound* of the subrange type, and the definition is acceptable only if

```
lowerbound ≤ upperbound
```

Standard Pascal permits the lower bound to be equal to the upper bound but, as the resulting type has only one value, definitions of this kind are seldom used.

Subrange variables are declared in the usual way in the variable declaration section.

```
var
    counter, entry : index;
    firstchar, lastchar : letter;
```

The two declarations necessary for a subrange variable can be combined into one. We can write

```
var
    counter, entry : 1..20;
    firstchar, lastchar : 'a'..'z';
```

In most cases, as we have already seen, it is preferable to keep the type definition and the variable declaration separate.

Any operator that may be used with a variable of a particular type may also be used with a subrange of that type. Furthermore, different subranges of a type may be mixed in the same expression. We could declare

```
var
    radix : 1..10;
    smallnumber : 0..100;
    result : integer;
```

and then write the expression

```
result + smallnumber div radix
```

Subrange variables may also be used on both sides of assignment statements. After the same declarations we could also write

```
radix := smallnumber;
smallnumber := result
```

Attempting to assign a value to a subrange variable beyond its range, however, will cause a run-time error.

All the functions defined for the host type may be used with the subrange type. The value of a function is not necessarily a member of the subrange to which its argument belongs. For example, the value of

```
sqr (smallnumber)
```

is not restricted to the range 0..100.

The procedures *read* and *write* may be used with subranges of the types *integer* and *char* and have the expected results.

Range-checking is an important and often neglected aspect of computer programming. Subranges take the burden of range-checking from the programmer and pass it on to the compiler. You should use subranges, particularly subranges of *integer*, as frequently as possible. In fact, the type *integer* rarely appears in well-written Pascal programs because it is not often that the range of values of an integer variable is completely unpredictable. The use of subrange definitions also improves the readability of the program; by explicitly stating the range of values that a variable can take, you give the reader of the program important information about the variable.

The standard types (*integer*, *char*, *boolean*), enumerated types, and subrange types constitute the *ordinal types* of Pascal. The ordinal types have a finite number of values, are ordered, and can be represented by integers. The type *real* is not an ordinal type.

5.3   SETS

A *set* is a collection of objects of the same type. If *S* is a set of objects of type *T*, then any object of type *T* is either a member of *S* or is not a member of *S*. We may define a *set* type to correspond to any ordinal type. Values of the set type are sets of values of the ordinal type. We can define the enumerated type

```
type
    ingredients = (apples, strawberries, bananas, nuts, icecream,
                   chocolatesauce, cream, pastry, sugar, ice);
```

and the set type

```
type
    dessert = set of ingredients;
```

Variables of the type *dessert* are declared in the variable declaration section in the usual way.

```
var
    sundae, applecrumble, feast : dessert;
```

The type *dessert* is the *associated set type* of the type *ingredients*. Conversely, *ingredients* is the *base type* of the type *dessert*.

The values of a constant or a variable of the type *dessert* are subsets of the set of ingredients. A set is represented by a list of its members, enclosed in square brackets. These are constants of the type *dessert*.

```
[icecream, chocolatesauce]
[icecream, bananas, cream]
[icecream]
```

If the members of a set are consecutive values of the base type, only the first and last need be specified, and so

```
[apples, strawberries, bananas, nuts]
```

may be written

```
[apples..nuts]
```

A set may have no members at all, in which case it is called the *empty set* and is written

        [ ]

There are 2^{10} = 1024 possible values of dessert. In general, if the base type has n values, the associated set type has 2^n values.

The *union* of two sets is a set containing the members of both sets. The union operator is " + ", and the value of

        `[apples] + [pastry, sugar]`

is [*apples, pastry, sugar*]. The *intersection* of two sets is a set containing only the objects that are members of both sets. The intersection operator is "*", and the value of

        `[bananas, icecream, cream] * [icecream, nuts]`

is [*icecream*]. The *difference* of two sets is a set containing all the members of the first set that are not members of the second set, and it is denoted by the symbol " – ". The value of

        `[apples, strawberries, bananas] - [strawberries, cream]`

is [*apples, bananas*].

The relational operators may be used to compare sets.

$$= \quad \text{denotes set equality}$$
$$\neq \quad \text{denotes set inequality}$$
$$\leqslant \quad \text{denotes ``is contained in''}$$
$$\geqslant \quad \text{denotes ``contains''}$$

A set, *X, contains* a set, *Y,* if every member of *Y* is also a member of *X.* The following expressions are *true.*

        `[icecream, chocolatesauce] = [chocolatesauce, icecream]`
        `[icecream] ≠ [ice, cream]`
        `[strawberries] ≤ [strawberries, cream]`
        `[apples..ice] ≥ [icecream..cream]`

The symbol **in,** which is a reserved word in Pascal, is used to test set membership. The left operand of **in** is an expression, and the right operand is an expression of the set type associated with the left operand. The expression

        `apples in [apples, pastry, sugar]`

is *true,* but the expression

        `apples in [strawberries, cream]`

is *false.*

	TABLE 5.1	
MEANING	**CONVENTIONAL SYMBOL**	**PASCAL SYMBOL**
Set	{ ... }	[...]
Union	∪	+
Intersection	∩	*
Contains	⊃	≥
Is contained by	⊂	≤
Inclusion	∈	**in**
Empty set	∅	[ ]

The assignment statement may be used with set variables and set expressions in the usual way.

```
applecrumble := [apples, pastry, sugar];
feast := applecrumble + [icecream]
```

If you are familiar with set algebra, you will have noticed that the conventional symbols for set operations are not used in Pascal. This is because the set operation symbols are not available on most hardware. Table 5.1 shows the relationship between the conventional symbols and the Pascal symbols.

APPLICATION: TONE ROWS

If we represent the twelve tones of a chromatic octave by the type

```
type
    tonevalues = 1..12;
```

then the tones in a *tone row*, which consists of several tones, can be represented by the associated set type

```
type
    row = set of tonevalues;
```

In some kinds of serial music, a tone row must contain exactly one occurrence of each tone. Using the variables

```
var
    tone : tonevalues;
    sequence : row;
```

we can initialize a sequence by giving it no tones.

```
sequence := [ ]
```

Each time we add a new tone we can include it in the sequence by using the union operator:

```
sequence := sequence + [tone]
```

A tone is permitted in the sequence only if it has not been used already; that is

```
if not (tone in sequence)
```

The sequence is complete when it contains each of the twelve tones.

```
sequence = [1..12]
```

These ideas, used in conjunction with the random-number generator of Chapter 4, lead to Program *tonerows* which generates a specified number of random tone rows. The second number read by the program is used to initialize the random-number generator.

```
{ Print random tone rows. }
program tonerows (input, output);
  const
    rowlength = 12;     { Length of a tone row }
  type
    tonevalues = 1..rowlength;
    row = set of tonevalues;
  var
    seed, counter, cycles : integer;
    tone : tonevalues;
    sequence : row;
  { Generate a random tone in the range 1,2,...,12. }
  procedure randomtone (var randomtone, randval : integer);
    begin
      randomtone := randval div (65536 div 12) + 1;
      randval := (25173 * randval + 13849) mod 65536
    end; { randomtone }
  begin { tonerows }
    read (cycles, seed);
    for counter := 1 to cycles do
```

```
begin
  sequence := [ ];
  repeat
    randomtone (tone, seed);
    if not (tone in sequence)
      then
        begin
          write (tone);
          sequence := sequence + [tone]
        end { then }
  until sequence = [1..rowlength];
  writeln
end { for }
end. { tonerows }
```

INPUT		OUTPUT										
5 20000	4	5	2	10	8	11	9	3	1	6	12	7
	8	2	12	10	7	11	6	1	4	5	9	3
	9	3	2	7	1	12	5	10	4	11	6	8
	10	3	12	7	11	4	9	1	6	2	8	5
	9	6	1	3	5	12	7	8	2	11	10	4

APPLICATION: A COMBINATORIAL PROBLEM

As another example of the use of sets, we will consider a simple combinatorial problem. Suppose that we have a bag containing r numbered balls and that we are interested in possible ways of drawing k balls from it. The *number* of possible ways is easy to calculate using the appropriate binomial coefficient. A more interesting problem is to generate the selections one at a time. The bag may contain none, some, or all of the balls at any one time, and it may be represented appropriately by a set.

```
const
  capacity = 20;
type
  object = 1..capacity;
  container = set of object;
var
  bag : container;
  ball : object;
```

Now suppose that we have to select *total balls* from the bag and that we have already selected *drawn* of them. Consider the problem of drawing the next one: either *drawn* < *total* and we have to look in the bag for another ball, or *drawn* = *total* and we have finished. This is done by the recursive procedure *select* in the program *selections*. As each ball is drawn, its number is printed. An entry in the third column of the output listing indicates that the ball with that number was the third to be selected. It also indicates the level of recursion.

```
{ Use recursion to enumerate subsets of a set. }
program selections (input, output);
  const
    capacity = 20;
  type
    counter = 0..capacity;
    object = 1..capacity;
    container = set of object;
  var
    numballs, samplesize : counter;

  { Print all ways of drawing sample-drawn balls from the set bag. }
  procedure select (bag : container;
                    sample, drawn : counter);
    var
      ball : object;
    begin
      if drawn < sample
        then
          for ball := 1 to capacity do
            if ball in bag
              then
                begin
                  writeln (ball : 3 * drawn);
                  select (bag - [ball], sample, drawn + 1)
                end { then }
    end; { select }

begin
  read (numballs, samplesize);
  if numballs ⩾ samplesize
  then select ([1..numballs], samplesize, 0)
  else writeln ('The number of balls must be ',
                'greater than the sample size.')
end. { selections }
```

INPUT	OUTPUT		
4 3	1		
		2	
			3
			4
		3	
			2
			4
		4	
			2
			3
	2		
		1	
			3
			4
		3	
			1
			4
		4	
	....		

APPLICATIONS OF SETS

Character sets have many uses. For example, Program *convert* in Chapter 3 and Program *calculator* in Chapter 4 use the expression

$$('0' \leqslant ch) \text{ and } (ch \leqslant '9')$$

Using set notation, we can write this expression more succinctly in the form

$$ch \text{ in } ['0'..'9']$$

If we declare

```
type
   charset = set of char;
```

we can write a procedure, *skipchars*, that skips over characters in a given set.

```
procedure skipchars (var ch : char; skipset : charset);
   begin
     while ch in skipset do
        read (ch)
   end;
```

The statement

```
skipchars (ch, ['a'..'z'])
```

skips over letters, and the statement

```
skipchars (ch, [',', '.', ';', ':'])
```

skips over punctuation marks.

It is often easier to work with symbols than with characters. In a Pascal program, each of the following is regarded as a single symbol.

```
begin
end
varname
1235.685
:=
```

A procedure, called a *lexical scanner*, is used to read characters from the input file and assemble them into symbols. The symbols are classified by a type definition. In a simple case, we might have

```
type
  symboltype = (reservedword, identifier, number, becomes);
  setofsymbol = set of symboltype;
```

We can write a procedure, *getsymbol*, that reads the next symbol and returns its type and value, and a procedure, *skipsymbols*, that skips over unwanted symbols in the same way as *skipchars* skips over characters.

During the execution of a large program, many kinds of errors may be detected. When an error is identified, an error code is printed. At the end of the run, explanations of the errors that occurred are printed. To implement this, we declare

```
const
  maxerrorcode = 50;
type
  errorcode = 1..maxerrorcode;
  errorset = set of errorcode;
var
  cumerror : errorset;
  error : errorcode;
```

During the initialization of the program, we set

```
cumerror := [ ]
```

When an error is identified, we call a procedure of the following form.

```
procedure reporterror (error : errorcode);
   begin
      writeln ('Error', error : 3);
      cumerror := cumerror + [error]
   end;
```

At the end of the run, we execute this loop.

```
for error := 1 to maxerrorcode do
   if error in cumerror
      then write description of error
```

TYPE DENOTER SYNTAX

Figure 5.1 shows the syntax for a type denoter. A *type identifier* is one of the standard identifiers, *integer, real, boolean,* or *char,* or it is an identifier defined in a previous type definition.

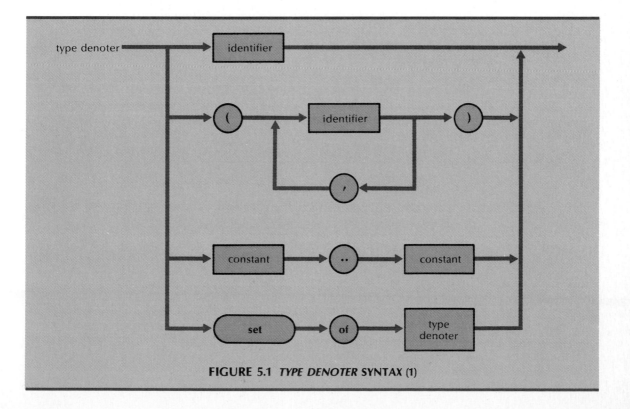

FIGURE 5.1 *TYPE DENOTER* SYNTAX (1)

5.4   RELATIONSHIPS BETWEEN TYPES

Types that we can define ourselves are a very important part of Pascal, but their use introduces some subtle problems. Consider the following declarations.

```
type
  facesofdie = 1..6;
var
  throw : facesofdie;
  toss : 1..6;
  score : integer;
```

These declarations suggest various questions. Do *throw* and *toss* have the same type? Can we write statements such as

```
score := score + throw + toss
```

in which "different" types are used? These questions have already been answered informally. In this section we describe the way in which Pascal is supposed to resolve type conflicts.

There are three relationships that can exist between two types: identity, compatibility, and assignment-compatibility. Types that are used at two or more places in the text of a program are *identical* if at least one of the following statements is true.

- The same type identifier is used at each place.
- The type identifiers are different, *T1* and *T2* for instance, but they have been defined as equivalent by a declaration of the form *T1 = T2*.

Two types are *compatible* if at least one of the following statements is true.

- They are identical.
- One is a subrange of the other.
- They are both subranges of the same type.
- They are set types with compatible base types.

An expression, *E*, of type *T2* is *assignment-compatible* with a type, *T1*, if at least one of the following statements is true.

- *T1* and *T2* are identical.
- *T1* is *real* and *T2* is *integer* or a subrange of *integer*.
- *T1* and *T2* are compatible ordinal types and the value of *E* is a permissible value of the type *T1*.
- *T1* and *T2* are compatible set types and every member of the set *E* is a permissible value of the base type of *T1*.

The purpose of these definitions is to ensure that relationships between types are precisely defined in all circumstances and that types behave in a reasonable way. We will clarify the definitions by considering some examples.

```
type
    T1 = 0..100;
    T2 = T1;
    T3 = 0..100;
    T4 = 0..10;
    T5 = (A, B, C, D, E);
    T6 = A..C;
    T7 = D..E;
    S1 = set of T5;
    S2 = set of T6;
var
    U, V : T1;
    W : T2;
    X : T5;
    Y : T6;
    Z : T7;
```

The variables U and V have identical types because the same type identifier, $T1$, is used for each. The type of W is identical to the type of U and V because $T2$ is defined by $T2 = T1$. Although the type $T3$ allows the same values as $T1$, it is *not* identical to $T1$.

If a procedure or a function has a variable formal parameter, the type of the corresponding actual parameter must be identical to the type of the formal parameter. An important consequence of this is that the type of a variable formal parameter must always be specified by a type identifier; in no circumstances can we write something like

```
procedure wrong (var arg : 1..5);
```

If two types are identical, they are also compatible. Thus $T1$ and $T2$ are compatible. $T1$ and $T3$ are also compatible because both are subranges of *integer*. $T6$ is compatible with both $T5$ and $T7$ because $T6$ and $T7$ are subranges of $T5$. The set types $S1$ and $S2$ are compatible because their base types are compatible.

Identity and compatibility are symmetric relations: if type X is identical to, or compatible with, type Y, then Y is identical to, or compatible with, type X.

Assignment-compatibility is not symmetric; it is defined in terms of an expression and a type. The rules of assignment-compatibility determine whether the statement

$$V := E$$

is legal or not. It is legal if the type of E is assignment-compatible with the type of V. Identity and compatibility can always be determined by the compiler, but assignment-compatibility may not be known until the program is executed because, in general, the compiler is not able to determine the value of the expression E. Using the declarations above, the statement

$$X := Y$$

can always be executed successfully because X can be assigned any value that Y may possess. On the other hand, the statement

$$Y := X$$

may cause a run-time error. For example, the value of X might be D, which cannot be assigned to Y.

The rule of assignment-compatibility is also used to determine the validity of an actual value parameter. The value of an actual value parameter must be assignment-compatible to the type of the corresponding formal parameter. If we have declared

```
procedure play (toy : plaything);
```

and we call

```
play (ball)
```

then the expression *ball* must be assignment-compatible with the type *plaything*.

5.5   THE case STATEMENT

The **if** statement allows a process to select one of two possible choices of action according to the value of a *boolean* expression. The **case** statement is a generalization of the **if** statement. It enables the process to execute one of several actions according to the value of a scalar or subrange expression.

As an introductory example, suppose that there is a toll bridge at which bicycles and motorcycles cross free of charge, cars are charged 25 cents, cars with trailers are charged 50 cents, and trucks are charged 25 cents per ton. We are required to write a program to calculate tolls. First we make some declarations.

```
const
  maxweight = 50;
  maxtoll = 1250;
type
  vehicletype = (cycle, car, carandtrailer, truck);
var
  weight : 1..maxweight;
  toll : 0..maxtoll;
  vehicle : vehicletype;
```

We can use an **if** statement to calculate the toll.

```
if vehicle = cycle
  then toll := 0
else if vehicle = car
  then toll := 25
else if vehicle = carandtrailer
  then toll := 50
else toll := 25 * weight
```

The case statement enables us to express this calculation in a more natural way.

```
case vehicle of
  cycle : toll := 0;
  car : toll := 25;
  carandtrailer : toll := 50;
  truck : toll := 25 * weight
end
```

In this statement, the variable *vehicle* is a case *selector*. The different values that the case selector can have appear in the **case** statement as case *labels*. In the example, these values are *cycle, car, carandtrailer,* and *truck*. After each label, there is a single statement. When the **case** statement is executed, the case selector is evaluated. If there is a case label with the same value as the case selector, the statement following this label is executed. If there is no such label, a run-time error occurs.

When the same action is required for several different values of the case selector, these values may be written in a list.

```
type
  month = (jan, feb, mar, apr, may, jun,
           jul, aug, sep, oct, nov, dec);
  year = 1900..2000;
  lenmonth = 28..31;
var
  yy : year;
  mm : month;
  len : lenmonth;
....
  case mm of
    jan, mar, may, jul, oct, dec : len := 31;
    apr, jun, sep, nov : len := 30;
    feb : if yy mod 4 = 0
                    then len := 29
                    else len := 28
  end { case }
```

Sometimes there are values of the case selector for which no action is required, as for the value *sunday* in the following example.

```
var
  day : (sunday, monday, tuesday, wednesday,
         thursday, friday, saturday);
....
  case day of
    sunday : ;
    monday, tuesday, wednesday, thursday, friday :
      begin
        gotowork;
        work;
        comehome
      end;
    saturday : washcar
  end { case }
```

If there is one action for which a long label list is required, the **case** statement can be combined with an **if** statement.

```
var
  control : 1..20;
....
  if control in [2, 3, 5, 7, 8, 11, 17, 20]
    then
```

```
        case control of
          2, 5 : action (1);
          3, 7, 11 : action (2);
          8, 17 : action (3);
          20 : action (4)
        end { case }
      else writeln ('Illegal control value')
```

If there is no case label corresponding to the value of the case selector, the program fails. Some compilers permit the use of a special case label or clause, such as **otherwise**, to catch values of the case selector for which there is no case label. This is an extension to the standard language.

APPLICATION: *SNAKES AND LADDERS*

The object of the children's game *Snakes and Ladders* is to move a token from the first cell to the last cell of a square board containing 100 cells. Each player throws a die to determine the number of cells traversed during a move. Snakes and ladders drawn on the board make the game more exciting than it otherwise would be. A player whose token lands on the head of a snake moves it to the tail of the snake, and a player whose token lands at the foot of a ladder moves it to the head of the ladder and has an extra turn. In Pascal, we can use sets to represent the cells at which snakes and ladders start and a **case** statement to calculate the cells at which they end.

The following program is organized around a **repeat** statement. During each iteration, the program requests a number corresponding to a throw of the die and calculates the new position of the token.

```
{ Snakes and ladders game for one player }
program snakesandladders (input, output);
  const
    lastcell = 100;
  type
    celltype = 1..lastcell;
    setofcell = set of celltype;
  var
    snakes, ladders : setofcell;
    position : celltype;
    throw : integer;
  begin
    snakes := [42,55,83,86,96];
    ladders := [7,9,15,43,69];
    position := 1;
```

```
repeat
  write ('You are at cell ', position:1, '. Enter throw: ');
  read (throw);
  if not (throw in [1..6])
    then writeln ('The die has only six sides: try again.')
  else if position + throw ≤ lastcell
    then
      begin
        position := position + throw;
        if position in snakes
          then
            begin
              writeln ('You''ve been swallowed by a snake.');
              case position of
                42 : position := 3;
                55 : position := 25;
                83 : position := 59;
                86 : position := 47;
                96 : position := 18
              end { case }
            end { then }
        else if position in ladders
          then
            begin
              writeln ('You''ve climbed a ladder.');
              case position of
                 7 : position := 73;
                 9 : position := 50;
                15 : position := 36;
                43 : position := 84;
                69 : position := 93
              end { case }
            end { then }
      end { then }
until position = lastcell;
writeln ('Congratulations: you''ve finished!')
end. { Snakesandladders }
```

case STATEMENT SYNTAX

Figure 5.2 is a syntax diagram for the **case** statement. The reserved words **case**
and **end** act as brackets around the statement. The last statement in the case

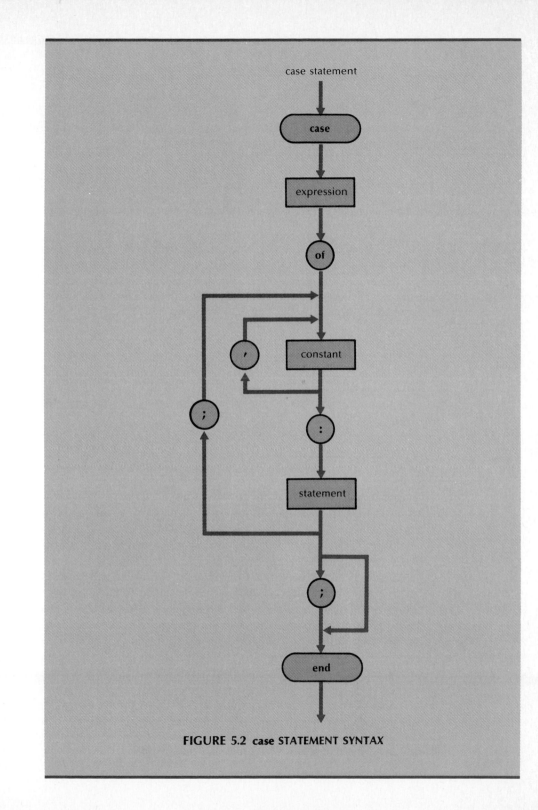

FIGURE 5.2 case STATEMENT SYNTAX

list need not be followed by a semicolon. There is no provision in Fig. 5.2 for a case label without an action because the complete syntax of Pascal, given in Appendix B, allows a statement to be empty.

5.6   APPLICATION: POCKET CALCULATOR SIMULATION REVISITED

We conclude this chapter by presenting a second version of Program *calculator* of Chapter 4. The new version illustrates the programming techniques introduced in this chapter and a variation in programming style. The principal changes introduced in this version of the program are listed below, and a discussion of their relative merits follows.

- All constants are defined globally.
- The variables *nextchar* and *nextpos* are declared globally. They are altered directly by the procedures that use them rather than being passed as parameters.
- The variables *nextpos*, *count*, and *scale* are declared with appropriate subrange types.
- The new identifiers *digits*, *addingops*, *multops*, and *terminators* denote constant character sets.
- **Case** statements replace **if** statements in appropriate contexts.

Because the two versions of Program *calculator* perform the same task, we are interested in the effect of these changes on the ease with which we can read and understand the program. The use of subrange types, set notation, and **case** statements clearly improves the clarity of the program. These features of Pascal should be used in all appropriate circumstances.

The variables *nextchar* and *nextpos* are used throughout both versions. In the first version they are passed as parameters to each procedure, and in the second version they are accessed directly by the procedures. We can argue for or against either method. The advantage of passing parameters is that fully parametrized procedures are self-contained entities that can be understood without reference to the surrounding text. The disadvantage is that, as we enhance the modularity of the program, we obscure the relationships between its parts.

In the second version, the constant definitions appear in a group at the beginning of the program and all constants have global scope. The use of global constants is conventional and, in this example, it is also appropriate for the program. In a large, modular program, it would be appropriate to define constants only within the modules in which they were used.

The new version of *calculator* reveals some shortcomings of Pascal. First, we note that Pascal does not provide literals for types other than the simple types. We would like to write

```
const
    digits = ['0'..'9'];
```

but instead we have to declare a variable

```
var
    digits : set of char;
```

and then assign a value to it:

```
digits := ['0'..'9']
```

This circumlocution obscures the fact that *digits* is never changed after the initial assignment. Another shortcoming of Pascal is that we have limited control over the scope of identifiers. If a variable is accessed from several different parts of the program by different procedures, it must be declared globally.

Discussions of programming style must be conducted in the context of particular programs and programming environments. Program *calculator* is a small program of about 150 lines. Large programs, consisting of thousands of lines, can be completed successfully only if careful attention is paid to coding conventions and disciplines. If the program is written by a team of programmers rather than by an individual, these considerations become even more important.

```
{ The second version of a program that calculates expressions }
program calculator (input, output);
    const
        radix = 10;      maxscale = 20;      maxlinelen = 80;
        blank = ' ';     separator = ',';    terminator = ';';
        point = '.';     plus = '+';         minus = '-';
        multiply = '*';  divide = '/';       marker = '↑';
        leftparen = '('; rightparen = ')';
    type
        position = 0..maxlinelen;
        charset = set of char;
    var
        nextchar : char;
        nextpos : position;
        result : real;
        digits, addingops, multops, delimiters : charset;
```

```
{ Read one character from the keyboard; return nextchar,
  the character, and nextpos, its position on the line. }
procedure readchar;
  begin
    repeat
      if eoln
        then
          begin
            nextpos := 0;
            nextchar := blank;
            readln
          end { then }
        else
          begin
            nextpos := nextpos + 1;
            read (nextchar)
          end { else }
    until nextchar ≠ blank
  end; { readchar }
{ Report an error by displaying '↑' under the offending character.
  Skip to the next expression or the end of the input, whichever
  comes first. }
procedure reporterror;
  begin
    writeln (marker : nextpos);
    while not (nextchar in delimiters) do
      readchar
  end; { reporterror }
{ Read a number. On entry, the current character is a digit.
  Return the value of the number in numvalue. }
procedure readnumber (var numvalue : real);
  type
    scalefactor = 0..maxscale;
  var
    count, scale : scalefactor;
  begin
    numvalue := 0;
    while nextchar in digits do
```

```pascal
    begin
      numvalue := radix * numvalue + ord (nextchar)
                                  - ord ('0');
      readchar
    end; { while }
  if nextchar = point
    then
      begin
        readchar;
        scale := 0;
        while nextchar in digits do
          begin
            numvalue := radix * numvalue + ord (nextchar)
                                        - ord ('0');
            readchar;
            scale := scale + 1
          end; { while }
        for count := 1 to scale do
          numvalue := numvalue / radix
      end { then }
  end; { readnumber }
{ Read an expression. An expression consists of
  one or more terms separated by either '+' or '-'. }
procedure readexpression (var exprvalue : real);
  var
    addop : char;
    nexttermval : real;

  { Read a term. A term consists of one or
    more factors separated by '*' or '/'. }
  procedure readterm (var termvalue : real);
    var
      mulop : char;
      nextfacval : real;

    { Read a factor. A factor is a number
      or an expression enclosed in parentheses. }
    procedure readfactor (var factorvalue : real);
```

```
      begin
        if nextchar in digits + [leftparen]
          then
            case nextchar of
              '0', '1', '2', '3', '4', '5', '6', '7', '8', '9' :
                readnumber (factorvalue);
              leftparen :
                begin
                  readchar;
                  readexpression (factorvalue);
                  if nextchar = rightparen
                    then readchar
                    else reporterror
                end
            end { then and case }
          else
            begin
              reporterror;
              factorvalue := 0
            end { else }
      end; { readfactor }
  begin { readterm }
    readfactor (termvalue);
    while nextchar in multops do
      begin
        mulop := nextchar;
        readchar;
        readfactor (nextfacval);
        case mulop of
          multiply :
            termvalue := termvalue * nextfacval;
          divide :
            if nextfacval ≠ 0
              then termvalue := termvalue / nextfacval
              else reporterror
        end { case }
      end { while }
  end; { readterm }
```

```
begin { readexpression }
  readterm (exprvalue);
  while nextchar in addingops do
    begin
      addop := nextchar;
      readchar;
      readterm (nexttermval);
      case addop of
        plus :
          exprvalue := exprvalue + nexttermval;
        minus :
          exprvalue := exprvalue - nexttermval
      end { case }
    end { while }
end; { readexpression }

begin { calculator }
  digits := ['0'..'9'];
  addingops := [plus, minus];
  multops := [multiply, divide];
  delimiters := [separator, terminator];
  nextpos := 0;
  readchar;
  while nextchar ≠ terminator do
    begin
      readexpression (result);
      if nextchar in delimiters
        then
          begin
            writeln (result);
            if nextchar = separator
              then readchar
          end { then }
        else reporterror
    end { while }
end. { calculator }
```

5.7 EXERCISES

5.1 Show how a **case** statement may be used to print values of a scalar variable.

5.2 In the following program fragment, identify statements that
   a) will execute correctly;
   b) may cause a run-time error;
   c) should cause a compile-time error.

Assume that a statement that will certainly fail if it is executed is a compile-time error. Assume also that variables that are not defined in these fragments have been assigned values elsewhere in the program.

```
const
  min = - 100;
  zero = 0;
  max = 100;
type
  counter = 1..maxint;
  zeromin = min..zero;
  zeromax = zero..max;
  coin = (penny, nickel, dime, quarter, halfdollar);
var
  count : counter;
  small : zeromin;
  big, value : zeromax;
  change : coin;
  flipflop : boolean;
  slot : set of coin;
begin
  ...
  count := 0;
  small := big;
  change := penny;
  repeat
    write (change : 10);
    change := succ (change)
  until change > halfdollar;
  dime := 2 * nickel;
  count := count + ord (flipflop);
  slot := slot + [halfdollar];
```

```
            case coin of
              penny :
                value := 1;
              nickel :
                value := 5;
              dime :
                value := 10;
              quarter :
                value := 25;
            end;
            ...
          end.
```

5.3 Given that

```
    type
      numberset = set of min..max;
```

and *min* and *max* are integer constants, write a procedure, *printset*, that prints the value of a variable of type *numberset*. For example, the set whose members are 3, 7, 11, and 19 should be printed as

    [3,7,11,19]

5.4 Write a program that counts, in any given text, the words that contain at least four different vowels.

5.5 Determine experimentally the form of the function $p(k, N)$ defined as follows. Declare

```
    var
      x, y : set of 1..N;
```

Generate random values of x and y such that each has k elements. Then

$$p(k, N) = \text{probability that } x \text{ and } y \text{ are disjoint sets}$$
$$= prob(x * y = [\ \ ])$$

5.6 Write a program that plays a game according to the following rules.

> The computer constructs a set of random letters. The object of the game is for the player to enter from the keyboard a set of letters identical to the set chosen by the computer. Each time the player enters a trial set, the computer displays the number of letters the two sets have in common.

5.7 The date calculation in Section 5.5 assumes that the year, *yy*, is a leap year if *yy* is a multiple of four. This is sometimes incorrect at the end of a century. The year *dd*00 is a leap year only if *dd* is a multiple of four. For example, 1900 was not a leap year but 2000 will be a leap year. Correct the example.

5.8 Rewrite Program *snakesandladders* as a game that can be played by two people.

5.9 Enhance Program *calculator* so that the letter "p" may be used to obtain the value of the previous expression. For example, the calculation

$$3*3, \; p*p;$$

should produce the result

$$9$$
$$81$$

6

ARRAYS
AND RECORDS

With the exception of set types, the variable types we have encountered so far have all been simple types. In this chapter and the next we introduce structured types. A structured type differs from a simple type in that variables of a structured type have more than one component. Each component of a structured type is a variable that may have a simple or structured type. At the lowest level, the components of a structured variable have simple types. These may be assigned values and used in expressions in the same way as simple variables. The important thing about a structured variable is the way in which its components are accessed. In this chapter we introduce variables of the types *array* and *record*, which permit us to use the computer's memory in more flexible ways than we have been able to do. In the next chapter we introduce files, which enable programs to access information stored on external media. We use the terms *simple variable* and *structured variable* to denote variables whose types are simple and structured respectively.

6.1   ARRAYS

An *array* is an ordered collection of variables all of which have the same type. For example, we can use an array of characters to represent a line of text and an array of reals to represent a vector. A matrix consists of columns, each of which is a vector, and can be represented by an array of vectors.

An array type is defined in terms of an *index type* and a *component type*.

```
type
   vec = array [1..3] of real;
```

The index type of *vec* is 1..3 and the component type is *real*. It is usually preferable to use a type identifier for the index type, as in the following definition.

```
type
   axis = 1..3;
   vec = array [axis] of real;
```

We can also use an enumerated type as an index type.

```
type
   direction = (x, y, z);
   vector = array [direction] of real;
```

We can declare variables of the type *direction* and *vector* in the usual way.

```
var
   s, t : direction;
   u, v : vector;
```

A variable of type *vector* has three components, one corresponding to each of the three values of the type *direction*. The three components of the vector *v* are

$$v [x], v [y], v [z].$$

The conventional mathematical notation for vectors uses subscripts to denote the components of a vector. The components of *v* are written in the form

$$v_x, v_y, v_z.$$

For this reason, the values of an index type are sometimes called *subscripts*.

Each of the components of *v* is a *real* variable that may be used in any context where a *real* variable may be used. For example, the *norm* of a vector is the sum of the squares of its components. We could calculate the norm of *v* with either of the statements

$$norm := sqr\ (v\ [x]) + sqr\ (v\ [y]) + sqr\ (v\ [z])$$

or

```
begin
  norm := 0;
  for s := x to z do
    norm := norm + sqr (v [s])
end
```

The value of one array may be assigned to another array of the same type by a single assignment statement. The statement

```
v := u
```

in which *u* and *v* are both vectors, is equivalent to the assignments

```
v [x] := u [x];
v [y] := u [y];
v [z] := u [z]
```

An array may also be passed to a procedure or a function as a value parameter or as a variable parameter. For example, the *inner product* of two vectors, *u* and *v*, is the number

$$u\ [x] * v\ [x] + u\ [y] * v\ [y] + u\ [z] * v\ [z].$$

The function *innerproduct* calculates the inner product of two vectors.

```
function innerproduct (u, v : vector) : real;
  var
    ip : real;
    s : direction;
  begin
    ip := 0;
    for s := x to z do
      ip := ip + u [s] * v [s];
    innerproduct := ip
  end;
```

The *outer product* of two vectors is itself a vector. We cannot write a function that calculates an outer product because Pascal does not allow functions to return structured values. We can, however, write *outerproduct* as a procedure which evaluates *w*, the outerproduct of *u* and *v*.

```
procedure outerproduct (u, v : vector;
                             var w : vector);
    begin
        w [x] := u [y] * v [z] - u [z] * v [y];
        w [y] := u [z] * v [x] - u [x] * v [z];
        w [z] := u [x] * v [y] - u [y] * v [x]
    end;
```

Arrays may be passed as value parameters or as variable parameters. In most cases, the choice should be made according to the rules given in Chapter 4. There is, however, an additional factor that we must consider when arrays are passed as value parameters. Whenever an object is passed to a procedure by value, a local copy of it is made. If the object is a large array, the copying operation will make the program slower and will increase its memory requirements. If a procedure receives a large array and does not alter any component of it, we may save space and time by passing the array as a variable parameter.

ARRAY SYNTAX

An *array type* is a kind of type denoter. Figure 6.1, which shows the syntax of an *array type*, should therefore be regarded as an additional part of Fig. 5.1, the syntax diagram for *type denoter.*

The index type of an array must be an ordinal type. Remember that *real* is not an ordinal type. The component type of an array may be any type, even a structured type.

A *component* of an array has the same properties as a variable of the component type and is a variety of factor. Figure 6.2 shows the syntax of an *array component*.

APPLICATION: CONVERSION OF NUMBERS TO STRINGS

Program *convert* in Chapter 3 performed a conversion from a string of digits to a number in the computer's internal form. We now consider the inverse problem, converting a variable to a string of digits. The value of each digit in the string can be obtained easily enough by repeated remaindering and division.

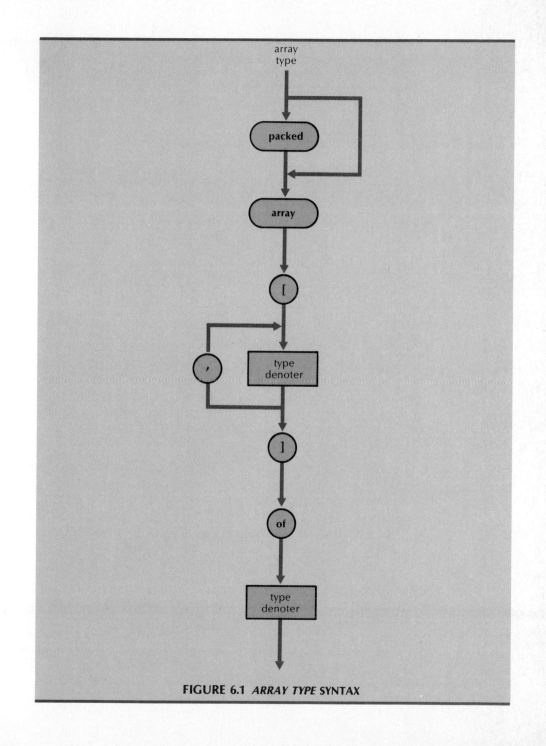

FIGURE 6.1 *ARRAY TYPE* SYNTAX

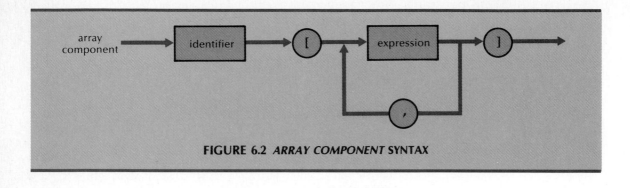

FIGURE 6.2 *ARRAY COMPONENT* SYNTAX

```
var
   datum, digit : integer;
....
   repeat
     digit := datum mod 10;
     datum := datum div 10
   until datum := 0
```

Unfortunately, this simple program produces the numbers in the reverse order to that in which we want to print them. Suppose, for example, that *datum* = 123. During the execution of the repeat statement, *digit* takes the values 3, 2, and 1, in that order. We can get around this problem by storing the successive digits in an array and then writing them from the array in reverse order. We declare

```
const
   maxlen = 32;
   rad = 10;
var
   jp, kp : 0..maxlen;
   buffer : array [1..maxlen] of char;
   num : integer;
```

The conversion loop takes this form:

```
   kp := 0;
   repeat
     kp := kp + 1;
     buffer [kp] := chr (num mod rad + ord ('0'));
     num := num div rad
   until num = 0
```

The digits can then be written in the correct sequence.

```
for jp := kp downto 1 do
  write (buffer [jp])
```

There is an alternative solution to this problem: we can store integer values instead of characters in the buffer. Three changes are required. First, we change the declaration of *buffer* to

```
var
  buffer : array [1..maxlen] of 0..9;
```

Second, the assignment to *buffer* becomes

```
buffer [kp] := num mod rad
```

Third, we change the **for** loop that prints the digits.

```
for jp := kp downto 1 do
  write (chr (buffer [jp] + ord ('0')))
```

We have chosen 10 as the divisor in the example because we are accustomed to using the decimal system. It is just as easy for the computer to use another divisor and print numbers in a different scale. Program *numberscales* reads a number using the standard procedure *read*, which performs a decimal conversion. The program then performs the inverse conversion for each of the scales 2 through 10 in turn.

```
{ Read a number and write its representation
  in number scales from 2 through 10. }
program numberscales (input, output);
  const
    maxradix = 10;          { Largest possible number base }
    maxlen = 32;            { Longest possible representation }
  type
    radix = 2..maxradix;
  var
    datum : integer;
    scale : radix;

  { Write the representation of num in the scale rad. }
  procedure writenumber (num : integer; rad : radix);
    var
      jp, kp : 0..maxlen;
      buffer : array [1..maxlen] of char;
```

```
      begin
        if num < 0
          then
            begin
              write ('-');
              num := abs (num)
            end; { then }
        kp := 0;
        repeat
          kp := kp + 1;
          buffer [kp] := chr (num mod rad + ord ('0'));
          num := num div rad
        until num = 0;
        for jp := kp downto 1 do
          write (buffer [jp])
      end; { writenumber }
  begin { numberscales }
    read (datum);
    for scale := 2 to maxradix do
      begin
        writenumber (datum, scale);
        writeln
      end { for }
  end. { numberscales }
```

INPUT	OUTPUT
100	1100100
	10201
	1210
	400
	244
	202
	144
	121
	100

APPLICATION: SORTING AN ARRAY

The word *sorting* is used in computer science to denote the process of arranging objects in the order of their size. This is possible if there is an *ordering* associated with the type of the objects. A collection of integers, such as

$$4 \quad 1 \quad -7 \quad 2 \quad 3 \quad -4 \quad 4 \quad 9 \quad 0 \quad 2$$

can be sorted because there is an ordering associated with the type *integer*. Integers may in fact be sorted into either ascending or descending order:

$$-7 \quad -4 \quad 0 \quad 1 \quad 2 \quad 2 \quad 3 \quad 4 \quad 4 \quad 9$$
$$9 \quad 4 \quad 4 \quad 3 \quad 2 \quad 2 \quad 1 \quad 0 \quad -4 \quad -7$$

Before we discuss algorithms for sorting, we need a precise definition of a sorted sequence. Using Pascal notation, we can declare an array, a, and an index, i.

```
var
  a : array [I] of T
  i, j : I;
```

If there is an ordering associated with the type T, the array a is sorted in ascending order if

$$i > j \quad \text{implies that} \quad a[i] \geqslant a[j],$$

and it is sorted in descending order if

$$i > j \quad \text{implies that} \quad a[i] \leqslant a[j].$$

The problem of sorting an array is one of the classical problems of computer science. Although the first programs for sorting were written by von Neumann in 1945, the major advances in sorting theory did not occur until over twenty years later.

Sorting is still an important aspect of computer science, but its importance is diminishing. Increasingly, computer systems are designed to provide immediate access to stored information. A system that sorts the information once a day or once a week cannot provide immediate access efficiently. Most modern systems are therefore designed in such a way that information is always stored in sorted form.

The algorithm we use to sort an array was invented in 1959 by Donald L. Shell. It is called the *Shell sort* or the *diminishing increment sort*. The Shell sort is an *interchange sort*, which means that sorting is accomplished by exchanging pairs of numbers in the array until the array is sorted. The efficiency of an interchange sort depends entirely on the way in which we choose the numbers to be exchanged.

In any sort, an object has an initial position and a final position, and during the sorting process it moves from one to the other. In the simplest varieties of interchange sort, the objects move only one step at a time. The observation that led to Shell sort is that the process could be speeded up by allowing the objects to take large jumps at first and smaller jumps as they approached their destination. Although the idea is very simple, the mathematical analysis of it turns out to be very complicated. It is not easy to decide how large the first jumps should be, and it is even harder to discover how the jump size should diminish. We use a straightforward version of the Shell sort, in which the jump size is initially half the array length and is halved at the end of each iteration.

The program we will construct reads numbers from an input file, stores them in an array, sorts the array, and then prints it. The sort consists of three nested loops. The outermost loop controls the jump size. Within this loop, the array is scanned repeatedly until no more interchanges are possible with the current jump size. The innermost loop actually does the scanning. These loops are shown in the following schema. *Length* is the number of components in *row*, the array that we are sorting.

```
jump := length;
while jump > 1 do
  begin
    jump := jump div 2;
    repeat
      for m := 1 to max do
        begin
          n := m + jump;
          if row [m] > row [n]
              then interchange row [m] and row [n]
        end
    until no more interchanges possible
  end
```

The value of *max* in the **for** loop must be chosen so that the program does not attempt to access components beyond the end of the array. Accordingly,

$$max + jump \leqslant length$$

and a suitable value for *max* is

$$length - jump.$$

Interchanging two values in a computer program always requires a temporary variable. We introduce the variable *temp* for the interchange of *row* [m] and *row* [n]:

```
temp := row [m];
row [m] := row [n];
row [n] := temp
```

The **repeat** loop must continue scanning the array until a complete scan without interchanges is performed. A *boolean* variable, *alldone,* is set to *true* at the be-

TABLE 6.1										
Original Sequence	9	8	1	7	6	3	4	5	4	1
Jump = 5	3	8	1	7	6	9	4	5	4	1
	3	4	1	7	6	9	8	5	4	1
	3	4	1	4	6	9	8	5	7	1
	3	4	1	4	1	9	8	5	7	6
Jump = 2	1	4	3	4	1	9	8	5	7	6
	1	4	1	4	3	9	8	5	7	6
	1	4	1	4	3	5	8	9	7	6
	1	4	1	4	3	5	7	9	8	6
	1	4	1	4	3	5	7	6	8	9
Jump = 1	1	1	4	4	3	5	7	6	8	9
	1	1	4	3	4	5	7	6	8	9
	1	1	4	3	4	5	6	7	8	9
	1	1	3	4	4	5	6	7	8	9
Final Sequence	1	1	3	4	4	5	6	7	8	9

ginning of each iteration and is changed to *false* if an interchange is performed. The loop is executed until, at the end of an iteration, *alldone* is *true*.

Table 6.1 shows how the sort works. The top row of numbers in the table represents the unsorted array. The bottom row shows the same array after sorting. Each intermediate row contains two underlined numbers. These are the numbers that were interchanged during the previous iteration. The distance between the two underlined numbers is the value of *jump*. This value decreases during the sort, as the column of numbers at the left of the table shows.

The Shell sort demonstrates the way in which subscripts can be calculated and used to access the components of an array in a nonlinear sequence. It also demonstrates two general properties of an interchange sort. First, the storage required consists of the array itself and one extra component, *temp*, used for interchanging. This is significant because faster methods of sorting usually require more storage: this is the price paid for increased speed. Second, the direction of the sort is determined solely by the expression

$$row\ [m] > row\ [n]$$

In order to sort the numbers in descending order, we need only change this expression to

$$row\ [m] < row\ [n]$$

```
{ Read a list of numbers, sort the list, and print it.
  The first number read is the length of the list.
  The list must not contain more than 1000 numbers. }
program shellsort (input, output);
  const
    maxlength = 1000;
  type
    index = 1..maxlength;
    rowtype = array [index] of integer;
  var
    inrow : rowtype;
    count : 0..maxlength;
    ix : index;

{ Sort the array row containing length numbers. }
procedure sort (var row : rowtype; length : index);
    var
      jump, m, n : index;
      temp : integer;
      alldone : boolean;
    begin
      jump := length;
      while jump > 1 do
        begin
          jump := jump div 2;
          repeat
            alldone := true;
            for m := 1 to length - jump do
              begin
                n := m + jump;
                if row [m] > row [n]
                  then
                    begin
                      temp := row [m];
                      row [m] := row [n];
                      row [n] := temp;
                      alldone := false
                    end { then }
              end { for }
          until alldone
        end { while }
    end; { sort }
```

```
begin { shellsort }
  read (count);
  for ix := 1 to count do
    read (inrow [ix]);
    sort (inrow, count);
  for ix := 1 to count do
    write (inrow [ix])
end. { shellsort }
```

INPUT	OUTPUT
10	
9 8 1 7 6 3 4 5 4 1	1 1 3 4 4 5 6 7 8 9

6.2 MULTIDIMENSIONAL ARRAYS

The component type of an array may itself be an array. In the following declarations, the component type of *matrix* is *column*.

```
const
  size = 10;
type
  subscript = 1..size;
  column = array [subscript] of real;
  matrix = array [subscript] of column;
```

We can incorporate the declaration of *column* into the declaration of *matrix*.

```
type
  matrix = array [subscript] of
             array [subscript] of real;
```

This rather unwieldy expression can be further simplified to the more convenient form

```
type
  matrix = array [subscript, subscript] of real;
```

Now declare some variables.

```
var
  a, b, c : matrix;
  r, s, t : subscript;
```

Column s of matrix a is the component

$$a\ [s]$$

The component t of column s is a real variable that may be written

$$a\ [s]\ [t]$$

By analogy with the abbreviated declaration, we can simplify this to

$$a\ [s, t]$$

The array a is called a *two-dimensional array* because we can imagine that it is stored in this form:

$a[1, 1]$	$a[1, 2]$	$a[1, 3]$	$\ldots$	$a[1, 10]$
$a[2, 1]$	$a[2, 2]$	$a[2, 3]$	$\ldots$	$a[2, 10]$
$a[3, 1]$	$a[3, 2]$	$a[3, 3]$	$\ldots$	$a[3, 10]$
$\ldots$				
$a[10, 1]$	$a[10, 2]$	$a[10, 3]$	$\ldots$	$a[10, 10]$

The two-dimensional array is an abstraction; the memory of the computer is one dimensional. The compiler has to perform a mapping from the abstract, two-dimensional array to the actual, one-dimensional array that constitutes the computer's memory.

The *unit matrix* is defined by

$$a\ [s, t] = 1 \quad \text{if } s = t;$$
$$a\ [s, t] = 0 \quad \text{if } s \neq t.$$

We can give a this value by executing either the statement

```
for s := 1 to size do
  for t := 1 to size do
    if s = t
      then a [s, t] := 1
      else a [s, t] := 0
```

or the more efficient statement

```
for s := 1 to size do
  for t := 1 to size do
    a [s, t] := 0;
for s := 1 to size do
  a [s, s] := 1;
```

The product, *c*, of two matrices, *a* and *b*, is obtained by executing the statement

```
for r := 1 to size do
  for s := 1 to size do
    begin
      c [r, s] := 0;
      for t := 1 to size do
        c [r, s] := c [r, s] + a [r, t] * b [t, s]
    end
```

The component *c* [*r*, *s*] is accessed 2 * *size* times within the innermost loop. If you use a good compiler, this will not matter, but if your compiler is simple-minded, you could help it by referring to *c* [*r*, *s*] only once.

```
for r := 1 to size do
  for s := 1 to size do
    begin
      sum := 0;
      for t := 1 to size do
        sum := sum + a [r, t] * b [t, s];
      c [r, s] := sum
    end
```

APPLICATION: FREQUENCIES OF LETTER PAIRS

As an example of the use of multidimensional arrays, we present a program that measures the frequencies of pairs of adjacent letters in words. It tells us, for example, whether "EA" occurs more or less often than "IE". The program counts only within-word pairs, so that, given "THE CAT", it will count "TH", "HE", "CA", and "AT" but not "EC". The counters are stored in a two-dimensional array whose index type is *letter*. We declare

```
type
  letter = 'a'..'z';
var
  conmat : array [letter, letter] of integer;
```

We need a "window" two characters wide through which to look at the text. The window moves along, one character at a time, and whenever both characters in the window are letters, the appropriate component of *conmat* is incremented. The central loop of the program has the form

```
while not eof do
  begin
    read (thischar);
    if [thischar, prevchar] ≤ ['a'..'z']                              (6.1)
      then
        conmat [thischar, prevchar]
          := conmat [thischar, prevchar] + 1;
    prevchar := thischar
  end
```

Thischar and *prevchar* are the two characters visible through the window. Note, incidentally, that the use of sets considerably simplifies the *boolean* expression (6.1), which would otherwise be

```
('a' ≤ thischar) and (thischar) ≤ 'z')
and ('a' ≤ prevchar) and (prevchar ≤ 'z')
```

```
{ Read a text and construct a matrix of letter pairs from it. }
program contingencies (input, output);
  const
    numwidth = 4;
    blank = ' ';
  type
    letter = 'a'..'z';
  var
    conmat : array [letter, letter] of integer;
    across, down : letter;
    thischar, prevchar : char;
  begin
    for across := 'a' to 'z' do
      for down := 'a' to 'z' do
        conmat [across, down] := 0;
    prevchar := blank;
    while not eof do
      begin
        read (thischar);
        if [thischar, prevchar] ≤ ['a'..'z']
          then
            conmat [thischar, prevchar] :=
              conmat [thischar, prevchar] + 1;
        prevchar := thischar
      end; { while }
```

```
      write (blank : 2);
      for down := 'a' to 'z' do
        write (blank : numwidth - 1, down);
      writeln; writeln;
      for across := 'a' to 'z' do
        begin
          write (blank, across):
          for down := 'a' to 'z' do
            write (conmat [across, down] : numwidth);
          writeln
        end { for }
  end. { contingencies }
```

6.3   PACKED ARRAYS

The components of an array are stored in consecutive words of the computer's memory. This is an efficient way of storing integer and real components because on many computers an *integer* or *real* requires at least a whole word of memory. It is not always an efficient way of storing variables of other types, however, because space may be wasted. The amount of space wasted may be reduced by *packing* several components of an array into each word. The compiler will do this for you if you declare the array as packed. For example, the array *longstring*, declared as

```
    var
      longstring : array [1..1000] of char;
```

occupies 1000 words of memory. The array declared as

```
    var
      longstring : packed array [1..1000] of char;
```

occupies 100 words of memory on a CDC 6000 series computer that stores ten characters per word and 250 words of memory on an IBM 360/370 computer that stores four characters per word.

A packed array is used in a program in the same way as an unpacked array with one important exception: in many Pascal implementations, a component of a packed array cannot be passed as a variable parameter to a procedure or to a function. A program using a packed array will execute somewhat more slowly than the same program using an unpacked array. This is because a component of an unpacked array can be accessed more efficiently than a component of a packed array. The decision as to whether to pack a particular array or not depends on many factors, including available memory size, processor speed, required response time, and volume of data. A valid choice for one environment may be quite inappropriate to another. Packing is not particularly useful on byte-oriented machines and is not usually provided by Pascal implementations for microcomputers.

In many cases, the extra time required for accessing packed arrays can be reduced by packing or unpacking all the components in a single operation rather than one at a time. This can be accomplished using the standard procedures *pack* and *unpack*. Suppose that we are reading text from a file and decide to store a word of the text in the variable *word*, a packed array of 20 characters. Rather than copying characters from the file directly into *word*, we copy them into a temporary buffer that is not packed. The declarations for these variables are

```
const
  wordsize = 20;
var
  buffer : array [1..wordsize] of char;
  word : packed array [1..wordsize] of char;
```

When *buffer* contains a complete word, we use the procedure call

```
pack (buffer, 1, word)
```

to pack all the characters in *buffer* into the packed array *word*. The inverse operation is

```
unpack (word, buffer, 1)
```

that transfers characters from the packed array *word* to the unpacked array *buffer*.

In the general case, suppose that we have declared an array, A, of type T, and a corresponding packed array, P, also of type T.

```
var
  A : array [m..n] of T;
  P : packed array [i..j] of T;
```

In these declarations, i, j, m, and n are scalar constants, and

$$n - m \geqslant j - i.$$

The statement

```
for k := i to j do
  P [k] := A [k − i + m]
```

may be abbreviated to

```
pack (A, m, P)
```

and read as "pack components $A[m]$ through $A[j - i + m]$ of A into components $P[i]$ through $P[j]$ of P." The statement

```
for k := i to j do
    A [k - i + m] := P [k]
```

may be abbreviated to

```
unpack (P, A, m)
```

read as "unpack components $P[i]$ through $P[j]$ of P to components $A[m]$ through $A[j - i + m]$ of A."

6.4 *boolean* ARRAYS

An array with base type *boolean* has the same properties as a set. Each component of the array corresponds to a potential member of the set, which may be absent (*false*) or present (*true*). If we declare

```
type
    index = 1..20;
var
    ix : index;
    xset : set of index;
    xarr : array [index] of boolean;
```

then the operations

```
xarr [ix] := false
xarr [ix] := true
```

are equivalent to

```
xset := xset - [ix]
xset := xset + [ix]
```

and the *boolean* expression

```
xarr [ix]
```

is equivalent to

```
ix in xset
```

The operators $\leqslant$ and $\geqslant$, which test whether one set contains another, cannot be applied to *boolean* arrays. In most circumstances, set notation is easier to read than the corresponding *boolean* notation, so whenever possible a set should be used in preference to a *boolean* array. In many implementations of

Pascal, however, a *boolean* array can have more components than a set. When we need a very large set, say of 10,000 or 100,000 components, the program will probably be easier to write (and read) if we use a single *boolean* array rather than an array of sets. A considerable amount of space can be saved, at the expense of additional execution time, by packing the array.

APPLICATION: PRIME NUMBER GENERATION

The classical algorithm for enumerating prime numbers is the *Sieve of Eratosthenes*. Suppose that we want to find the prime numbers less than 10. We start by writing down the numbers from 2 to 10.

2   3   4   5   6   7   8   9   10

We then remove the lowest number, claim that it is prime, and remove its multiples. After the first step, we have 2 as a prime and the sieve contains only odd numbers.

3   5   7   9

After the second step, we know that 3 is a prime and only 5 and 7 remain in the sieve. The process terminates when the sieve is empty. We declare

```
const
  maximum = 100000;
var
  sieve : packed array [2..maximum] of boolean;
```

Initially we set each component of *sieve* to *true*, indicating that all the numbers are present. As we remove numbers, we set the corresponding components to *false*. The program consists of two nested loops, one to find the lowest number still in the sieve and the other to remove its multiples. The termination condition for the outer loop is that there are no numbers left in the sieve. We maintain a count, *leftin*, of the numbers left in the sieve; when *leftin* reaches zero, the outer loop terminates.

```
{ Find and print prime numbers from 2 to maximum. }
program primenumbers (input, output);
  const
    firstprime = 2;
    maximum = 100000;
  var
    sieve : packed array [firstprime..maximum] of boolean;
    leftin, range, factor, multiple : 0..maximum;
```

```
begin
  read (range);
  for factor := firstprime to range do
    sieve [factor] := true;
  leftin := range - firstprime + 1;
  factor := firstprime - 1;
  repeat
    factor := factor + 1;
    if sieve [factor]
      then { factor is prime }
        begin
          writeln (factor);
          for multiple := 1 to range div factor do
            if sieve [factor * multiple]
              then { remove multiple }
                begin
                  sieve [factor * multiple] := false;
                  leftin := leftin - 1
                end { then }
        end { then }
  until leftin = 0
end. { primenumbers }
```

INPUT	OUTPUT
50	2
	3
	5
	7
	11
	13
	17
	19
	23
	29
	31
	37
	41
	43
	47

6.5   STRINGS

We are already familiar with the use of characters and variables of type *char*
in Pascal programs. A string is a sequence of characters. These are strings.

> First catch your hare.
> Isabella Beeton's "Book of Household Management"

When a literal string is used in a Pascal program, it is enclosed by apostrophes.
We can do this easily enough for the first string.

```
'First catch your hare.'
```

The second string presents a problem because it contains an apostrophe. We
indicate to the compiler that the apostrophe is actually a part of the string by
writing another apostrophe immediately after it.

```
'Isabella Beeton''s "Book of Household Management"'
```

A constant string may be defined in a constant definition or used in a *write*
statement.

```
const
  message = 'Time to go home';
  ....
  write (message);
  write ('Time to go home')
```

The two *write* statements have exactly the same effect.

Suppose that the value of *s* is a string of *n* characters. The statement

```
write (s : m)
```

has the following effect: if $m \geqslant n$, $(m - n)$ blanks followed by *s* are written to the
output file; if $m < n$, only the first *m* characters of *s* are written. The following
statement uses the case $m \geqslant n$ to plot a graph of damped harmonic motion.

```
for t := 0 to 60 do
  writeln ('*' : round (60 * (1 + exp ( - t / 30) * sin (t / 3))))
```

A string may contain any character, but a string must not extend over more
than one line. The characters in a string represent *themselves*, in contrast to
other characters in a program that represent numbers, identifiers, reserved
words, or other symbols. Therefore

'begin'	has nothing to do with **begin**
'123'	is not a number
' + '	is not an operator

A *string variable* is a packed array of characters. These are string type definitions.

```
type
    cardimage = packed array [1..80] of char;
    lineimage = packed array [1..150] of char;
    longstring = packed array [1..1000] of char;
```

The length of a string is determined by its type and is fixed. Standard Pascal therefore offers less opportunity for string manipulation than do some other programming languages which allow strings to vary in length during execution. Many implementations of Pascal, however, provide additional string processing features such as concatenation and substring extraction.

Most of the properties of strings carry over from the usual properties of arrays. For example, strings of the same type may be copied by assignment statements or compared using the operators " = " and " ≠ ". Strings have the additional property that they are ordered. The ordering is determined by comparing each character of the string in turn, starting with the first, until unequal characters are found. The unequal characters are then used to define the order. This is the conventional "dictionary" order if the strings contain only letters. When the strings contain other characters, the order will depend on the computer's representation of the characters. For example,

```
'periapt' < 'perigee'
```

because

```
'a' < 'g'
```

The standard procedure *read* does not automatically read strings from the input device. If you want to read a string, you must read one character at a time, in a loop.

In general, array types are compatible only if they are identical. This rule is relaxed for string types, which are compatible if the strings have the same length.

6.6 RECORDS

Arrays and records are abstractions of modes of data storage used at the machine-language level. A *record*, like an array, is a structured variable with several components. The components of a record may have different types, however, and they are accessed by name, not by subscript.

A description of a planet might include the following information.

>   name
>   visible to the naked eye (yes/no)
>   diameter
>   mean orbital radius

We can use a string for the name. A *boolean* variable suffices for "visible to the naked eye." The other two quantities are *real*. We can define the type *planet* as follows.

```
type
    planet =
      record
        name : packed array [1..7] of char;
        visible : boolean;
        diameter, orbitrad : real;
      end;
```

A record definition is similar to a variable declaration section. The variable declarations are bracketed by **record** and **end**. The semicolon between *real* and **end** may be omitted.

Variables with this type can be declared in the usual way.

```
var
    inner, outer : planet;
```

A *component* of a record is selected by using the name of the record variable and the name of the component, separated by a period.

>   *inner.name*   is the name of the planet *inner*
>
>   *outer.diameter*   is the diameter of the planet *outer*

These names are called *record selectors*, and they are used in a program in exactly the same way as variables of the same type. We can write assignment statements such as

```
inner.name := 'Venus  ';
inner.visible := true;
inner.diameter := 12104; { kilometers }
inner.orbitrad := 108.2; { gigameters }
outer.name := 'Neptune';
outer.visible := false;
outer.diameter := 49500;
outer.orbitrad := 4496.6;
```

The structured types array and record can be combined. Using the same definition of *planet*, we can further define

```
const
  furthest = 9;
type
  planet = { as above }
var
  solarsystem : array [1..furthest] of planet;
  numplan : 1..furthest;
```

We can then execute statements like these:

```
write ('I live on ', solarsystem [3].name);
for numplan := 1 to furthest do
  if solarsystem [numplan].orbitrad < 4000
    then solarsystem [numplan].visible := true
    else solarsystem [numplan].visible := false
```

The second of these statements can be simplified, as you may already have realized, to

```
for numplan := 1 to furthest do
  solarsystem [numplan].visible                                    (6.2)
    :=solarsystem [numplan].orbitrad < 4000
```

The names of the components must be unique within the record. We could not use *name* more than once in the definition of *planet*, but we could use it to denote a variable or a component of another record. There are no operators which may be used with records as operands. In particular, there is no ordering associated with records. The value of a record can, however, be assigned to another record by an assignment statement. Using the example above, the single statement

```
inner := outer
```

is equivalent to the assignments

```
inner.name := outer.name
inner.visible := outer.visible
inner.diameter := outer.diameter
inner.orbitrad := outer.orbitrad
```

A record may be passed as a parameter to a procedure or a function. In Standard Pascal the value of a function cannot be a record.

THE with STATEMENT

It is often necessary to access the same component of a record, or different components of the same record, several times in a small section of the program. The **for** statement (6.2) is an example: the record *solarsystem* [*numplan*] appears twice on consecutive lines. Using **with**, we can write this statement in the form

```
for numplan := 1 to furthest do
  with solarsystem [numplan] do
    visible := orbitrad < 4000
```

The general form of the **with** statement is

```
with record identifier do
  S
```

Within the statement *S*, components of the record may be referred to by field name only: the compiler supplies the record name. In addition to saving some writing, the **with** statement may be helpful to the compiler because the record need be located only once. On the other hand, if the statement *S* is long or the program contains many different kinds of record, the program may be hard to read if it contains many **with** statements. The **with** statement is a useful shorthand but it must be used with discretion.

APPLICATION: TEXT CONCORDANCE

This example illustrates the use of an array whose components are records. It also illustrates the use of packed arrays. The program reads a text and then prints a list. Each list entry consists of a word of the text together with the number of times it was found. A list of this kind is called a concordance of the text. The form of the output suggests that the program should maintain a table, each entry of which contains a word and a counter. We start by defining

```
const
  tablesize = 1000;
type
  tableindex = 1..tablesize;
  entrytype =
    record
      word : wordtype;
      count : counttype
    end;
  tabletype = array [tableindex] of entrytype;
```

We use a packed array to represent a word of the text and a positive integer to represent the counter for that word.

```
const
  maxwordlen = 20;
type
  charindex = 1..maxwordlen;
  wordtype = packed array [charindex] of char;
  counttype = 1..maxint;
```

The program will have three sections. First, the table is initialized; second, the text is read and entries are made in the table; and third, the contents of the table are printed. When the program has read a word from the text, either the word has been encountered before, in which case its counter is incremented, or it is a new word that must be entered into the table. Clearly, the efficiency of the program will depend on the technique we use to look for the word in the table. In this program we use a simple *linear search*. The word being read is compared with each table-entry in turn. The variable, *nextentry*, is the index of the next free space in the table when there are already *nextentry* $- 1$ words in the table. We read a word and put it into this free space. The linear search then takes the form

```
entry := 1;
while table [entry].word ≠ table [nextentry].word do
  entry := entry + 1
```

The loop will always terminate provided that *nextentry* $\geqslant 1$. We can ensure this by initializing *nextentry* to 1, which means that there are 0 entries in the table, and incrementing *nextentry* when we add a new entry to the table. The loop will terminate with

```
entry < nextentry
```

if the word is already in the table, or

```
entry = nextentry
```

if it is a new word. In the latter case, the word is already in the correct place, the next free space, so all we have to do is increment *nextentry* and initialize the counter.

The program uses two procedures: *readword* assembles a word of the text into a buffer and then packs it; and *printword* unpacks a word and prints it.

```
{ Count occurrences of each word in a text. }
program concordance (input, output);
  const
    tablesize = 1000;
    maxwordlen = 20;
  type
    charindex = 1..maxwordlen;
    counttype = 1..maxint;
    tableindex = 1..tablesize;
    wordtype = packed array [charindex] of char;
    entrytype =
      record
        word : wordtype;
        count : counttype
      end; { entrytype }
    tabletype = array [tableindex] of entrytype;
  var
    table : tabletype;
    entry, nextentry : tableindex;
    tablefull : boolean;
    letters : set of char;
{ Read one word from the text. A "word" is a string of letters.
  Words are separated by characters other than letters. }
procedure readword (var packedword : wordtype);
  const
    blank = ' ';
  var
    buffer : array [charindex] of char;
    charcount : 0..maxwordlen;
    ch : char;
  begin
    if not eof
      then
        repeat
          read (ch)
        until eof or (ch in letters);
    if not eof
      then
```

```
            begin
              charcount := 0;
              while ch in letters do
                begin
                  if charcount < maxwordlen
                    then
                      begin
                        charcount := charcount + 1;
                        buffer [charcount] := ch
                      end; { then }
                  if eof
                    then ch := blank
                    else read (ch)
                end; { while }
              for charcount := charcount + 1 to maxwordlen do
                buffer [charcount] := blank;
              pack (buffer, 1, packedword)
            end { then }
      end; { readword }
  { Print a word. }
  procedure printword (packedword : wordtype);
    const
      blank = ' ';
    var
      buffer : array [charindex] of char;
      charpos : 1..maxwordlen;
    begin
      unpack (packedword, buffer, 1);
      for charpos := 1 to maxwordlen do
        write (buffer [charpos])
    end; { printword }
    begin { concordance }
      letters := ['a'..'z'];
      tablefull := false;
      nextentry := 1;
      while not (eof or tablefull) do
        begin
          readword (table [nextentry].word);
          if not eof
            then
```

```
          begin
            entry := 1;
            while table [entry].word ≠ table [nextentry].word do
              entry := entry + 1;
            if entry < nextentry
              then table [entry].count := table [entry].count + 1
              else if nextentry < tablesize
                then
                    begin
                      nextentry := nextentry + 1;
                      table [entry].count := 1
                    end { then }
                else tablefull := true
            end; { then }
        end; { while }
    if tablefull
      then writeln ('The table is not large enough.')
    else
      for entry := 1 to nextentry − 1 do
        with table [entry] do
          begin
            printword (word);
            writeln (count)
          end { else, for, and with }
  end. { concordance}
```

6.7   VARIANT RECORDS

Records of the same type do not necessarily contain the same components. We can illustrate this with an example from coordinate geometry. Suppose we need a program that will perform calculations with points, lines, and circles. We start with the definition

```
          type
            coordinate =
              record
                xcoor, ycoor : real
              end;
```

A point is easily represented by its coordinates.

```
type
  point =
    record
      position : coordinate
    end;
```

A line is best represented by the coefficients in its equation

$$Ax + By + C = 0,$$

and we define

```
type
  line =
    record
      xcoeff, ycoeff, con : real
    end;
```

A circle may also be represented in terms of its equation

$$(x - p)^2 + (y - q)^2 = r^2$$

and in this case we have the simple interpretation that the circle has radius r and center (p, q).

```
type
  circle =
    record
      center : coordinate;
      radius : real
    end;
```

The record types *point*, *line*, and *circle* can be condensed into a single definition of a record type which we call *figure*.

A record with variants, such as *figure*, has two parts. The first is called the *fixed part* and the second is called the *variant part*. In this example, the fixed part of the record type *figure* is simply a *tag* that tells us what kind of figure the record represents, and the variant part contains the definitions of *point*, *line*, and *circle* we have already used. The complete definition for *figure* is

```
type
  coordinate =
    record
      xcoor, ycoor : real
    end;
```

```
shape = (point, line, circle);
figure =
  record
    tag : shape;
    case shape of
      point : (position : coordinate);
      line : (xcoeff, ycoeff, con : real);
      circle : (center : coordinate; radius : real)
  end;
```

This definition contains several points of interest. The use of **case** is reminiscent of the **case** statement of Chapter 5, and we will find that the **case** statement is useful for manipulating record variants. There are important differences between the two uses of **case**, however. First, the case selector in a record definition is a *type*, not a variable. In this example, the case selector is the type *shape*. Second, the **case** does not require a matching **end** because the **end** required by the **record** definition also suffices to terminate the **case**.

Because the variant part must follow the fixed part, there can never be any fields after the **case** clause. The identifiers used in different variants must be unique within the record: a field identifier cannot be used in two variants of the same record, nor can it be used in both the fixed and the variant parts of the same record. The same field identifier may, however, be used in more than one record definition.

If these rules seem confusing, consider the definitions (6.3) below. The record *r1* is illegal and would be rejected by the compiler because the field identifier *switch* occurs twice. Both *r2* and *r3*, on the other hand, are legal record-definitions, although the field identifiers *x* and *y* occur in both.

```
type
  r1 =
    record
      switch : boolean;
      case boolean of
        num : integer;
        switch : real
    end;
  r2 =
    record
      x, y : real
    end;
```

(6.3)

```
r3 =
  record
    x, y : integer
  end;
```

Although we are not required by Pascal syntax to include a tag field in a variant record, it is clear that in most cases we are going to need it so that we can distinguish one variant from another. Accordingly, the preceding definition for *figure* may be abbreviated to the following equivalent form.

```
type
  figure =
  record
    case tag : shape of
      point : (position : coordinate);
      line : (xcoeff, ycoeff, con : real);
      circle : (center : coordinate; radius : real)
  end;
```

The tag must be an ordinal type. It is not necessary to define a record variant for every possible value of the tag, although in the interests of program security it is obviously desirable.

The **case** clause used in the declaration of a record with variants is often paralleled by a **case** statement in the body of the program. The following procedure has a record of type *figure* as its formal parameter and it prints values associated with the figure.

```
procedure printfigure (pic : figure);
  begin
    with pic do
      case tag of
        point :
          with position do
            write ('Point: (', xcoor, ',', ycoor, ')');
        line :
          write ('Line: ', xcoeff, ' * X +', ycoeff,
                 ' * Y +' , con, ' = 0');
        circle :
          with center do
            write ('Circle: Center (', xcoor, ',', ycoor,
                   ') Radius ', radius)
      end; { case }
      writeln
  end; { printfigure }
```

Here are some examples of figures printed by this procedure.

```
Line:   4 * X + 3 * Y + −5 = 0
Point:  (12, −4)
Circle:  Center  (0,0)  Radius  5
```

The technical term for a record with variants is *union type*. This term is used because a record with variants is in fact a union of two or more types. A union is *discriminated* if it has a tag field and *free* if it does not. Define

```
type
  thingtype = (int, re, bool);
  thing =
    record
      case thingtype of
        int : (intval : integer);
        re : (reval : real);
        bool : (boolval : boolean)
    end;
var
  something : thing;
```

Thing is a free union. *Something* is an object with three different names: *something.intval, something.reval,* and *something.boolval.* According to the name we use, this object will be treated as an *integer, real,* or *boolean* variable. There are situations in which free unions are appropriate, but they are rare. In most cases you should discriminate unions by providing a tag field. It is important to ensure that the value of the tag and the contents of the record are compatible at all times because the compiler cannot check this.

RECORD SYNTAX

Figure 6.3 shows the syntax for *record type denoter*. Records, like arrays, may be packed to conserve space at the expense of access time. A component of a packed record may not be passed as a variable parameter to a procedure or function. The syntax for *field list* shows that a record may contain a fixed part, a variant part, or both, but that if it contains both, the fixed part must come first. The syntax for *variant part* contains *field list,* thereby allowing variant records to be nested.

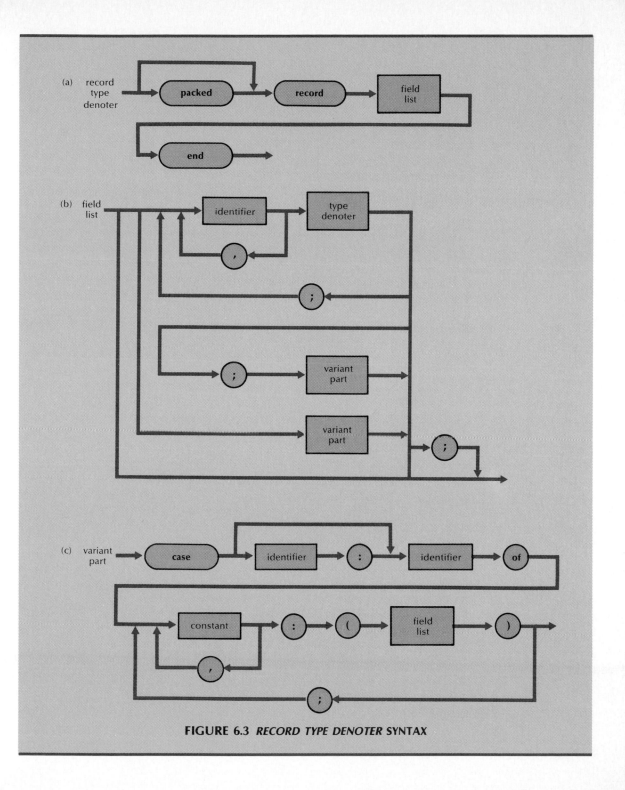

FIGURE 6.3 *RECORD TYPE DENOTER* SYNTAX

The following record definition contains three levels of nesting.

```
type
  mediumtype = (string, wind);
  methodtype = (struck, bowed);
  materialtype = (brass, wood);
  instrument =
    record
      case medium : mediumtype of
        string :
          (case method : methodtype of
            struck :
              (case keyboard : boolean of
                false : (range : integer);
                true : (numberofkeys : 1..100) );
            bowed :
              (size : (bass, cello, viola, violin)) );
        wind :
          (case material : materialtype of
            brass : (technique : (keyed, slide));
            wood : (reed : (single, double)) )
    end;
```

A variable of type *instrument* has either three or four simple components.

```
var
  trombone, piano : instrument;
begin
  ....
  trombone.medium := wind;
  trombone.material := brass;
  trombone.technique := slide;
  piano.medium := string;
  piano.method := struck;
  piano.keyboard := true;
  piano.numberofkeys := 88
  ....
```

A component of an array or record performs the same syntactic function as a variable. The Pascal Standard gives the name *variable access* to a variable, an array component, or a record component. The term *L-value*, mentioned pre-

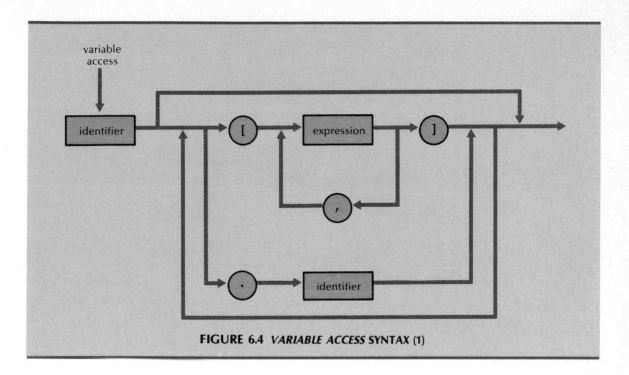

FIGURE 6.4 *VARIABLE ACCESS* SYNTAX (1)

viously in Chapter 4, has the same meaning as variable access. Figure 6.4 shows the syntax for *variable access*. The syntax allows variables such as these:

$$x$$
$$a.b$$
$$p.q \ [3]$$
$$a \ [x.y].f$$

When a component of a record is itself a record, the notation is extended in the obvious way. If *roundthing* is a *circle*, then

$$roundthing.center \qquad\qquad (6.4)$$

is the coordinate of its center and

$$roundthing.center.xcoor := 0$$

assigns zero to the *x*-coordinate of its center.

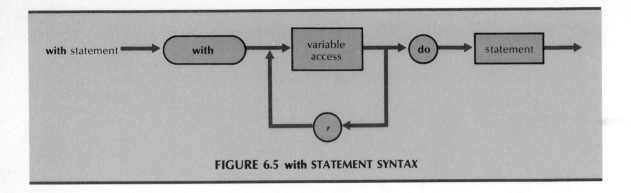

FIGURE 6.5 **with** STATEMENT SYNTAX

Figure 6.5 shows the syntax of the **with** statement. Note that several record identifiers may appear within a single **with** clause. The statement (6.4) can be written in any of the alternative forms:

```
with roundthing do
  with center do
    xcoor := 0
```

or

```
with roundthing, center do
  xcoor := 0
```

or

```
with roundthing.center do
  xcoor := 0
```

6.8   APPLICATION: CONSTRUCTING THE CIRCUMCIRCLE

We will use the declaration of the record type *figure* as a starting point for a program that constructs the circumcircle of a triangle, or equivalently, the circle that passes through three given points. We use the following algorithm. (See Fig. 6.6.)

Let the given points be $p1$, $p2$, and $p3$. Draw three circles, $c1$, $c2$, and $c3$, with centers $p1$, $p2$, and $p3$ and the same radius. (The radius is arbitrary but should be large enough to ensure that the circles intersect.) Draw the line $s1$ through the points of intersection of $c1$ and $c2$, and draw the line $s2$ through the points of intersection of $c2$ and $c3$. Then $s1$ and $s2$ meet at the circumcenter of the three points and the radius of the circumcircle is the distance from this point to any of the given points.

We can express this algorithm as a program schema.

```
choose a radius, r;
drawcircle (p1, r, c1);
drawcircle (p2, r, c2);
drawcircle (p3, r, c3);
intersect (c1, c2, s1);
intersect (c2, c3, s2);
meet (s1, s2, circumcenter);
circumradius := distance (p1, circumcenter);
drawcircle (circumcenter, circumradius, circumcircle)
```

Sometimes the construction will not work. Some or all of the points may coincide, in which case the construction is impossible; or the points may be colinear, in which case the lines s1 and s2 are coincident. Since we do not expect exact results from our computations, we should test for "very close" rather than "coincident," and "almost parallel" rather than "parallel." This will avoid potential problems of overflow and underflow and will prevent the construction from

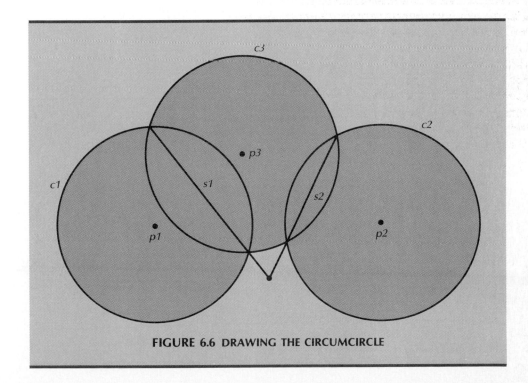

FIGURE 6.6 DRAWING THE CIRCUMCIRCLE

being performed when it might be inaccurate. We add the additional value
empty to the type *shape*. A procedure can then communicate failure by returning an empty figure. The new definitions are

```
type
  shape = (empty, point, line, circle);
  figure =
    record
      case tag : shape of
        empty : ( );
        point : (position : coordinate);
        line : (xcoeff, ycoeff, con : real);
        circle : (center : coordinate; radius : real)
    end;
```

The procedure *drawcircle* offers no particular difficulties.

```
procedure drawcircle (cen : figure;
                      rad : real;
                      var circ : figure);
begin
  with circ do
    if (cen.tag = point) and (rad > 0)
      then
        begin
          tag := circle;
          center := cen.position;
          radius := rad
        end
      else tag := empty
end;
```

The procedure *meet* finds the point of intersection of two lines, provided
they are not parallel. Suppose that the lines are *aline* and *bline:*

$$aline : Ax + By + C = 0.$$
$$bline : Dx + Ey + F = 0.$$

If $AE - BD = 0$, the lines are parallel or coincident, otherwise they meet at the
point

$$x = -\frac{(CE - BF)}{(AE - BD)}$$

$$y = \frac{(CD - AF)}{(AE - BD)}$$

The procedure *intersect* finds the line of intersection of two circles. Suppose that the circles are *acirc* and *bcirc*:

$$acirc : (x - A)^2 + (y - B)^2 = C^2$$
$$bcirc : (x - D)^2 + (y - E)^2 = F^2$$

By subtraction

$$-2Ax + A^2 + 2Dx - D^2 - 2By - B^2 + 2Ey - E^2 = C^2 - F^2$$

and the equation of the line of intersection is

$$x(A - D) + y(B - E) + ((C^2 - A^2 - B^2) - (F^2 - D^2 - E^2)) / 2 = 0.$$

This is actually the equation of the locus of a point equidistant from the centers of the circles. For our application it will give the correct line even if the circles do not in fact meet.

```
{ Read the coordinates of three points in a plane
  and construct the circle passing through them. }
program circles (input, output);
  const
    delta = 1e-6;   { Criterion for "very close" points }
  type
    shape = (empty, point, line, circle);
    coordinate =
      record
        xcoor, ycoor : real
      end; { coordinate }
    figure =
      record
        case tag : shape of
          empty :
            ( );
          point :
            (position : coordinate);
          line :
            (xcoeff, ycoeff, con : real);
          circle :
            (center : coordinate;
              radius : real)
      end; { figure }
  var
    p1, p2, p3, c1, c2, c3, s1, s2,
    circumcenter, circumcircle : figure;
    r, circumradius : real;
```

```
{ Print a figure of any type. }
procedure printfigure (pic : figure);
  begin
    with pic do
      case tag of
        empty :
          write ('Null figure');
        point :
          with position do
            write ('Point : (', xcoor, ',', ycoor, ')');
        line :
          write ('Line :', xcoeff, ' * X + ', xcoeff,
                    ' * Y + ', con, ' = 0 ');
        circle :
          with center do
            write ('Circle : center (', xcoor, ',', ycoor,
                                  ') radius : ', radius)
      end; { case }
    writeln
  end; { printfigure }
{ Read the coordinates of a point. }
procedure readpoint (var pnt : figure);
  begin
    with pnt, position do
      begin
        tag := point;
        read (xcoor, ycoor)
      end { with }
  end; { readpoint }
{ Calculate the distance between two points.
  The parameters are passed as figures: this
  function checks that they represent points. }
function distance (afig, bfig : figure) : real;
  begin
    if (afig.tag = point) and (bfig.tag = point)
      then distance := sqrt (sqr (afig.position.xcoor
                              - bfig.position.xcoor)
                          + sqr (afig.position.ycoor
                              - bfig.position.ycoor))
      else distance := 0
  end; { distance }
```

```
{ Return true if the given points are close together.
  This function does not check that its arguments
  represent points and will return true if they do not. }
function veryclose (afig, bfig : figure) : boolean;
  begin
    veryclose := distance (afig, bfig) < delta
  end; { veryclose }

{ Construct a circle given its center and radius. }
procedure drawcircle (cen : figure; rad : real;
                        var circ : figure);

  begin
    with circ do
      if (cen.tag = point) and (rad > 0)
        then
          begin
            tag := circle;
            center := cen.position;
            radius := rad
          end { then }
        else tag := empty
  end; { drawcircle }

{ Given two lines, return their point of intersection. }
procedure meet (aline, bline : figure;
                var pnt : figure);

  var
    den : real;
  begin
    if (aline.tag = line) and (bline.tag = line)
      then
        begin
          den := aline.xcoeff * bline.ycoeff
                  - aline.ycoeff * bline.xcoeff;
          if abs (den) < delta
            then pnt.tag := empty { parallel lines }
            else
              with pnt do
                begin
                  tag := point;
                  with position do
```

```
              begin
                xcoor := - (aline.con * bline.ycoeff
                          - aline.ycoeff * bline.con) / den;
                ycoor :=   (aline.con * bline.xcoeff
                          - aline.xcoeff * bline.con) / den
              end { with position }
            end { else and with pnt }
        end { then }
      else pnt.tag := empty
    end; { meet }
{ Find the two points at which the two given circles
  intersect and return the line joining them. }
procedure intersect (acirc, bcirc : figure;
                     var intline : figure);
    begin
      if (acirc.tag = circle) and (bcirc.tag = circle)
        then
          with intline do
            begin
              tag := line;
              xcoeff := acirc.center.xcoor - bcirc.center.xcoor;
              ycoeff := acirc.center.ycoor - bcirc.center.ycoor;
              con := ( (  sqr (acirc.radius)
                        - sqr (acirc.center.xcoor)
                        - sqr (acirc.center.ycoor) )
                      - (  sqr (bcirc.radius)
                        - sqr (bcirc.center.xcoor)
                        - sqr (bcirc.center.ycoor) ) ) / 2
            end { then and with intline }
        else intline.tag := empty
    end; { intersect }

begin { circles }
  readpoint (p1);
  readpoint (p2);
  readpoint (p3);
  if  veryclose (p1, p2)
    or veryclose (p2, p3)
    or veryclose (p3, p1)
    then writeln ('The points are not distinct.')
    else
```

```
        begin
          r := distance (p1, p2) + distance (p2, p3);
          drawcircle (p1, r, c1);
          drawcircle (p2, r, c2);
          drawcircle (p3, r, c3);
          intersect (c1, c2, s1);
          intersect (c2, c3, s2);
          meet (s1, s2, circumcenter);
          circumradius := distance (p1, circumcenter);
          drawcircle (circumcenter, circumradius, circumcircle);
          printfigure (circumcircle)
        end { else }
    end. { circles }
```

INPUT		OUTPUT
−1000	0	Circle: center (0, −499999.5) radius: 500000.5
1000	0	
0	1	

The main program in this example deals only with distances and figures. The representation of figures (by values in records of type *figure*) is not relevant to the main program and is not visible within it. We could rewrite the declaration of *figure*, and the procedures and functions of the program, using an entirely different representation—polar coordinates, for instance—without having to alter the main program at all. More importantly, at the level of the main program, we do not have to worry about the details of the representation, and we are free to think about the solution of the problem at the appropriate level of abstraction.

6.9 EXERCISES

6.1 An array is used to store descriptions of people. Each component of the array is a record with fields containing information about height, weight, hair color, eye color, and sex. Write appropriate declarations and use them in a program that can read a description or print a list of stored descriptions. Extend the program so that when a new description is added, the closest description already filed is located and printed.

6.2 The following definitions suggest a suitable representation for this book.

```
const
  linelen = 70;
  pagesize = 55;
  thickness = 330;
type
  line = array [1..linelen] of char;
  page = array [1..pagesize] of line;
  volume = array [1..thickness] of page;
var
  book : volume;
```

Identify the type and value of each of the following expressions.

```
book [25]
book [187] [30]
book [220] [18] [40]
```

Write a program to print the contents of *book* in an appropriate format.

6.3 Write a program that reads a text and prints a frequency distribution of word lengths. (How many words have one letter, how many have two letters, etc.?) The program should also print the mean and standard deviation of word lengths.

6.4 Write a program that prints a list of the numbers that are palindromes in both binary and decimal notation. (A palindromic number is unchanged if its digits are reversed: 79488497 is a decimal palindrome.)

6.5 If an array is already sorted, the linear search is not the best method of locating an entry in it. A better method is the *binary search*. Assume that the array *arr* is sorted in ascending order and that it contains a component whose value is *key*. *Lower* and *upper* are the bounds of a range of subscripts. After executing the statements

```
middle := (lower + upper) div 2;
if key > arr [middle]
  then lower := middle + 1
  else upper := middle - 1
```

either *arr* [middle] = *key* and we have found the component we want, or the bounds are set for a search over a smaller range. Write a recursive procedure and an iterative procedure to perform a binary search. What happens if the array does not contain the component sought? Modify your procedures to take this into account.

6.6 Extend Program *concordance* so that it prints two lists. In the first list, the words are in alphabetical order. In the second, they are in order of frequency of occurrence, with the most frequent first. The program should contain a sorting procedure based on procedure *sort* of Program *shellsort*. One of the parameters of this procedure should specify which sort is to be performed.

6.7 A text contains words of ten characters or less. Write a program that reads a text of up to 1000 words and then prints the same words arranged in a random order.

6.8 Write a procedure that reads and writes hexadecimal (scale of sixteen) numbers, using the 16 characters

$$0 \quad 1 \quad 2 \quad 3 \quad 4 \quad 5 \quad 6 \quad 7 \quad 8 \quad 9 \quad A \quad B \quad C \quad D \quad E \quad F$$

6.9 Write a program that converts integers from one scale to another. The symbols " < " and " > ", followed by a decimal integer between 2 and 10, set the input and output scales. For example, the input string

$$<8 >2$$

instructs the program to read octal numbers and print their binary equivalents.

6.10 *Clock-patience* is played with a standard deck of 52 cards. It is called clock-patience because the cards are dealt to the twelve positions corresponding to the numbers on the face of a clock. Cards are distributed face down into four-card piles around the thirteenth pile at the center of the "clock." The player starts the game by taking the top card from the center pile and placing it face up under the appropriate pile. The card for the next move is taken from this pile, and so on. For example, a six is placed under the pile at the six o'clock position and the next card is taken from the top of this pile. A jack is placed at eleven o'clock, a queen at twelve o'clock, and a king under the center pile. The game continues in this way until all the cards are face up or no further move is possible. Write a program that simulates clock-patience, using a pseudo-random number generator to "deal" the cards.

6.11 One way of overcoming Pascal's limited ability to handle strings of different lengths is to use a *string table*.

```
const
  tablesize = 10000;
  maxstringlen = 100;
type
  charindex = 1..tablesize;
  string =
    record
      first, last : charindex
    end;
```

```
var
    stringtable : packed array [charindex] of char;
    buffer : array [1..maxstringlen] of char;
```

If the string table contains

'TOOTHEATERRIBLE...'

the strings "TOO", "TOOTH", "THEATER", and "TERRIBLE" are represented by records (1,3), (1,5), (4,10), (8,15). Devise procedures that
a) determine whether the table contains a given string;
b) add a new string to the table;
c) compare strings;
d) generate substrings;
e) concatenate strings.

Assume that no individual string and no result of a concatenation may have more than *maxstringlen* characters.

6.12 The game of *Life,* invented by J. H. Conway, takes place on a rectangular grid of cells, each of which may contain an organism. Each cell has eight neighbors, and we use *occ* (*k*) to denote the number of cells adjacent to cell *k* that are occupied by an organism. The configuration of a new generation of organisms is obtained from the previous generation by applying two simple rules.
a) An organism in cell *k* survives to the next generation if $2 \leqslant occ\ (k) \leqslant 3$, otherwise it dies.
b) An organism is born in the empty cell *k* if *occ* (*k*) = 3, otherwise the cell remains empty.

Write a program that reads an initial configuration of occupied cells, calculates a series of generations according to the rules, and prints each configuration. Because all changes occur *simultaneously,* the program must maintain two copies of the configuration. Test your program with a seven-cell, U-shaped pattern, the first six generations of which are shown below.

```
* *
* *       ** **       ** **       ** **       ** **       ** **
***        * *        ** **        *   *        *   *        *   *
            *            *           ***          ***          ***
                                                   *            ***
```

6.13 An undirected graph with *maxvert* vertices can be represented by an array

graph : **array** [1..*maxvert*, 1..*maxvert*] **of** *boolean*;

in which *graph* [*u, v*] is *true* if vertices *u* and *v* are joined by an edge and *false* otherwise.

a) Describe an equivalent representation of an undirected graph using an array of sets.

b) A vertex, v, can be reached from a vertex, u, by traversing at most n edges if

$$graph^n[u, v] = true$$

where $graph^n$ is calculated by matrix "multiplication" in which the boolean operators **or** and **and** replace addition and multiplication. Can $graph^n$ be computed easily using the set representation?

c) Write a program that reads edge descriptors, each consisting of two numbers, and prints $graph^n$ for

$$n = 1, 2, \ldots, 5.$$

d) Can you find a way of terminating the program when n is the length of the longest path, rather than arbitrarily after five cycles?

6.14 If you did Exercise 4.12, you have a program that will evaluate complex expressions. You can now write it more elegantly using the declaration

```
type
  complex =
    record
      realpart, imagpart : real
    end;
```

6.15 Write a Pascal program for *Snakes and Ladders* (see Section 5.5) using an array to represent the snakes and ladders.

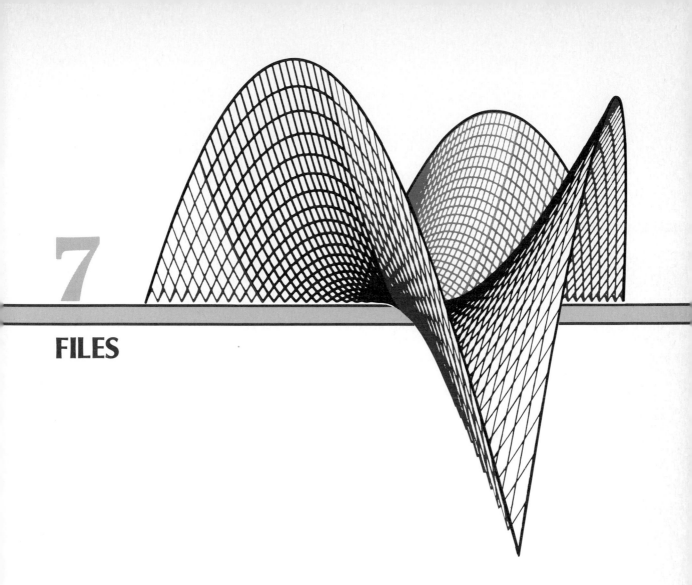

7

FILES

The programs we have studied have all produced some output, and in most cases they have also accepted some input. They have done this by means of the standard files *input* and *output*. In this chapter we consider these and other files in more detail.

Files are important for three reasons. First, a program can communicate with its environment only by means of files. Second, a program is usually short-lived: a program is loaded into memory and executed, and as soon as it terminates, the memory is used by another program. If the program does not alter a file during its execution, there will be no evidence that it ran at all. The third reason for the importance of files is that larger amounts of data may be stored in a file than in the memory of the computer.

In Pascal, a file is a variable. It is a somewhat anomalous sort of variable, however, because it may exist both before and after the program is executed, and because it may be larger than the program itself. For these reasons, the actions that a Pascal program can perform with a file are restricted in certain ways. In particular, the program can access only one component of a file at a time.

Since Pascal files are an abstraction of actual files, the program does not contain information about the physical nature of a file. For example, although you know that the effect of a call to the standard procedure *read* will be to transfer data from a file to a variable in your program, you do not have to state, or even know, whether the data will be obtained from a deck of cards, a disk file, or the keyboard of a terminal. It is a function of the operating system to assign actual files to your program at run-time. The operating system does this according to directions that are not part of your Pascal program.

The relationship between the formal files declared and referenced within the program and the actual files provided by the operating system at run-time is loosely analogous to the relationship between the formal parameters of a procedure and the actual parameters provided by the calling program when the procedure is executed. This analogy is reflected in the syntax of a Pascal program heading (Fig. 2.10), which is rather like a procedure heading (Fig. 4.3).

7.1   SEQUENTIAL FILES

We define a *file type* in a Pascal program by writing an appropriate type description.

$$
\begin{aligned}
&\textbf{const} \\
&\quad maxcol = 80; \\
&\textbf{type} \\
&\quad colindex = 1..maxcol; \\
&\quad card = \textbf{array } [colindex] \textbf{ of } char; \\
&\quad cardfile = \textbf{file of } card;
\end{aligned}
\tag{7.1}
$$

We declare the file as a variable.

```
var
    deck : cardfile;
```

Most Pascal compilers require that the name of the file be included in the program heading.

```
program cardshuffler (input, output, deck);
```

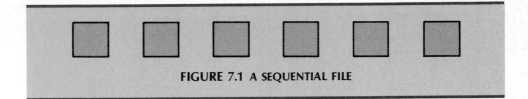

FIGURE 7.1 A SEQUENTIAL FILE

We do not declare the standard files *input* and *output* in the variable declaration section. *Input* must appear in the program heading if *read, readln, eof,* or *eoln* are used without a file name parameter. *Output* must appear in the program heading if *write* or *writeln* are used without a file name parameter. Some systems require *output* to be mentioned in the program heading even if the program contains no calls to *write,* so that there is always a destination for error messages.

The *component type* of the file *deck* defined in (7.1) is *card.* A *component* of the file is a variable of the component type. At any one time, exactly one component of the file is accessible to the program. The component of *deck* to which we have access is a variable of type *card* and is written

$$deck\uparrow$$

Sometimes we refer to a component of a file as a *record* of the file. This use of the word "record" is related to Pascal's use of the same word. In each case, a "record" denotes a logical grouping of data. Frequently we use a Pascal **record** type as the component type of a file.

Pascal files have sequential structure. We can visualize a file as a row of boxes, each box containing one component of the file (Fig. 7.1).

WRITING TO A FILE

A file is created or extended by *writing* to it. Each write operation adds a new component to the file. Components can be added only to the end of a sequential file. We can imagine a *marker,* associated with the file, that tells us where the next component will be placed. In Fig. 7.2 the marker is represented by an arrow. Figure 7.2(a) shows an empty file, with the marker indicating the position in which the first record will be placed. Figure 7.2(b) shows a file to which four records have been written, with the marker indicating where the fifth will be placed.

The procedure call

$$rewrite\ (deck)$$

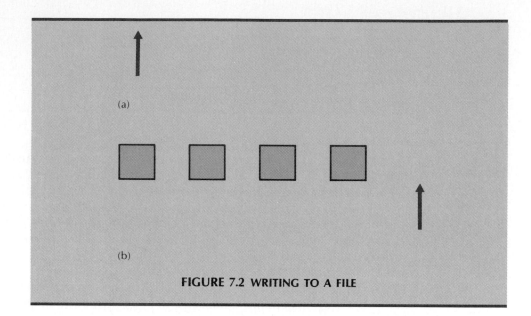

(a)

(b)

FIGURE 7.2 WRITING TO A FILE

performs the operations of setting the marker to the beginning of the file and preparing the file for writing. These operations also destroy any existing information in the file *deck*. After *rewrite* has executed, the situation is as shown in Fig. 7.2(a). In order to write a component to the file, we assemble the data into *deck*↑ and call the procedure *put*.

$$put \ (deck)$$

This has the effect of creating a new component of the file in the position indicated by the marker and moving the marker one place to the right.

Suppose that we have declared

> **var**
>   *buffer : card;*

and that *buffer* contains information to be written to the file. Then the statements

> *deck*↑ := *buffer;*
> *put* (*deck*)

may be abbreviated to

$$write \ (deck, \ buffer)$$

READING FROM A FILE

When we have created the file, we can read from it. Before starting to read the file *deck,* we execute

$$reset \ (deck)$$

which moves the marker to the beginning of the file as shown in Fig. 7.3(a). The procedure *reset* also transfers information from the first component of the file into the variable *deck↑*. In order to read the next component of the file, we call the procedure

$$get \ (deck)$$

This advances the pointer and copies information from the next component into *deck↑*. There comes a time when we move the pointer to the right and there is no

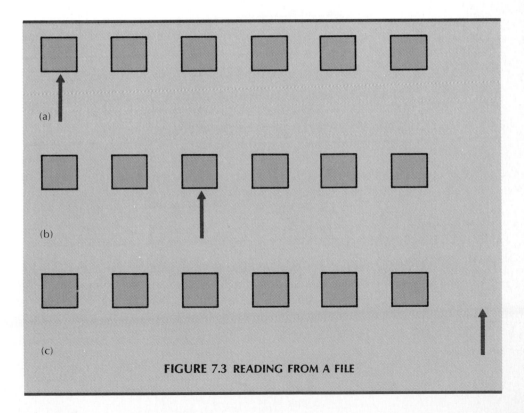

FIGURE 7.3 READING FROM A FILE

information there, as in Fig. 7.3(c). In this case, *deck↑* is undefined and the *boolean* function *eof* (*deck*) returns the value *true*. After calling *get,* we have one of two situations.

> *eof* (*deck*) = *false* and *deck↑* contains the next component

or

> *eof* (*deck*) = *true* and *deck↑* is undefined.

If the file happens to be empty when we read the first record, as in Fig. 7.2(a), then *eof* (*deck*) will be *true* immediately after *reset* has been called. For this reason, it is best to test *eof* before calling *get.* The procedure *read* may also be used.

```
read (deck, buffer)
```

is equivalent to

```
buffer := deck↑;
get (deck)
```

If *eof* is *true* after the *read, buffer* contains the last component of the file.

RESTRICTIONS ON READING AND WRITING

The Pascal type *file* is an abstraction of a magnetic tape. The operators *reset* and *rewrite* correspond to rewinding the tape and preparing to read from it or write to it. A *write* operation must not be followed by a *read* and a *read* operation must not be followed by a *write.* If a file is going to be used for both input and output, it must be rewound, written, rewound again, and read. The physical nature of the actual file may impose further restrictions. We can only read from a deck of cards or a keyboard, and we can only write to a printer or a display. Pascal forbids writing to the file *input* or reading from the file *output.*

APPLICATION: CARD COPYING

Files, unlike variables of other types, cannot be copied by an assignment statement. They must be copied one component at a time. The function of Program *copydeck* is to copy a deck of cards by reading from the file *indeck* and writing to the file *outdeck.* Blank cards in *indeck* are not copied to *outdeck.*

```
{ Copy a deck of card images from indeck to outdeck. }
program copydeck (indeck, outdeck, output);
  const
    maxcol = 80;     { Width of card image }
    blank = ' ';
```

```
type
    colindex = 1..maxcol;
    card = packed array [colindex] of char;
    cardfile = file of card;
var
    indeck, outdeck : cardfile;
    buffer, blankcard : card;
    column : colindex;
begin
    for column := 1 to maxcol do
        blankcard [column] := blank;
    reset (indeck);
    rewrite (outdeck);
    while not eof (indeck) do
        begin
            read (indeck, buffer);
            if buffer ≠ blankcard
                then write (outdeck, buffer)
        end { while }
end. { copydeck }
```

7.2   TEXT FILES

Pascal provides a standard type, *text*. A *text* is a file that contains characters organized into lines. Text files have useful properties that the definition

```
type
    text = packed file of char;
```

would not provide. In particular, we can use the function *eoln* to detect line breaks in text files and to read and write variables that are not of type *char*.

Input and *output* are standard identifiers implicitly declared by

```
type
    input, output : text;
```

Pascal also initializes these files by implicitly executing

```
reset (input);
rewrite (output);
```

These conventions apply only to the files *input* and *output:* you must explicitly declare and initialize any other *text* files your program uses.

AUTOMATIC CONVERSION

Text files are the most commonly used variety of file, and Pascal provides several special facilities to make text files easy to use. The most important of these is the implicit conversion performed by *read* and *write*. If a *text* file was actually a file of *char*, the statements

        read (x)

and

        write (x)

would be valid only if the type of *x* was *char*. As we saw in Chapter 2, however, the type of *x* may also be *integer* or *real* (or *boolean* in the case of *write*), and the procedures provide automatic conversion.

APPLICATION: DATA CONVERSION

Suppose that we have a text file containing statistical data. The data is in groups and each group contains ten real numbers. The file is large, containing perhaps several thousand such groups, and it must be processed many times. It is inefficient to keep such a file in text form because thousands of conversions must be performed every time it is read. It is more efficient to convert the numbers only once and to store them in another file in binary form for subsequent processing. Program *convertgroups* reads the text from file *datafile* and writes the data in binary form in file *binaryfile*. A component of *binaryfile* consists of an array of ten real values. The conversion is done implicitly by the call

        read (datafile, binaryfile↑[ix])

which reads one number in character form, converts it to internal *real* form, and stores the result directly in the component *binaryfile*↑.

```
{ Convert groups of data from decimal string to binary form. }
program convertgroups (datafile, binaryfile, output);
  const
    groupsize = 10;    { Number of components in each group }
  type
    index = 1..groupsize;
    group = array [index] of real;
  var
    datafile : text;
    binaryfile : file of group;
    ix : index;
    groupcount : integer;
```

```
begin
  reset (datafile);
  rewrite (binaryfile);
  groupcount := 0;
  while not eof (datafile) do
    begin
      groupcount := groupcount + 1;
      ix := 0;
      while (ix < groupsize) and not eof (datafile) do
        begin
          ix := ix + 1;
          read (datafile, binaryfile↑[ix])
        end; { while }
      if ix < groupsize
        then
          begin
            writeln ('Premature end of file.');
            writeln ('Group ', groupcount:1, ' has only ',
                      ix:1, ' members.');
            groupcount := groupcount - 1
          end
        else put (binaryfile)
    end; { while }
  writeln (groupcount:1, ' groups converted.')
end. { convertgroups }
```

PARAMETERS FOR *READ* AND *WRITE*

The procedures *read* and *write* may have several parameters when they are used with text files. Each parameter may be of the type *integer*, *real*, or *char*. The procedure *write* will also accept a parameter that is *boolean* or a packed array of characters. In these examples, *fn* is the name of a text file and *p1, p2, . . . , pn* are parameters.

$$read\ (fn,\ p1,\ p2,\dots,\ pn)$$

is equivalent to

```
read (fn, p1);
read (fn, p2);
. . . .
read (fn, pn)
```

and

```
write (fn, p1, p2,..., pn)
```

is equivalent to

```
write (fn, p1);
write (fn, p2);
....
write (fn, pn)
```

The filename parameter, *fn*, may be omitted. The compiler then supplies the default file *input* for *read, readln, eoln,* and *eof,* and the default file *output* for *write* and *writeln.*

LINE STRUCTURE

In many practical applications, text files are not mere streams of characters. They are programs, data, or prose, and they are structured in various ways. Text is most frequently structured by lines and pages. There are standard procedures and functions in Pascal that enable programs to generate files containing lines and pages and to recognize such structure in an input text file.

Lines are represented in different ways by different computers and operating systems. Pascal provides a standard *boolean* function, *eoln,* that is *true* at the end of a line of text and *false* everywhere else. In principle, this makes Pascal programs independent of the actual representation of line terminators used by any particular system. In practice, there are circumstances in which this abstraction is inconvenient.

The standard procedure *readln* skips over characters until the end of the current line. The call

```
readln (fn)
```

in which *fn* is the name of a text file, is equivalent to the statements

```
while not eoln (fn) do
   get (fn);
get (fn)
```

The next call to *read* will obtain the first character of the next line unless the end of the file has been reached. The file name may be omitted, in which case *input* is assumed. *Readln* may also be used with parameters.

$$readln\ (fn,\ p1,\ p2,\ldots,\ pn)$$

is equivalent to

```
read (fn, p1);
read (fn, p2);
....
read (fn, pn);
readln (fn)
```

Readln can be used to skip over redundant information, such as comments or units, in the input. Be careful not to skip over things that you intend to read.

The procedure *writeln* is used to terminate the current output line and to start a new one. The call

$$writeln\ (fn,\ p1,\ p2,\ldots,\ pn)$$

is equivalent to

```
write (fn, p1);
write (fn, p2);
....
write (fn, pn);
writeln (fn)
```

The properties of text files suggest a simple schema for processing or copying text files.

```
{ Process a text file. }
program copyfile (infile, outfile);
  var
    infile, outfile : text;
    ch : char;
  begin
    reset (infile);
    rewrite (outfile);
    while not eof (infile) do
      begin
        while not eoln (infile) do
          begin
            read (infile, ch);
            { Perform character processing. }
            write (outfile, ch)
          end; { while not eoln }
        readln (infile);
```

```
              { Perform line processing. }
              writeln (outfile)
        end; { while not eof }
      { Perform end of file processing. }
    end. { copyfile }
```

7.3   INPUT AND OUTPUT

It is the purpose of this section to give some guidelines for designing the input
and output sections of programs. In typical computer programs, as opposed to
the examples in this book, the input and output sections are often the largest.
For a program to be generally useful, all input must be fully validated and invalid data must be displayed with accurate and specific diagnostic messages.
Printed output must be neatly organized so that the significant results are immediately apparent to the reader. Moreover, a careful balance must be struck
between too little output, with useful or important results absent, and too much
output, in which potentially useful results are lost in a morass of useless detail.
To conserve space, the programs in this book are skeleton programs, bereft of
the flesh of good input and output.

The conventions used for input and output should be chosen according to
the mode in which the program is to be run. In general, programs intended to be
run in batch mode should produce more output than programs intended to be
run in interactive mode. In particular, a batch program should copy all or most
of its input file to the output file, along with suitable annotation. Many Pascal
compilers do this. The input file for the Pascal compiler is your Pascal program,
and its output is an annotated listing of your Pascal program, including headings, line numbers, code addresses, and error messages. The program listing is
an important part of the compiler's output. Without it, you would have to obtain
a listing of your program using a listing program, and it would be harder to relate the error messages to the program. (The Pascal compiler also generates
another file, of course, containing the machine-language translation of your
program.) Similar considerations apply to other programs; if your program
prints only answers, you may find yourself wondering in six months what the
questions were.

INPUT

A program that does not read data is useless because it does exactly the same
things each time it is run. It is sometimes tempting, especially if you are using a
system with good interactive editing facilities, to incorporate data into the pro-

gram itself, in the form of constant declarations, and then to alter these declarations before each run. This is bad programming practice. Constant declarations are intended to be used for defining values that are applicable to many different runs of the program. Any value that is changed every time the program is run is input data and belongs in the input file.

Input data may be in *free format* or *fixed format*. Pascal is more suited to reading data in free format because the procedure *read* can read one character at a time from the input buffer. Program *calculator* in Chapter 4 reads data in free format. When you are designing a program to read free format data, you will find it helpful to draw syntax diagrams for the permitted input data structures. These will simplify the design of the program and will also aid other users when they are preparing data for it.

Fixed-format input is the older method of reading input data. It originated when decks of cards were used extensively in data processing. The card, or input record, is divided into *fields* of fixed length, and each item of data is assigned a field. Table 7.1 shows a simple fixed-field card layout. One of the weak points of Pascal is that it does not provide facilities for reading fixed-field data. The easiest way to handle fixed-field records is to read the entire input record into a Pascal array and then validate and convert each field in turn.

Suppose that a program is to read 80-column cards with several unsigned numeric fields, and we have declared

```
const
  maxcol = 80;
type
  colindex = 1..maxcol;
  cardimage = array [colindex] of char;
var
  data : file of cardimage;
  inputcard : cardimage;
```

TABLE 7.1 FIXED-FIELD LAYOUT			
FIELD	**COLUMN**		**FORMAT**
	From	**To**	
Name	1	30	Alphabetic
Address	31	70	Alphanumeric
Reference Number	71	80	Numeric

We could use the following procedure to validate and convert selected fields.

```
procedure convertnumericfield (card : cardimage;
                               first, last : colindex;
                               var val : integer;
                               var error : boolean);
  const
    blank = ' ';
    radix = 10;
  var
    col : colindex;
  begin
    val := 0;
    error := false;
    col := first;
    while (card [col] = blank) and (col < last) do
      col := col + 1;
    if card [col] ≠ blank
      then
        for col := col to last do
          if card [col] in ['0'..'9']
            then val := radix * val + ord (card [col])
                                    - ord ('0')
          else error := true
  end; { convertnumericfield }
```

A problem arises when an input file is processed character by character. Responses and error messages are generated while a line of input is being read. If the program is running in batch mode and copying its input stream to the output file, the output file will get very confused. This can be avoided by reading and printing the input file a line at a time but passing only one character at a time back to the calling program. This requires a *line buffer*. In the main program, declare:

```
const
  maxlinelen = 100;
type
  buffer =
    record
      line : array [1..maxlinelen] of char;
      index, length : 0..maxlinelen
    end;
```

```
var
    inbuf : buffer;
    infile, outfile : text;
```

We provide two procedures, *initread* and *readchar*, written in such a way that the program may use a loop of the following form:

```
initread (inbuf, infile);
while not eof (infile) do
    begin
        readchar (ch, inbuf, infile);
        { process ch }
    end
```

The procedure *readchar* must handle empty lines correctly, and it must not set *eof* (*infile*) to *true* until after the last non-empty line has been processed. The program must call *initread* before attempting to use *readchar*, and it must test *eof* (*infile*) before each call to *readchar*.

```
procedure skipblanklines (var infile : text);
    begin
        while eoln (infile) and not eof (infile) do
            readln (infile)
    end; { skipblanklines }

procedure initread (var inbuf : buffer;
                    var infile : text);
    begin
        inbuf.index := 0;
        reset (infile);
        skipblanklines (infile)
    end; { initread }

procedure readchar (var ch : char;
                    var inbuf : buffer;
                    var infile : text);
    begin
        with inbuf do
            begin
                if index = 0
                    then
```

```
          begin
            length := 0;
            while not eoln (infile) do
              begin
                read (infile, ch);
                if length < maxlinelen
                  then
                    begin
                      length := length + 1;
                      line [length] := ch
                    end
              end; { while }
          end;
          index := index + 1;
          ch := line [index];
          if index = length
            then
              begin
                index := 0;
                skipblanklines (infile)
              end
        end { with }
    end; { readchar }
```

OUTPUT

All programs should write something to the output file, even if the bulk of the data written by the program goes to some other file. A program that merges two files, for example, should write a report of its activities, such as

14371	records read from file "MASTER"
7320	records read from file "TRANSACTIONS"
11	records occurred in both files
21680	records written to file "NEW MASTER"

A program that produces more than one page of output should display its results with page divisions and page numbers. A procedure can conveniently be used to generate page throws when necessary. The standard procedure *page* (*fn*) will generate a skip to the next page of the file *fn*. If the parameter *fn* is omitted, the compiler assumes that the file *output* is intended. In the main program declare

```
const
  pagesize = 60;
  maxpages = 1000;
type
  linecounter = 1..pagesize;
  pagecounter = 1..maxpages;
var
  linesonpage : linecounter;
  pagenumber : pagecounter;
```

and assign these initial values:

```
linesonpage := pagesize;
pagenumber := 1
```

Whenever a line of output has been assembled by *write* statements, use the statement

```
newline (linesonpage, pagenumber)
```

to signal the end of the line. The program should not use *writeln* anywhere other than within the procedure *newline*. The definition of *newline* follows.

```
procedure newline (var line : linecounter;
                   var pagenum : pagecounter);
const
  heading = 'My Results';
begin
  if line ≥ pagesize
    then
      begin
        page;
        writeln (heading, ' ': 60, 'Page', pagenum: 5);
        writeln; writeln;
        pagenum := pagenum + 1;
        line := 3
      end
    else
      begin
        writeln;
        line := line + 1
      end
end; { newline }
```

INTERACTIVE PROGRAMS

Interactive programs and batch programs use different conventions for input and output. The first and most obvious difference is that output from an interactive program should be minimal. The user does not want to sit and watch the program type or display long and predictable messages. In particular, an interactive program should not copy data from the input file to the output file; the user can already see the input.

An interactive program should report errors as soon as they are recognized. Users do not appreciate being told that there was an error in the first line, after they have already typed ten lines. Nor should interactive programs collapse when they encounter invalid data. The call

```
read (value)
```

where *value* is an integer or real variable, will cause the program to halt if the input file does not contain a syntactically correct number. This means that a useful interactive program written in Pascal cannot use automatic conversion and therefore must do its own conversion. Program *calculator* in Chapter 4 is intended for interactive use and does not use automatic conversion.

It is not difficult to write interactive programs in Pascal provided you follow a few simple rules. Remember that the procedure *readln* reads not to the end of the current line but to the first character of the next line. Consider this extract.

```
write ('Enter first number: ');
readln (first);
write ('Enter second number: ');
readln (second)
```

With some implementations of Pascal, this program will display "*Enter first number*: " and will read the value of *first*. The procedure *readln* does not return until the first character of the next line has been read, so the program will ask for *second* before it has displayed "*Enter second number*: ". It is not easy to provide a general solution for this problem because different implementations handle it in different ways. Here are some hints that may be useful.

- Put a *readln* immediately *before* reading a line of text other than the first line from a terminal.
- Do not use *readln* with parameters.
- Be sure to process an entire line of *input* before sending any messages to *output*.

7.4 APPLICATIONS: TABLE PROCESSING AND FILE UPDATING

It is difficult to work with computers for long without becoming acquainted with the fact that there are two schools of programming methodology and two kinds of programmers. One school is concerned with scientific programming and the other with commercial data processing. Programmers who work for the most part on one side of the divide tend to think that the problems of the other side are uninteresting, trivial, or useless. This schism is so deep that there are many languages, and even computers, designed to solve either commercial or scientific problems but not both. There is some justification for this. The commercial programmer requires efficient access to large amounts of data but does not indulge in "number crunching," whereas the scientific programmer is often involved with smaller amounts of data but more intensive calculation. Requirements differ even at the very basic level of number representation. Commercial programs require a small range of values but sufficient precision to ensure that they do not lose cents. Scientific programs often require a wider range of values at lower precision.

These dichotomies tend to mask the fact that the basic programming problems are actually rather similar. Although more recent programming languages have attempted to bridge the gap, they have done this by providing "scientific features" and "commercial features." The object of the examples in this section is to show that Pascal, with its relatively small number of basic constructs, can be used effectively to solve problems outside the domain of scientific programming.

APPLICATION: TABLE PROCESSING

The receivables file of a simple accounting system might be declared in the following way.

```
type
  receivable =
    record
      customerid, invoiceid : ident;
      invoicedate : date;
      balance : real
    end;
var
  recfile : file of receivables;
```

Table 7.2 shows a portion of this receivables file displayed in readable form. The file is maintained in ascending sequence by *customerid* and *invoiceid*.

TABLE 7.2 EXTRACT FROM RECEIVABLES FILE			
CUSTOMERID	**INVOICEID**	**INVOICE DATE**	**BALANCE**
CR1046	P1123	Apr 21	66.35
CR1046	P1127	Apr 23	78.00
CR1046	P1145	Apr 29	15.50
CU1214	P1009	Feb 16	216.95
CU1214	P1114	Apr 18	78.00
CU1214	S851	Jan 2	7.41
CY1249	P1110	Apr 18	23.90
CY1249	P1149	Apr 30	78.00

Because the company has several branch offices, the dates are not in the same sequence as the invoice numbers, and therefore the records are not sequenced chronologically. The problem is to write a program that lists all the transactions of a customer who has had any invoice outstanding for more than 90 days.

There are several ways of writing a program to do this. One way is to sort the file maintaining the ordering by *customerid* but arranging the records chronologically for each customer. We suppose, however, that the ordering by *invoiceid* is preferred for accounting purposes and that the file is too large to sort economically. Another approach would be to read the entire file, create a list of delinquent customers, and then read the file again, printing every transaction of a customer who was recorded in the list. There is a third way, which we adopt. This is to process the file by *groups* of customer records rather than by individual records. In order to do this, we need a data structure in memory large enough to hold all the records relating to any one customer. An array is a suitable structure. An array of records is often called a *table*.

We consider first a general algorithm for constructing and processing tables. We associate a key with each table. When we read a record from the file, we look at its key. If it is the same as the key of the current table, the new record is added to the table. If it is different, we process the current table and start a new one. In the following schema we use *customerid* as the key and *entrycount* to record the number of entries in the table.

```
            while not eof (recfile) do
              begin
                read (recfile, nextrec);
                if nextrec.customerid ≠ key
                  then
                    begin
                      processtable (table, entrycount);
                      key := nextrec.customerid;
                      entrycount := 0
                    end;
                if entrycount < tablesize
                  then
                    begin
                      entrycount := entrycount + 1;
                      table [entrycount] := nextrec
                    end
                  else table is full
              end
```

This schema works well enough in the middle of the file but it is unsatisfactory at the beginning and the end of the file. We start the program off on the right track by using the *customerid* of the first record as the initial value of *key*. We insert the following statements before the **while** statement.

```
            entrycount := 1;
            read (recfile, table [entrycount]);
            key := table [entrycount].customerid
```

At the end of the file there will be an unprocessed table in the memory, so we must conclude the schema with the statement

```
            processtable (table, entrycount)
```

In the program that follows, this schema is used to build tables of records that all have the same *customerid*. The procedure *processtable* prints all of these records if any one of them is more than ninety days old. The program calls a procedure, *readdate*, that returns the date of the day of processing. *Readdate* is not declared in the program because it is a request to the operating system and its form will vary between implementations.

```
{ Process receivables file. }
program tableprocessor (recfile, input, output);
  const
    tablesize = 100;   { Max # of entries with same customerid }
    idenlen = 10;      { Max length of invoice or customerid }
    maxage = 90;       { Age of invoices to be reported }
  { Calendar information }
    longestmonth = 31;
    feblen = 29;
    firstyear = 70;
    lastyear = 99;
    lenyear = 365;
    leap = 4;
  type
    month = (jan, feb, mar, apr, may, jun,
             jul, aug, sep, oct, nov, dec);
    day = 1..longestmonth;
    idenindex = 1..idenlen;
    tableindex = 0..tablesize;
    ident = array [idenindex] of char;
    date =
      record
        yy : firstyear..lastyear;
        mm : month;
        dd : day
      end; { date }
    receivable =
      record
        customerid, invoiceid : ident;
        invoicedate : date;
        balance : real
      end; { receivable }
    rectable = array [tableindex] of receivable;
  var
    recfile : file of receivable;
    table : rectable;
    entrycount : tableindex;
    nextrec : receivable;
    key : ident;
    today : date;
    lenmonth : array [month] of day;
```

```pascal
{ Request today's date. This is a system-dependent
  procedure not defined here. }
procedure readdate (var today : date);
  external;

{ Process a table of invoices with same customerid. }
procedure processtable (tab : rectable;
                        size : tableindex;
                        procdate : date);

var
  index : tableindex;
  oldtran : boolean;

  { Return days since 1/1/firstyear. }
  function age (dt : date) : integer;
    var
      mth : month;
      dys : integer;
    begin
      with dt do
        begin
          dys := dd - 1;
          if mm > jan
            then
              for mth := jan to pred (mm) do
                dys := dys + lenmonth [mth];
          if (mm > feb) and (yy mod leap = 0)
            then dys := dys + 1;
          dys := dys + lenyear * (yy - firstyear)
        end; { with }
      age := dys
    end; { age }

  { Print a receivables record. }
  procedure printrec (rec : receivable);

    { Print a customerid or invoiceid. }
    procedure printident (id : ident);
      var
        ix : 1..idenlen;
      begin
        for ix := 1 to idenlen do
          write (id [ix]);
        write (' ')
      end; { printiden }
```

```
begin { printrec }
  with rec do
    begin
      printident (customerid);
      printident (invoiceid);
      with invoicedate do
        begin
          write (ord (mm) + 1 : 2, '/');
          write (dd : 2, '/');
          write (yy : 2, ' ')
        end; { with invoicedate }
      writeln (balance : 12 : 2)
    end { with rec }
end; { printrec }

begin { processtable }
  oldtran := false;
  index := 0;
  while (index < size) and not oldtran do
    begin
      index := index + 1;
      if age (procdate) - age (table [index].invoicedate) > maxage
        then oldtran := true
    end; { while }
  if oldtran
    then
      for index := 1 to size do
        printrec (table [index])
end; { processtable }

begin { tableprocessor }
  lenmonth [jan] := 31; lenmonth [feb] := 28;
  lenmonth [mar] := 31; lenmonth [apr] := 30;
  lenmonth [may] := 31; lenmonth [jun] := 30;
  lenmonth [jul] := 31; lenmonth [aug] := 31;
  lenmonth [sep] := 30; lenmonth [oct] := 31;
  lenmonth [nov] := 30; lenmonth [dec] := 31;
  reset (recfile);
  readdate (today);
  entrycount := 1;
  read (recfile, table [entrycount]);
  key := table [entrycount].customerid;
  while not eof (recfile) do
```

```
begin
  read (recfile, nextrec);
  if nextrec.customerid ≠ key
    then
      begin
        processtable (table, entrycount, today);
        key := nextrec.customerid;
        entrycount := 0
      end; { then }
  if entrycount < tablesize
    then
      begin
        entrycount := entrycount + 1;
        table [entrycount] := nextrec
      end { then }
    else writeln ('Table overflowed.')
  end; { while }
  processtable (table, entrycount, today)
end. { tableprocessor }
```

APPLICATION: SEQUENTIAL UPDATE

We consider a second example of file processing, updating a sequential file. We suppose that there is a master file containing many records and a transaction file containing relatively few records. The sequential update program reads from an old master file, *oldfile*, and a transaction file, *transfile*, and creates an updated master file, *newfile*. Each step in the execution of the program involves either copying a record from *oldfile* to *newfile* or applying a transaction to an *oldfile* record to create a *newfile* record. There are three kinds of transaction: *change, delete,* and *insert*. A *change* alters the value of a master record. A *delete* deletes a master record. *Insert* creates a new master record. The information required for *change* and *insert* is contained in the transaction file. The *change* transaction is actually redundant because it can be accomplished by a deletion and an insertion, but we include it for completeness.

Some way of identifying the records to be affected is clearly necessary. We will assume that both master records and transaction records contain a *key* and that both have been sorted into ascending sequence on this key. As a simple example, suppose that the master file contains descriptions of cars and that each record has an integer key. Here is a portion of the master file.

KEY	DATA		
2	Chevrolet	red	81
3	Pontiac	green	69
4	Buick	blue	74
6	Oldsmobile	brown	82
7	Cadillac	black	76

The following transactions are to be applied to this master file.

3	change	Pontiac	green	70
5	insert	Porsche	gray	74
7	delete			

After these transactions have been applied, the new master file contains these records:

2	Chevrolet	red	81
3	Pontiac	green	70
4	Buick	blue	74
5	Porsche	gray	74
6	Oldsmobile	brown	82

If our program is to be useful, we must allow more than one transaction to affect a single master record. We should allow, for example, the following transactions:

4	change	Buick	gray	74
4	change	Lamborghini	red	84

We must also check the validity of transactions. A master record can only be changed or deleted if it already exists. Conversely, we cannot insert a record if the master file already contains a record with that key. For example, the following transactions cannot be applied to our original master file.

3	insert	Jaguar	white	83
5	delete			

Although the transaction code is redundant in the old and new master files, we assume that all three files have the same structure and that this structure can be represented by the following declarations.

```
const
  desclen = 30;
type
  transtype = (change, delete, insert);
  description = array [1..desclen] of char;
  filerec =
    record
      transaction : transtype;
      key : integer;
      model, color : description;
      year : 0..99
    end;
  editfile = file of filerec;
var
  oldfile, transfile, newfile : editfile;
  oldbuf, transbuf, newbuf : filerec;
```

At this point we can make two observations that simplify the subsequent development. First, we will be comparing keys in order to decide from which file to read. Second, we cannot tell in advance which file will end first. We must allow for the possibility that either file might be empty. If we append to each file a dummy record containing a high key-value but no data, all the tests we will require can be written in terms of key comparisons. These records need not physically exist in the file; they can be supplied by a procedure within the program.

```
procedure readrecord (var infile : editfile;
                      var buffer : filerec);
  begin
    if eof (infile)
      then buffer.key := highkey
      else read (infile, buffer)
  end;
```

It is clear that the main program will contain a loop and that this loop must not terminate until both *oldfile* and *transfile* have been read to the end. The form of this loop will be

```
while (oldbuf.key < highkey) or (transbuf.key < highkey) do
  process at least one record
```

We must process at least one record during each iteration because otherwise the program might not terminate. The problem is to decide how much to do during each iteration. The solution to this problem is to choose one key-value and to process all records that possess that key. For a given key-value, there may be zero or one record in *oldfile* and zero or more records in *transfile*. We choose a key-value by inspecting the next record of each file and choosing the one with the smaller key. If the *oldfile* record has the smaller key, it is copied directly to *newfile*. If the *transfile* record has the lower key, the transaction type must be *insert*. If the keys are equal, the transaction is applied to the master record. The transaction, however, may be followed by more transactions with the same key. We therefore require an inner loop to process all transactions with the selected key. The result of processing all records with the chosen key is that there may or may not be a record to be written to *newfile* but there certainly cannot be more than one. If there is a new record to be written, it is stored in *newbuf*; if there is not, *newbuf.key* is set to *highkey*. The program has this structure.

```
readrecord (oldfile, oldbuf);
readrecord (transfile, transbuf);
while (oldbuf.key < highkey) or (transbuf.key < highkey) do
  begin
    select currentkey;
    initialize newbuf;
    process all transactions with transbuf.key = currentkey;
    if newbuf.key < highkey
       then write (newfile, newbuf)
  end
```

If *currentkey* turns out to be the key of *oldbuf*, we can immediately copy *oldbuf* to *newbuf* and read the next record from *oldfile*. If *currentkey* is less than *oldbuf.key*, we initialize *newbuf* to *highkey*, indicating that it does not yet contain valid data. In this case, the first transaction applied must be *insert*.

When a transaction record is processed, one of the following conditions must be true.

- There is data in *newbuf* (*newbuf.key* < *highkey*) and the transaction is *change* or *delete*.
- There is no data in *newbuf* (*newbuf.key* = *highkey*) and the transaction is *insert*.

If neither condition is satisfied, we print an error message and process the next transaction.

```
{ Apply transactions in transfile to
  records in oldfile giving newfile. }
program update (output, oldfile, transfile, newfile);
  const
    desclen = 30;
    highkey = maxint;
  type
    transtype = (change, delete, insert);
    description = array [1..desclen] of char;
    filerec =
      record
        transaction : transtype;
        key : integer;
        model, color : description;
        year : 0..99
      end; { filerec }
      editfile = file of filerec;
  var
    oldfile, transfile, newfile: editfile;
    oldbuf, transbuf, newbuf : filerec;
    currentkey : integer;

  { Read one record from the input file or the transaction file. }
  procedure readrecord (var infile : editfile;
                        var buffer : filerec);
    begin
      if eof (infile)
        then buffer.key := highkey
        else read (infile, buffer)
    end; { readrecord }

  begin { update }
    reset (oldfile);
    reset (transfile);
    rewrite (newfile);
    readrecord (oldfile, oldbuf);
    readrecord (transfile, transbuf);
    while (oldbuf.key < highkey) or (transbuf.key < highkey) do
      begin
        if oldbuf.key < transbuf.key
          then
```

```
            begin
              currentkey := oldbuf.key;
              newbuf := oldbuf;
              readrecord (oldfile, oldbuf)
            end { then }
          else
            begin
              currentkey := transbuf.key;
              newbuf.key := highkey
            end; { else }
        while transbuf.key = currentkey do
          begin
            if newbuf.key < highkey
              then
                case transbuf.transaction of
                  change : newbuf := transbuf;
                  delete : newbuf.key := highkey;
                  insert : writeln ('Insertion error.')
                end { then and case }
              else if transbuf.transaction = insert
                then newbuf := transbuf
                else writeln ('Change or delete error.');
            readrecord (transfile, transbuf)
          end; { while }
        if newbuf.key < highkey
          then write (newfile, newbuf)
    end { while }
end. { update }
```

7.5 SUBFILE STRUCTURE

A backing-store device, such as a tape or a disk, has a large capacity. It would be wasteful to store only one file on a tape or a disk unless the file was unusually large. A disk is a random-access device that cannot be represented accurately in a Pascal program. A multifile tape, on the other hand, is simpler in structure and can be represented by standard Pascal types.

It is possible to write on a tape a special character, called a *tape-mark*, which is distinguishable from ordinary data. Several files, separated by tape-marks, may be written on a tape. These files are usually called *subfiles* of the tape. In order to read the *n*th subfile, we execute

```
reset (tape);
for m := 1 to n - 1 do                    (7.2)
    skip to tape-mark
```

The tape unit is able to recognize tape-marks without transferring information in the intervening subfiles into the computer's memory. Skipping to a tape-mark is therefore a more efficient operation than reading a subfile. The subfile structure may be represented in Pascal by declaring a file whose components are files.

```
var
    tape : file of file of T;
```

T is the type of a component of a subfile. Note that all subfiles must be of the same type. The variable *tape↑* is a subfile. The operation *get (tape)* is equivalent to the operation *skip to tape-mark* used in (7.2). The function *eof (tape)* becomes *true* at the end of the tape. The variable *tape↑↑* is of type T and is one record of the subfile. The operation *get (tape↑)* reads one item from the subfile, and the function *eof (tape↑)* becomes *true* at the end of a subfile. The operation *put (tape↑)* writes one record to a subfile, and the operation *put (tape)* terminates a subfile by writing a tape-mark.

The type **file of file of** T is an appropriate abstraction for a file with subfiles but it is not supported by all Pascal implementations. Even if it is supported, the compiler may not be clever enough to apply it to tape-marks.

Files with a subfile structure are not as restricted as sequential files, since subfiles may be skipped without being read. They are less useful, however, than true random-access files. Most modern computer systems use disks to provide random-access storage, and magnetic tape only for archiving, for storing very large amounts of data, and for sending data to other installations. In view of the widespread and increasing use of random-access techniques, the lack of random-access facilities in Standard Pascal is something of an anachronism.

7.6 EXERCISES

7.1 Write programs to generate test data for Programs *update* and *processtable*.

7.2 Modify Program *processtable* so that it calculates the age of each record as soon as the record has been read and does not execute *processtable* at all if there is no item more than 90 days old.

7.3 Write a program that generates an *aged receivables report*. Assume that the input file contains records of the type *receivable* used in Program *processtable*.

The report lists the customer number, invoice number, and date in fixed columns at the left of the page. The amount is printed in one of four columns according to the age of the receivable item: current (less than 31 days old), 31 to 60 days old, 61 to 90 days old, and over 90 days old. At the end of the report, the total amount for each column and the total of all columns are printed.

7.4 Two files of the same type contain records sorted by a key. Write a program that reads the two files and *merges* them, producing a single output file sorted by the key. Write a program that generates test data for this program.

7.5 You have a tape that is to be sorted and a computer with three tape units and a small memory. The records on the tape are so large that only two of them will fit in the memory at the same time. Write a program that sorts the input tape and leaves the sorted file on one of the other two tapes.

7.6 Write a program that reads text that consists of words separated by blanks and writes the same text formatted for a specified page size. For example, the page size might be given as 40 lines with each line containing at most 50 characters. Words longer than the specified line length may be rejected. The program should print a page heading and a number at the top of each page.

7.7 Write a line-oriented *text editor*. This program reads text from an *input file* and an *edit file*. It writes to an *output file* that is a copy of the input file except where directives on the edit file were encountered. The edit file contains directives of the form

*R *m* *n*
lines of text

that means "replace lines *m* through *n* of the input file by the following text," and

*I *m*
lines of text

which means "insert the following text after line *m* of the input file." Give a full specification of your program, including restrictions on the sequencing of commands and the contents of textual insertions.

7.8 Extend Program *update* so that it prints a report showing the number of changes, deletions, and insertions made, and the number of records in *oldfile* and *newfile*. Provide an option so that the user can obtain a list of the records inserted or changed during the run.

7.9 We used the same type for master and transaction records in Program *update*. This decision simplified the development of the program but would be unacceptable in a production program because space is wasted in the master files. Modify the program so that transaction and master records have structures appropriate to their functions.

8

DYNAMIC
DATA STRUCTURES

A static structure is a data structure that remains fixed in size throughout its lifetime. The type constructors **array** and **record** allow us to create static structures in a Pascal program. We can always determine the size of a static structure by examining the constant definitions in the program. Dynamic data structures, on the other hand, change in size during the execution of the program. In this chapter we will discuss how dynamic data structures can be created and used.

In order to see why dynamic data structures might be useful, we consider the problem of maintaining a list. Each component of the list can be represented by a variable of the type *object*. The type *object* may be a simple type, such as *char* or *real*, or a structured type, such as array or record. We could represent the list by an array

```
var
    list : array [1..listsize] of object;
```

but there are several problems with this representation. In the first place, because we have to define the value of *listsize,* we have to decide how many components the list will eventually contain before we start. The next problem concerns the insertion of a new component into the list. We can append a new component to the end of the list but this does not help if we are maintaining a sorted list. We can insert a component into the middle of a list but this requires moving some of the existing components. Finally, if we delete a component, we have a "hole" in the list that we must mark in some way.

In order to solve these problems elegantly and efficiently, we need a data structure that will permit us to insert and delete components without having to worry about where new components fit or what happens to the empty space left by a deletion. The tool to create such a data structure is called a *pointer.*

8.1   POINTERS

Pointer is a simple type like *integer, real,* and *boolean.* "Pointer" is not, however, a standard identifier. Instead, pointers are defined in this way.

```
type
    link = ↑ object;
```

This definition is read:

> "The type *link* is a pointer to an *object.*"

The arrow "↑" tells us that *link* is a pointer type. A variable of the type *object* may be associated with a pointer of the type *link.* Figure 8.1(a) illustrates the as-

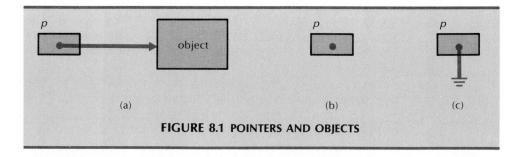

(a)   (b)   (c)

FIGURE 8.1 POINTERS AND OBJECTS

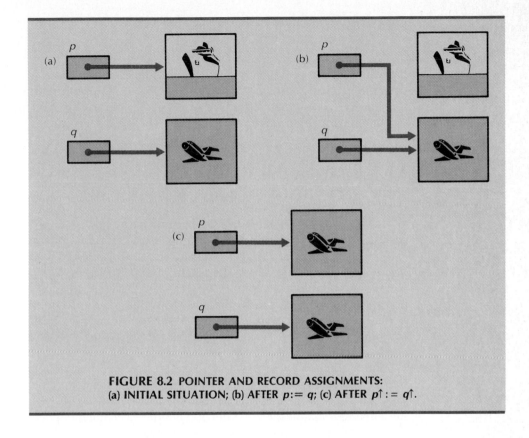

FIGURE 8.2 POINTER AND RECORD ASSIGNMENTS:
(a) INITIAL SITUATION; (b) AFTER $p := q$; (c) AFTER $p\uparrow := q\uparrow$.

sociation of a variable with a pointer. The variable p in this diagram is of type *link* and the object with which it is associated is designated $p\uparrow$.

Sometimes we have a pointer that is not associated with any *object.* In this case we write

$$p := \textbf{nil}$$

Figure 8.1(b) establishes the convention that we use in this book for drawing **nil**. Some books use the electrical "ground" symbol to represent **nil** pointers, as in Fig. 8.1(c). The symbol "Λ", capital lambda, is sometimes used in theoretical discussions of data structures to denote a **nil** pointer. The symbol **nil** is a reserved word in Pascal.

It is important to understand the distinction between pointers and the things to which they point. Figure 8.2(a) shows two variables, p and q, of type *link,* pointing to different objects. The assignment

$$p := q$$

has the effect of assigning the value of the pointer q to the pointer p. After this assignment, the situation is as shown in Fig. 8.2(b). Both pointers point to the airplane. If p was the only pointer to the ship before the assignment, the ship can no longer be accessed by the program. The statement

$$p\uparrow := q\uparrow$$

has quite a different effect. We are now copying the *value* of the object $q\uparrow$ to the object $p\uparrow$. The result is shown in Fig. 8.2(c). The pointers are unchanged but the value of $p\uparrow$ has been altered.

A pointer is sometimes called a *reference* because it *refers to* an object rather than representing the object directly. Consequently, you will sometimes see the operation performed in Pascal by "↑" referred to as *dereferencing*. In Fig. 8.2(a), p is a reference. The result of dereferencing p is $p\uparrow$, the ship.

A dynamic data structure consists of a number of components linked by pointers. We can add new components to the structure or delete old components from it as the program runs. Because the logical relationships between components are maintained by pointers rather than by relative positions in memory, the actual addresses of components are unimportant.

Each component in a dynamic data structure must contain one or more fields pointing to other components. Thus a component could be a pointer, an array, or a record. We can rule out pointer types because they cannot contain any information apart from the value of a pointer. The components of an array must all be of the same type, a rather serious restriction, and the only remaining candidate is a record. We can define an object containing a pointer and some other information by using a record in the following way.

```
type
    object =
        record
            next : link;
            data : datatype
        end;
```

Now we are confronted by a chicken-and-egg problem: do we declare *link* or *object* first? Fortunately the designers of Pascal anticipated this problem, and we are allowed to define a pointer to an object before we have defined the object itself. We can therefore write

```
type
  link = ↑ object;
  object =
    record
      next : link;
      data : datatype
    end;
```

In the next section, we will see how these declarations can be used to solve the list-maintenance problem with which we introduced this chapter. There is one more thing that we must know about pointers before we proceed. A pointer is *bound* to the variables of the type for which it was declared. Following the declarations

```
type
  P = ↑ A;
  Q = ↑ B;
var
  p : P;
  q : Q;
```

in which *A* and *B* are different types, the assignments

$$p := q$$

and

$$q := p$$

are illegal. The first one, for example, would require *p*, a pointer to an object of type *A*, to point to an object of type *B*. This is not allowed in Pascal.

The pointer **nil** is unusual in that it can be assigned to a pointer variable of any type. The assignments

```
p := nil;
q := nil
```

are both legal.

8.2   LINKED LISTS

The *linked list* is the simplest type of dynamic data structure. It provides a solution to the problem of maintaining a list in which components may be added or deleted at random.

Figure 8.3 shows a data structure built from a single pointer variable, *top*, and three components of type *object*. This data structure is a *linked list*. We now demonstrate how the structure of Fig. 8.3 can be assembled by a program.

Suppose that we want to use the pointer variable *top* as an anchor for the list, as in Fig. 8.3. Initially we want the list to be empty, so we write

$$top := \mathbf{nil}$$

We now need a component to insert into the list. Components are created dynamically by the standard procedure *new*, whose argument is a pointer. Declare

```
var
   p : link;
```
and call

$$new\ (p)$$

This will create a component of type *object* whose name is *p↑*. Figure 8.4(a) shows the situation. The next step is to assign some information to the new component. Because *p↑* is a record, the field *data* of *p↑* is designated *p↑.data*, and, assuming that a single character can be stored in data, we write

$$p{\uparrow}.data := \text{'X'}$$

The result of this assignment is shown in Fig. 8.4(b). The next step, for which the reason will shortly become apparent, is the assignment

$$p{\uparrow}.next := top$$

The current value of *top* is **nil,** and the effect of this statement is to set *p↑.next* to **nil,** as shown by Fig. 8.4(c). Finally, we assign

$$top := p$$

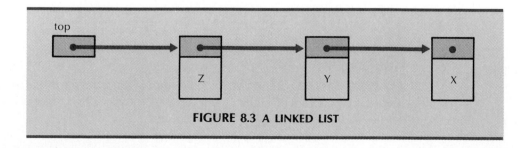

FIGURE 8.3 A LINKED LIST

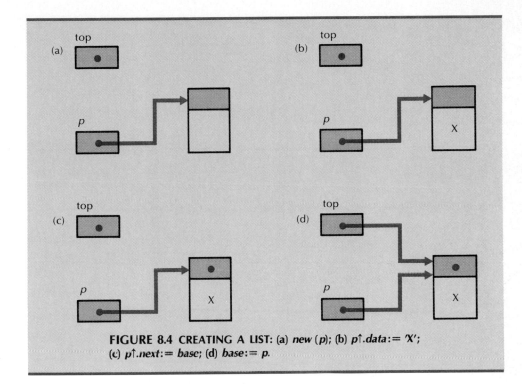

FIGURE 8.4 CREATING A LIST: (a) *new (p)*; (b) *p↑.data:= 'X'*;
(c) *p↑.next:= base*; (d) *base:= p.*

to obtain the desired result shown in Fig. 8.4(d). We have constructed a list containing one component. The value of *top↑.data* is "X" and the value of *top↑.next* is **nil.**

We can insert another component into the list in the same way. First we create the new component:

```
new (p);
p↑.data := 'Y'
```

As Figs. 8.5(a) and (b) show, we can insert the new component by using the same statements we used to insert the first component.

```
p↑.next := top;
top := p
```

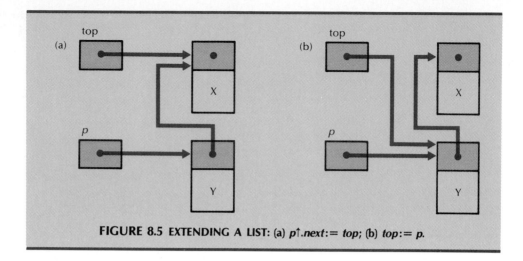

FIGURE 8.5 EXTENDING A LIST: (a) $p{\uparrow}.next := top$; (b) $top := p$.

LINKED LIST TRAVERSAL

We can now turn to the problem of accessing the components of a list. Consider again the list shown in Fig. 8.3. It is easy to access the first component because it is $top{\uparrow}$. We have

$$top{\uparrow}.data = \text{'Z'}$$

We can access the second component using the pointer field, $next$, of the first component. The second component is $top{\uparrow}.next{\uparrow}$, so

$$top{\uparrow}.next{\uparrow}.data = \text{'Y'}$$

We could continue in this way but the method is clearly unsuitable for accessing the components of a list of unknown length. To do this we need a general algorithm. The key to this algorithm lies in the fact that, if p points to a component of the list, the assignment

$$p := p{\uparrow}.next$$

alters p so that it points to the next component of the list. The assignment can be repeated until p becomes **nil**, which indicates that we are at the end of the list. Accordingly, the algorithm for *traversing* a list is

```
p := top;
repeat
   p := p↑.next
until p = nil
```

We can improve on this slightly. If we write

```
p := top;
while p ≠ nil do
  p := p↑.next
```

we have an algorithm that will not fail if the list happens to be empty.

If we use this algorithm to traverse the list shown in Fig. 8.5(b), we encounter the component containing "Y" first. We can easily see that the first component of a list, the component to which *top* points, is always the one most recently inserted. A simple linked list is a *last-in/first-out*, or *LIFO*, structure. A structure with this property is called a *stack*, which suggests a stack of plates: if we move one plate at a time, we can access only the top plate of the stack.

Program *reverselist* uses the list insertion and traversal techniques we have discussed to read a string of characters, store them in a list, and print them in reverse order.

```
{ Read a list of numbers and print it backwards. }
program reverselist (input, output);
  type
    link = ↑ object;
    object =
      record
        next : link;
        data : char
      end; { object }
  var
    top, p : link;
  begin
    top := nil;
    while not eof do
      begin
        new (p);
        read (p↑.data);
        p↑.next := top;
        top := p
      end; { while }
    p := top;
    while p ≠ nil do
      begin
        write (p↑.data);
        p := p↑.next
      end { while }
  end. { reverselist }
```

QUEUES

The simple linked list is useful in some applications. Its disadvantage is that only the first component of the list is readily accessible. It is not difficult to arrange a list so that it can be used as a *queue*. Although a queue is similar to a list, it differs from a list in that only the component that has been in the queue for the longest time can be retrieved. Thus a queue is a *first-in/first-out, or FIFO,* structure. The term "queue" is used by analogy to a queue of people; newcomers join the rear of the queue, and the person at the front of the queue is served first. The data structure is a list of the kind we have used already, with an additional pointer to its last component, as shown in Fig. 8.6(b). We can declare

```
type
    link = ↑ object;
    object =
        record
            next : link;
            data : datatype
        end;
var
    front, rear : link;
```

The procedure *retrieve* removes the first component from the queue and sets the pointer *first* pointing to it. When the last component of the queue is removed and the queue becomes empty (Fig. 8.6a), special action is needed.

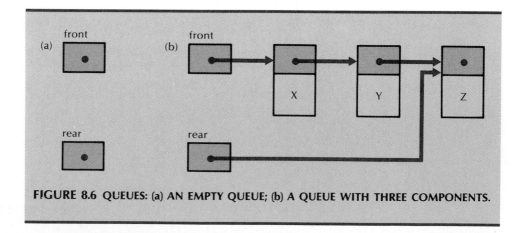

FIGURE 8.6 QUEUES: (a) AN EMPTY QUEUE; (b) A QUEUE WITH THREE COMPONENTS.

```
         procedure retrieve (var first, front, rear : link);
           begin
             first := front;
             if front ≠ nil
               then
                 begin
                   front := front↑.next;
                   if front = nil
                     then rear := nil
                 end
           end;
```

If the queue is empty when *retrieve* is called, it will return *first* = **nil**, indicating that there is nothing to retrieve. When the queue becomes empty as a result of a *retrieve*, both *front* and *rear* become **nil**.

The procedure *enterqueue* places a new component at the rear of the queue. *Arrival* is a pointer to the new component provided by the caller. Once again it is necessary to take special action when the queue is empty.

```
         procedure enterqueue (arrival : link;
                                     var front, rear : link);
           begin
             if front = nil
               then front := arrival
               else rear↑.next := arrival;
             rear := arrival
           end;
```

INSERTION AND DELETION

We now consider the problem of inserting and deleting components which may be in the middle of a list. It is not difficult to insert a component into the middle of a list if we have a pointer to the component that will precede the new component in the restructured list. Suppose that we have a list containing the component *tom*↑ and we want to insert *dick*↑ after *tom*↑. The procedure *insertafter* will do this.

```
         procedure insertafter (tom, dick : link);
           begin
             dick↑.next := tom↑.next;
             tom↑.next := dick
           end;
```

Figure 8.7 illustrates the effect of procedure *insertafter*. Figure 8.7(a) shows the situation prior to the execution of the procedure, and Fig. 8.7(b) shows the situa-

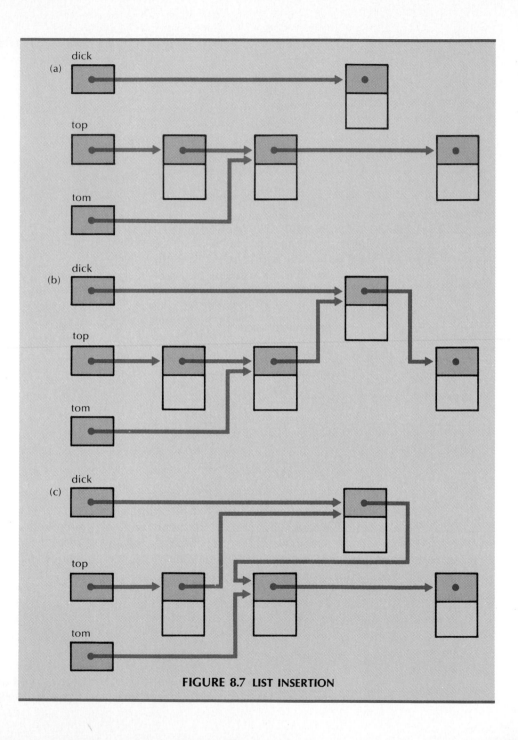

FIGURE 8.7 LIST INSERTION

tion after. *Insertafter* will work if *tom*↑ is the last component of the list but it will fail if *tom* = **nil**.

The procedure *insertbefore* is used when we have a pointer to the component that is to follow the new component in the new list. It is more difficult to implement than *insertafter* because we cannot directly access the pointer that we must alter in order to restructure the list. The situation we hope to reach after executing the procedure call *insertbefore* (*tom*, *dick*) is shown in Fig. 8.7(c). The initial conditions are the same as in Fig. 8.7(a). We first have to traverse the list.

```
var
  here : link;
....
  while here↑.next ≠ tom do
    here := here↑.next
```

If we assume that *tom* is not **nil**, the list cannot be empty. The first component of the list, however, might be *tom*↑, and in this case the traversal suggested above would not find him. Therefore we have to check for the special case in which *tom*↑ is the first component of the list.

```
procedure insertbefore (tom, dick : link;
                                 var top : link);
var
  here : link;
begin
  if tom = top
    then
      begin
        dick↑.next := tom;
        top := dick
      end
    else
      begin
        here := top;
        while here↑.next ≠ tom do
          here := here↑.next;
        here↑.next := dick;
        dick↑.next := tom
      end
end;
```

There is another way of implementing *insertbefore* which can be used when the amount of information in each component is not large. We can use the procedure *insertafter* to insert the new component in the wrong place in the list and then interchange the *contents* of *tom*↑ and *dick*↑.

```
procedure insertbefore (tom, dick : link);
  var
    tempstore : datatype;
  begin
    dick↑.next := tom↑.next;
    tom↑.next := dick;
    tempstore := tom↑.data;
    tom↑.data := dick↑.data;
    dick↑.data := tempstore
  end;
```

If the list may be very long, this version of *insertbefore* is better than the earlier version because it does not traverse the list. If the list is short but each component is large, the earlier version of *insertbefore* may be preferable. This method, and indeed any method that involves changing the contents of a record, must not be used if there may be other pointers to the record.

We encounter a similar problem when we want to delete a component of a list. The deletion is simple enough if we have a pointer to the component preceding the component to be deleted, called, say, *predecessor*.

```
predecessor↑.next := predecessor↑.next↑.next
```

It is more likely, however, that we will have a pointer to the component itself, and in this case we have to traverse the list in order to find its predecessor. Special treatment is required for the case in which the first component of the list has to be deleted.

```
procedure delete (tom : link;
                      var top : link);
  var
    here : link;
  begin
    if tom = top
      then top := tom↑.next
      else
        begin
          here := top;
          while here↑.next ≠ tom do
            here := here↑.next;
          here↑.next := tom↑.next
        end
  end;
```

RECURSIVE LIST PROCESSING

A linked list is a simple example of a *recursive* data structure. We can illustrate the recursive characteristics of linked lists in three ways. First, we can define lists recursively.

> A list is empty, or it consists of a record
> that contains a pointer to a list.

Second, we can represent a list by a recursive data structure. The definition of *link* refers to the definition of *object* and vice versa. In principle, we could write a simple recursive definition of a list in this way:

```
type
  list = record
           data : datatype;
           next : list
         end;
```

This form of definition, however, is not allowed in Pascal. As we have seen, we must introduce a pointer type as well, so that we can represent the empty list by a **nil** pointer.

Third, we can write a recursive procedure to process a list. The structure of the procedure corresponds to the definition in that the procedure will contain an **if** statement. One branch of the **if** statement performs the actions appropriate for an empty list. The other branch performs the actions appropriate to a single component and then calls the procedure recursively to process the remainder of the list. Two recursive procedures are used in the program below to read a string of characters and print them in the order in which they were read. The purpose of this program is to illustrate recursive list processing; there are much simpler ways to copy a list of characters.

```
{ Read a list and print it. }
program copylist (input, output);
  type
    link = ↑ object;
    object =
      record
        next : link;
        data : char
      end; { object }
  var
    top : link;
```

```
{ Read a datum, create a record containing it,
  and append the new record to the list ptr. }
procedure append (var ptr : link);
  begin
    if ptr = nil
      then
        begin
          new (ptr);
          ptr↑.next := nil;
          read (ptr↑.data)
        end { then }
        else append (ptr↑.next)
  end; { append }
{ Print the list ptr. }
procedure writelist (ptr : link);
  begin
    if ptr ≠ nil
      then
        begin
          write (ptr↑.data);
          writelist (ptr↑.next)
        end { then }
  end; { writelist }
begin { copylist }
  top := nil;
  while not eof do
    append (top);
  writelist (top)
end. { copylist }
```

DOUBLY LINKED RINGS

We can eliminate the inconvenience of having to check for special cases by elaborating the structure of the list. We can use two pointers in each component, one pointing to the preceding component and one to the following component. The definition becomes

```
type
  link = ↑ object;
  object =
```

```
record
    fptr, bptr : link;
    data : datatype
end;
```

Fptr is the pointer to the following component and is called the *forward pointer*. *Bptr* is the pointer to the preceding component and is called the *backward pointer*. We can complete the symmetry of the structure by linking together the first and last components. The result, illustrated in Fig. 8.8(b), is called a *doubly linked ring*. The procedures for manipulating rings are simplified if we define the empty ring to be a ring with a single dummy component linked to itself, as shown in Fig. 8.8(a).

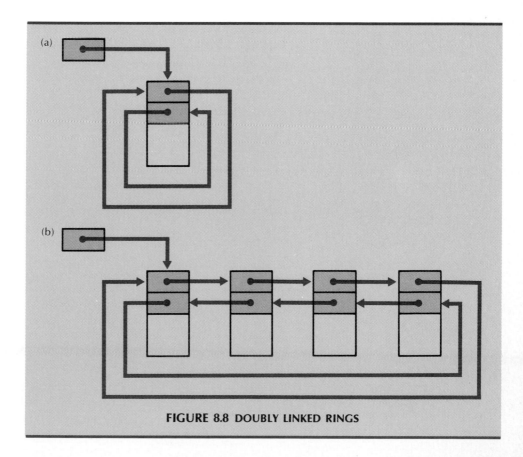

FIGURE 8.8 DOUBLY LINKED RINGS

Procedures for inserting and deleting components from rings follow.

```
{ Insert dick↑ after tom↑. }
procedure insertafter (tom, dick : link);
  begin
    dick↑.fptr := tom↑.fptr;
    dick↑.bptr := tom;
    tom↑.fptr↑.bptr := dick;
    tom↑.fptr := dick
  end;
{ Insert dick↑ before tom↑. }
procedure insertbefore (tom, dick : link);
  begin
    dick↑.fptr := tom;
    dick↑.bptr := tom↑.bptr;
    tom↑.bptr↑.fptr := dick;
    tom↑.bptr := dick
  end;
{ Delete tom↑. }
procedure delete (tom : link);
  begin
    tom↑.fptr↑.bptr := tom↑.bptr;
    tom↑.bptr↑.fptr := tom↑.fptr
  end;
```

Traversing a ring is not quite the same as traversing a list because we cannot look for a **nil** pointer. Instead, we have to remember the place from which we started. In the example below, *start* and *round* are pointers.

```
round := start↑.fptr;
while round ≠ start do
  begin
    S;
    round := round↑.fptr
  end
```

The statement *S* will be executed once for each component of the ring. At the time of execution of *S, round* points to the current component. If the ring is empty (Fig. 8.8(b)), *S* will not be executed at all. The ring can be traversed in the opposite direction using *bptr* instead of *fptr*.

It is interesting to compare simple lists and doubly linked rings. The procedures for rings do not need to know the value of *base*, the "anchor" of the ring, provided they have a pointer to at least one component of the ring. There is a price to pay for this convenience. Components of a ring are larger than components of a list because they contain an extra pointer. The procedures for rings are slower in some cases than the procedures for lists because there are more pointers to update. Overall, the doubly linked ring is a more elegant structure than the list because no traversals are necessary for simple operations and there is no need to consider special cases.

OPERATIONS ON POINTERS

Pascal does not permit us to use a pointer variable for anything except to point at something or, if the pointer is **nil**, to point at nothing. We cannot, for example, add, multiply, compare, or write pointers. This is a reasonable restriction because such operations are meaningless and machine-dependent. Occasionally, however, we would like to be able to write the value of a pointer, for example in a postmortem dump procedure. In many implementations, the value of a pointer is a memory address and it can be regarded as an integer. If this is the case, we can use the following procedure to write a pointer value.

```
procedure writepointer (pnt : pointer);
  type
    rep = (pointerrep, integerrep);
    aliastype =
      record
        case rep of
          pointerrep : (pointerval : pointer);
          integerrep : (integerval : integer)
      end; { aliastype }
  var
    alias : aliastype;
  begin
    alias.pointerval := pnt;
    write (alias.integerval)
  end;
```

You will recall from Chapter 6 that a variant record without a tag field is a free union. It is a programming device that may not work on all implementations. It may fail in certain cases, if the pointer is **nil,** for example. It is machine-dependent. We mention it because there are situations in which printing a pointer value is useful, particularly in program development. Do not allow procedures of this kind to remain in finished programs, and do not in any circumstances use them in a program that may be run at another installation.

Compared to other programming languages, Pascal is relatively strict. We have seen that this strictness enables the compiler to report errors that could not otherwise be detected. If a language is too strict, however, we are prevented from doing things which are occasionally necessary. Thus Pascal contains a few loopholes, such as free unions, that allow us to bend the rules slightly. The cumbersome definition of *aliastype* serves as a warning that something special is happening.

POINTER SYNTAX

Figure 8.9 is a complete syntax diagram for *type denoter*, including sets, arrays, records, files, and pointers. Figure 8.10 is a complete syntax diagram for *variable access*. These are examples of variable accesses:

$$a\uparrow.b \qquad c[3]\uparrow \qquad c[3]\uparrow[n] \qquad z\uparrow.y\uparrow.z$$

8.3 APPLICATION: DISCRETE EVENT SIMULATION

Computers are used frequently to simulate natural and artificial phenomena. Provided that the underlying theoretical model is adequate, useful results can be obtained from simulations in circumstances where experiments would be expensive or impossible. In this application we construct a program that simulates a bus service. Although in reality a bus service is a continuous process, we can design an abstract model of it using parameters that change only at discrete times. For example, we assume that a bus is traveling or stationary and that a passenger is waiting for a bus, boarding a bus, or sitting in a bus.

The bus company provides a service that consists of *bustotal* buses traveling around a circular route consisting of *stoptotal* bus stops. The bus company has done its utmost to ensure regularity of service by allowing fixed amounts of time for a bus to travel from one stop to the next and for a passenger to board a bus. The service would be entirely regular but for the fact that passengers arrive at bus stops at random intervals.

In the simulation we consider three kinds of events.

- A person joins the queue at a bus stop.
- A bus arrives at a bus stop.
- A person boards the bus.

We ignore disembarking passengers, assuming that they get out at the back faster than boarding passengers get in at the front. For each of the events above, we can specify another event that must follow.

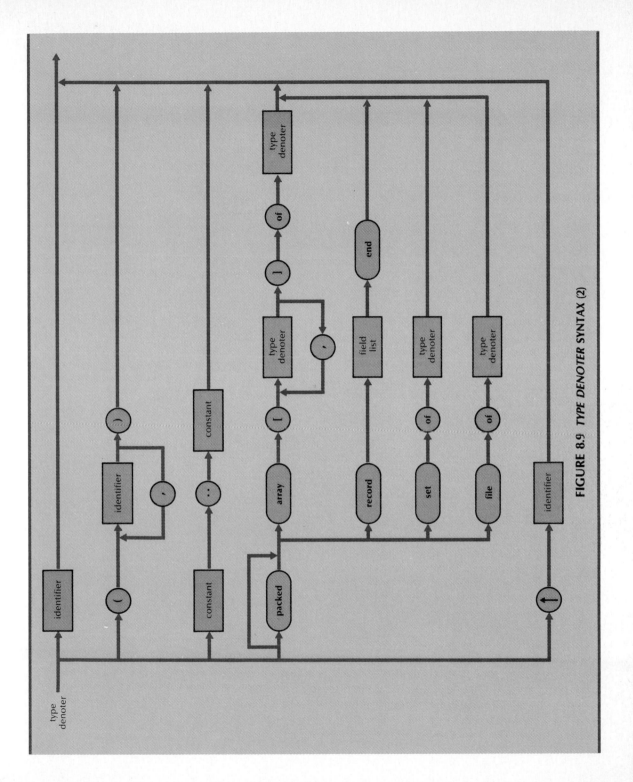

FIGURE 8.9 *TYPE DENOTER SYNTAX (2)*

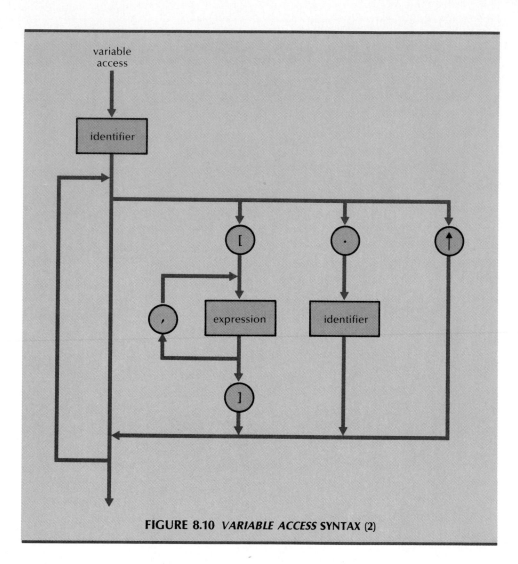

FIGURE 8.10 *VARIABLE ACCESS* SYNTAX (2)

- After a random interval, another person joins the queue.
- If there is a queue of people waiting at the bus stop, the next event is that the first person in the queue boards the bus. If there are no people waiting at the bus stop, the bus proceeds to the next stop.
- The length of the queue diminishes by 1. If the queue is now empty, the bus proceeds to the next stop, otherwise the next passenger boards the bus.

We represent an event by a record.

```
type
  eventkind = (person, arrival, boarder);
  event =
    record
      kind : eventkind
    end;
var
  currentevent : event;
```

We can now write a provisional schema for the program.

```
repeat
  get the current event;
  case currentevent.kind of
    person :
      begin
        queuelength := queuelength + 1
        schedule (person)
      end;
    arrival :
      if queuelength = 0
        then schedule (arrival)
        else schedule (boarder);
    boarder :
      begin
        queuelength := queuelength - 1;
        if queuelength = 0
          then schedule (arrival)
          else schedule (boarder)
      end
  end { case }
until end of simulation
```

In this schema we have assumed the existence of a procedure, *schedule*, that will schedule an event that is to occur at some time in the future. We have also written the statement "get the current event." This suggests that we will need a data structure to store events in chronological order so that the "next" event is immediately accessible. A queue is not an adequate structure because events are not generated in chronological order. A more appropriate structure is a ring in which each component is an event. The parameters of an event are: its *eventkind*, the time at which it will occur, the number of a bus stop, and the

number of a bus. We can write the following more detailed declarations for the
event record and the event ring.

```
type
  link = ↑ event;
  event =
    record
      fptr, bptr : link;
      kind : eventkind;
      time : real;
      stopnum : stopnumber;
      busnum : busnumber
    end;
var
  base : link;
  currentevent : link;
```

Figure 8.11(a) identifies the various fields of an event record and Fig. 8.11(b)
shows the form of the ring during the simulation. The events are ordered chronologically. In accordance with the conventions described in Section 8.2, we include a dummy event in the ring and consider the ring to be empty when it contains no components other than the dummy component. The current event is

```
currentevent := base↑.fptr
```

and the current time is

```
currentevent↑.time
```

When we have processed the current event, we delete it so that the next event
becomes the current event. The following assignments suffice to delete the current event; their effect is depicted in Fig. 8.11(c).

```
base↑.fptr := currentevent↑.fptr;
currentevent↑.fptr↑.bptr := base
```

We use an integer to represent the number of people in the queue at a bus stop.
The lengths of all the queues can be summarized in an array.

```
queue : array [stopnumber] of integer;
```

Using these declarations, we can write a refined version of the main program.

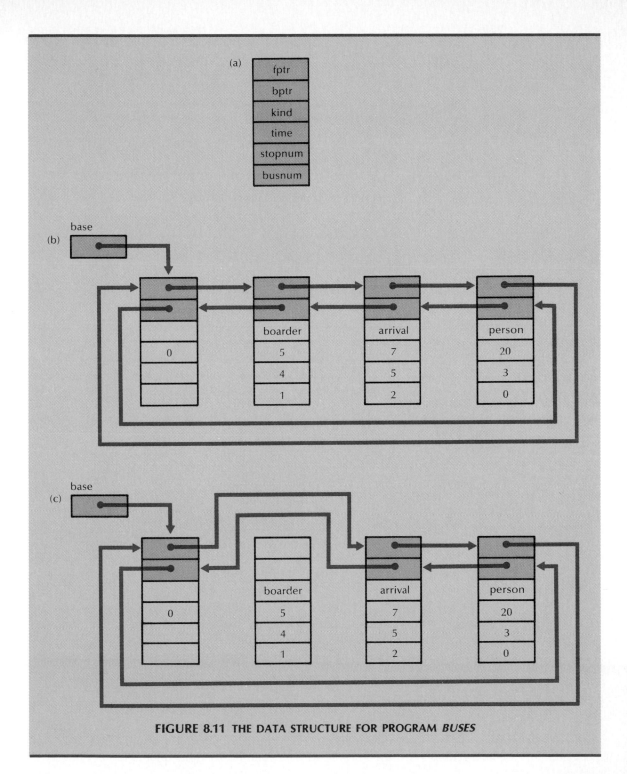

FIGURE 8.11 THE DATA STRUCTURE FOR PROGRAM *BUSES*

```
repeat
  currentevent := base↑.fptr;
  with currentevent↑ do
    case kind of
      person :
  begin
    queue [stopnum] := queue [stopnum] + 1;
    schedule (person, time, stopnum, 0)
  end;
      arrival :
        if queue [stopnum] = 0
          then schedule (arrival, time, nextstop, busnum)
          else schedule (boarder, time, stopnum, busnum);
      boarder :
        begin
          queue [stopnum] := queue [stopnum] - 1;
          if queue [stopnum] > 0
            then schedule (boarder, time, stopnum, busnum)
            else schedule (arrival, time, nextstop, busnum)
        end
    end; { with case }
  base↑.fptr := currentevent↑.fptr;
  currentevent↑.fptr↑.bptr := base
until base↑.fptr↑.time > maxtime
```

When a bus departs from a bus stop, we call

```
schedule (arrival, time, nextstop, busnum)
```

to generate an event representing the arrival of the bus at the next stop. If we suppose that the *stoptotal* bus stops are numbered 1 through *stoptotal*, we have

```
nextstop = (stopnum mod stoptotal) + 1
```

The procedure *schedule* has to calculate the time at which the new event will occur, construct the event, and insert it into the event ring. The time for which the new event is scheduled depends on what kind of event it is. There are three kinds of events and three different times. We can store the times in an array.

```
var
  evtime : array [eventkind] of real;
```

Evtime [*arrival*] and *evtime* [*boarder*] are constants, but the arrival of a person at a bus stop is a random event, so *evtime* [*person*] must be multiplied by a random variable each time it is used. The random variable should have a negative exponential distribution. If random events occur with a mean rate, R, the time between consecutive events is a random variable, t, where

$$t = \frac{-\ln(x)}{R}$$

and x is a random variable uniformly distributed between 0 and 1. The new event is inserted into the ring by searching the ring backwards until the event chronologically preceding the new event is found. This will always work provided that we assign time zero to the dummy event.

```
    { Schedule the event predicted by the current event. }
procedure schedule (evkind : eventkind;
                    newtime : real;
                    stop : stopnumber;
                    bus : busnumber);
  var
    ev, newev : link;
    delay : real;
  begin
    { Calculate time to next event. }
    if evkind = person
      then delay := evtime [evkind] * random
      else delay := evtime [evkind];
    { Construct the new event. }
    new (newev);
    with newev↑ do
      begin
        kind := evkind;
        time := newtime + delay;
        stopnum := stop;
        busnum := bus
      end;
    { Find a place for it in the queue. }
    ev := base;
    repeat
      ev := ev↑.bptr
    until newev↑.time ≥ ev↑.time;
    { Insert the event in the queue. }
    newev↑.fptr := ev↑.fptr;
    newev↑.bptr := ev;
    ev↑.fptr↑.bptr := newev;
    ev↑.fptr := newev
  end; { schedule }
```

The initial conditions of a simulation must be considered carefully if the simulation is to give useful results. The bus simulation starts with the buses distributed uniformly over the route and no one waiting at a bus stop. The purpose of the simulation is to discover whether the uniform spacing between buses is maintained or not. The simulation confirms what commuters already know: buses tend to bunch together. This is intuitively reasonable. As a bus gets closer to the bus in front of it, the queues at the bus stops get shorter and the second bus moves faster. Conversely, a bus that is a long way behind the bus in front will move slowly because it will encounter long queues. In the version of the simulation described above, the bunching effect is so strong that the buses rapidly form a convoy and never split up. The program given below eliminates convoys by a simple mechanism that is prohibited by many bus companies.

```
{ Bus service simulation }
program buses (input, output);
  const
    stopmax = 100;      { Maximum number of stops }
    busmax = 100;       { Maximum number of buses }
    queuemax = 100;     { Maximum length of queue }
  type
    stopnumber = 0..stopmax;
    busnumber = 0..busmax;
    queuelength = 0..queuemax;
    eventkind = (person, arrival, boarder);
    link = ↑ event;
    event =
      record
        fptr, bptr : link;
        kind : eventkind;
        time : real;
        stopnum : stopnumber;
        busnum : busnumber
      end; { event }
  var
    queue : array [stopnumber] of queuelength;
    atstop : array [stopnumber] of boolean;
    evtime : array [eventkind] of real;
    gap, stop, stoptot : stopnumber;
    bus, bustot : busnumber;
    maxtime : real;
    currentevent, base : link;
    randomseed : integer;
    evindex : eventkind;
```

```
{ Return a random variable with a
  negative exponential distribution. }
function random (var seed : integer) : real;
  begin
    random := − ln ((seed + 1) / 65536);
    seed := (25173 * seed + 13849) mod 65536
  end; { random }

{ Schedule the event predicted by the current event. }
procedure schedule (evkind : eventkind;
                    newtime : real;
                    stop : stopnumber;
                    bus : busnumber);
  var
    ev, newev : link;
    delay : real;
  begin
    if evkind = person
      then delay := evtime [evkind] * random (randomseed)
      else delay := evtime [evkind];
    new (newev);
    with newev↑ do
      begin
        kind := evkind;
        time := newtime + delay;
        stopnum := stop;
        busnum := bus
      end; { with }
    ev := base;
    repeat
      ev := ev↑.bptr
    until newev↑.time ≥ ev↑.time;
    newev↑.fptr := ev↑.fptr;
    newev↑.bptr := ev;
    ev↑.fptr↑.bptr := newev;
    ev↑.fptr := newev
  end; { schedule }
```

```
begin { buses }
  { Read simulation parameters. }
  read (stoptot, bustot);
  for evindex := person to boarder do
    read (evtime [evindex]);
  read (maxtime, randomseed);
  { Create an empty event ring. }
  new (base);
  with base↑ do
    begin
      fptr := base;
      bptr := base;
      time := 0
    end; { with }
  { Distribute buses evenly along the route. }
  if stoptot < bustot
    then gap := 1
    else gap := stoptot div bustot;
  stop := 1;
  for bus := 1 to bustot do
    begin
      schedule (arrival, 0, stop, bus);
      if stop + gap ≤ stoptot
        then stop := stop + gap
        else stop := 1
    end; { for }
  { Create a queue at each bus stop. }
  for stop := 1 to stoptot do
    begin
      queue [stop] := 0;
      schedule (person, 0, stop, 0);
      atstop [stop] := false
    end; { for }
  { Run the simulation until time limit. }
  repeat
    currentevent :=base↑.fptr;
    with currentevent↑ do
      case kind of
        person :
```

```
              begin
                queue [stopnum] := queue [stopnum] + 1;
                schedule (person, time, stopnum, 0)
              end; { person }
            arrival :
              if atstop [stopnum] or (queue [stopnum] = 0)
                then schedule (arrival, time,
                                (stopnum mod stoptot) + 1, busnum)
                else
                  begin
                    atstop [stopnum] := true;
                    schedule (boarder, time, stopnum, busnum);
                    write (time : 8 : 3);
                    write (' ' : 3 * stopnum);
                    writeln (busnum : 1)
                  end; { arrival and else }
            boarder :
              begin
                queue [stopnum] := queue [stopnum] - 1;
                if queue [stopnum] > 0
                  then schedule (boarder, time, stopnum, busnum)
                  else
                    begin
                      atstop [stopnum] := false;
                      schedule (arrival, time,
                                (stopnum mod stoptot) + 1, busnum)
                    end { else }
              end { boarder }
          end; { with and case }
        base↑.fptr := currentevent↑.fptr;
        currentevent↑.fptr↑.bptr := base
      until base↑.fptr↑.time ≥ maxtime
  end. { buses }
```

The event ring is a useful data structure because it permits us to simulate
concurrent events using a single processor. Program *buses* is a single sequential process but it accurately models the behavior of an arbitrary number of
buses and queues. We can generalize the requirements of a simulation of concurrent processes.

- For each process being simulated, there must be a record that represents the current status of that process.
- The processor must serve each process in turn. When a process has been served, either its updated process record is returned to the event ring or, as in Program *buses*, a new process record is created.
- There must be a means of scheduling processes. In Program *buses*, the scheduling is controlled by event times.

8.4   TREES

Pointers can be used in representations of structures more general than lists and rings. Suppose we have a structure consisting of records linked by pointers. This is a representation of a *directed graph*. The *vertices*, or *nodes*, of the graph are represented by records, and the *edges* of the graph are represented by pointers. A *tree* is a particular kind of graph. It has two important properties: the substructures linked to any node are disjoint, and there is a node, called the *root*, from which every node in the tree can be reached by traversing a finite number of edges. Figure 8.12 is a diagram representing a tree of which *A* is the

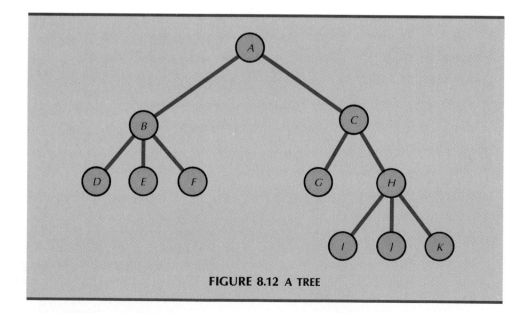

FIGURE 8.12 A TREE

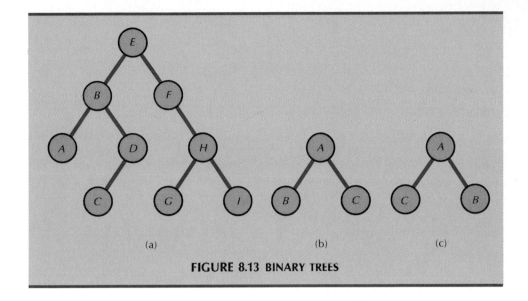

FIGURE 8.13 BINARY TREES

root. The nodes D, E, F, G, I, J, and K are *terminal nodes*, or *leaves*, of the tree. The nodes B, C, and H are *internal nodes* of the tree.

You may feel that Fig. 8.12 is upside down because the root, A, is at the top. A computer science convention is that trees are drawn upside down. We are accustomed to starting a drawing at the top of the page and drawing downwards, and it is easier to draw the root of the tree before we draw its leaves.

Like a list, a tree is a recursive structure. We can define a tree recursively.

A tree is empty, or it consists of a node
containing pointers to disjoint trees.

This definition is similar to the recursive definition of a list. Whereas lists may be manipulated easily by either recursive or iterative algorithms, we will see that trees are manipulated most easily by recursive algorithms.

BINARY TREES

In a binary tree, each node has at most two offspring. If both offspring are present, they are called the *left* and *right* offspring. In a binary tree, the offspring are not interchangeable. Figure 8.13 shows three different binary trees: Figs. 8.13(b) and 8.13(c) do not represent the same tree. We use a Pascal record to represent a node of a binary tree.

```
type
  link = ↑node;
  node =
    record
      left, right : link;
      data : datatype
    end;
```

We can define binary tree traversal recursively: at each node there are three things to do. We use the term "visit" to denote an operation to be applied to each node of the tree.

- Visit the node.
- Traverse the left subtree.
- Traverse the right subtree.

We can arrange these three steps in six different ways which correspond to six different ways of traversing the tree. These six ways can be reduced to three if we always traverse the left subtree before the right subtree. These three traversals have names. *Preorder* traversal visits the first node and then the subtrees. *Inorder* traversal visits first the left subtree, then the node, and finally the right subtree. *Postorder* traversal visits the subtrees and then the node. Here is a recursive procedure that traverses a binary tree.

```
procedure traverse (tree : link);
  begin
    if tree ≠ nil
      then
        begin
          visit (tree);
          traverse (tree↑.left);
          traverse (tree↑.right)
        end
  end;
```

This version of *traverse* performs a preorder traversal. The other orderings are obtained by permuting the three components of the compound statement. Traversals of the tree of Fig. 8.13(a) visit the nodes in the sequences

```
Preorder:   E  B  A  D  C  F  H  G  I
Inorder:    A  B  C  D  E  F  G  H  I
Postorder:  A  C  D  B  G  I  H  F  E
```

The inorder traversal produces an ordered sequence. This is not a coincidence: Fig. 8.13(a) was drawn so that this would occur. The tree shown in Fig. 8.13(a) is called a *binary search tree*. The binary search tree is a very useful structure, as we shall see from the procedures that follow.

Procedure *insert* adds a node to a binary search tree, preserving the ordering. The key to writing procedures of this kind is to consider one node at a time and to assume that on entry to the procedure, the parameter *tree* may point to any node in the tree or be **nil**. Insertion then consists of a case analysis: if *tree* is **nil**, we have found the appropriate place for the new node; otherwise we compare the data we want to insert with the data to which *tree* points.

```
procedure insert (var tree : link;
                      newdata : datatype);
begin
  if tree = nil
    then
      begin
        { Create a new entry. }
        new (tree);
        with tree↑ do
          begin
            left := nil;
            right := nil;
            data := newdata
          end { with }
      end
    else
      with tree↑ do
        if newdata < data
          { Search left subtree. }
          then insert (left, newdata)
        else if newdata > data
          { Search right subtree. }
          then insert (right, newdata)
        else { duplicate entry }
end;
```

The following function returns a pointer to a node in the tree that contains the given data or returns **nil** if there is no such node. It is similar to *insert* but returns **nil** if the tree does not contain a matching node.

```
function find (tree : link;
                   key : datatype) : link;
    begin
      if tree = nil
        then find := nil
        else
          with tree↑ do
            if key < data
              then find := find (left, key)
            else if key > data
              then find := find (right, key)
            else find := tree
end;
```

Although the use of recursion in *find* is natural, as it is in the other algorithms, it is unnecessary in this case. We can write *find* as a simple loop. On exit from the loop, the pointer *tree* either points to the matching node or is **nil**.

```
function find (tree : link;
                   key : datatype) : link;
    var
      finished : boolean;
    begin
      finished := false;
      repeat
        if tree = nil
          then finished := true
          else
            with tree↑ do
              if key < data
                then tree := left
              else if key > data
                then tree := right
              else finished := true
      until finished;
      find := tree
    end;
```

The entries in a binary search tree can be listed in sequence by inorder traversal. The only operation that is not easy to perform on a binary tree is the deletion of a node that is not a leaf. We must be careful to ensure that the new entries do not arrive in ascending or descending order because if they do, the tree will degenerate into a linear list. In practice, entries usually arrive in a random order, and a reasonably efficient search tree will be constructed.

The binary search tree is a more efficient structure than an array for storing and retrieving data. In a random binary search tree with N nodes, the time required to insert or delete a node is proportional to $\log(N)$, whereas the corresponding time for an array, using linear search, is proportional to N.

8.5 APPLICATION: WORD CONCORDANCE

Program *concordance*, which appeared in Chapter 6, reads a text and prints a list of the words in the text together with the number of occurrences of each. The following program does the same thing but stores the words in a binary search tree rather than in an array. The new program has two advantages over the earlier version. It will be faster, because a tree search is more efficient than a linear search, and it prints the words in alphabetical order without having to sort them. On the other hand, this version of the program will require more memory for a given table size because each entry now contains two pointers as well as the word and its counter.

```
{ Read a text and report the frequency
  with which each word in it is used. }
program concordance (input, output);
  const
    maxwordlen = 20;
  type
    charindex = 1..maxwordlen;
    counttype = 1..maxint;
    wordtype = packed array [charindex] of char;
    pointer = ↑ entrytype;
    entrytype =
      record
        left, right : pointer;
        word : wordtype;
        count : counttype
      end; { entrytype }
  var
    wordtree : pointer;
    nextword : wordtype;
    letters : set of char;
{ Read one word of the text. Words consist of spaces
  and are separated by characters other than letters. }
procedure readword (var packedword : wordtype);
  { See page 202. }
```

```
{ Print one word of the text. }
  procedure printword (packedword : wordtype);
{ See page 203. }

{ Make an entry in the binary search tree. If the word has
  not been read before, a new entry is made for it.
  Otherwise, the counter for the word is incremented. }
  procedure makentry (var tree : pointer; entry : wordtype);
    begin
      if tree = nil
        then
          begin
            new (tree);
            with tree↑ do
              begin
                word := entry;
                count := 1;
                left := nil;
                right := nil
              end; { with }
          end { then }
        else
          with tree↑ do
            if entry < word
              then makentry (left, entry)
            else if entry > word
              then makentry (right, entry)
            else count := count + 1
    end; { makentry }

{ Print the binary tree in alphabetical
  order with word counts. }
  procedure printtree (tree : pointer);
    begin
      if tree ≠ nil
        then
          with tree↑ do
            begin
              printtree (left);
              printword (word);
              writeln (count);
              printtree (right)
            end { then and with }
    end; { printtree }
```

```
begin { concordance }
  letters := ['a'..'z'];
  wordtree := nil;
  while not eof do
    begin
      readword (nextword);
      if not eof
        then makentry (wordtree, nextword)
    end; { while }
  printtree (wordtree)
end. { concordance }
```

GENERAL TREES

We now consider the problem of representing a tree in which a node may contain pointers to more than two subtrees. If the largest number of subtrees is limited to some reasonably small value, it may be practical to use an array of pointers to point to subtrees. In this case, we could declare the data structure in this way:

```
const
  maxnodes = 6;
type
  link = ↑ node;
  node =
    record
      subnode : array [1..maxnodes] of link;
    end;
```

Having to preset the value of *maxnodes* is a serious limitation. If we make *maxnodes* too small, we will sooner or later encounter a tree we cannot represent. If we make *maxnodes* too large, the unused pointers will waste memory space. An alternative solution is to attach to each node of the tree a linked list of its offspring. Figure 8.14 shows the tree of Fig. 8.12 transformed in this way. This representation requires that each node contain two pointers, one to the eldest descendant of the node and one to the next sibling. Either of these pointers may be **nil**. In Fig. 8.14, parent–offspring links are drawn vertically and sibling links are drawn horizontally. We have in fact transformed the tree into a binary tree.

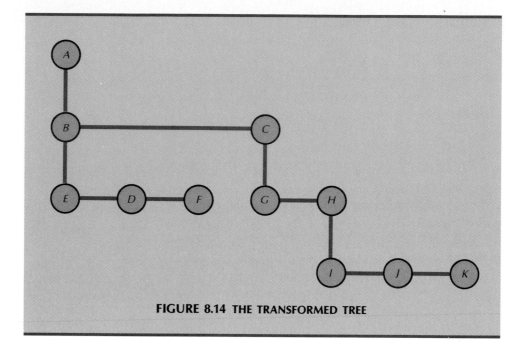

FIGURE 8.14 THE TRANSFORMED TREE

8.6 EXERCISES

8.1 Figure 8.7(a) illustrates the insertion of a new component, *dick*, into a list. What would happen if the record containing *dick* was already in the list?

8.2 Draw diagrams to illustrate the operations of insertion and deletion on a doubly linked ring. What is the effect of *delete* on an empty ring?

8.3 Show that in any binary tree, more than half of the pointer values are **nil**. (This is rather wasteful: programs that manipulate binary trees often use vacant fields to store pointers to nodes at higher levels.)

8.4 a) Draw diagrams of some of the possible forms a binary tree can assume. In particular, show the best and worst possible forms of a tree used for symbol storage and retrieval.

 b) Devise an algorithm for deleting a nonterminal node from a binary search tree without destroying the ordering.

8.5 The *level* of the root of a tree is defined to be 0. The level of any other node is defined to be one greater than the level of its parent. The *depth* of the tree is the level of the node whose level is the largest. The *internal path length* of a tree is the total number of edges within the tree. Write procedures that

a) find the level of a specified node in the tree;
b) find the depth of a given tree;
c) find the internal path length of a given tree.

8.6 There are several ways of representing binary trees on paper, other than the topological form of Fig. 8.13. For example, Fig. 8.13(a) can be described in either of two ways.

a) E(B(A,D(C,)),F(,H(G,I)))
b) E
     B
        A
        D
            C
    F
      H
        G
        I

Write a program that reads a binary tree in format (a) and then prints the same tree in format (b).

8.7 Algebraic expressions may be represented by binary trees. Each node of the tree contains an operator ($+$, $-$, $*$, or $/$) and pointers to two subexpressions. Figure 8.15 is the tree corresponding to the expression

$$(a * b) + c - a * (b + c).$$

Using Program *calculator* as a starting point, write a program that reads an expression and constructs the corresponding tree.

8.8 Program *buses* is run with 15 bus stops and 5 buses. Draw a graph showing the size of the event ring as a function of time.

8.9 Describe the mechanism used by Program *buses* to prevent buses from forming convoys. Explain its effect on a real bus service.

8.10 Write a procedure that takes a "snapshot" of the current situation in Program *buses*. The procedure should be activated once during initialization and should subsequently reactivate itself at regular intervals. Use this to plot the positions of buses as a function of time.

8.11 Modify Program *buses* to allow for disembarking passengers under one of the following conditions.

a) Passengers disembark at the same rate at which they join queues.
b) The journey length for any passenger is a random variable with a negative exponential distribution.

8.12 Design a data structure that models family relationships. Each person is represented by a record that contains his or her name and pointers to parents, spouse, and children. Write procedures that insert a new person into the structure and establish the relationships of the new person to existing members of

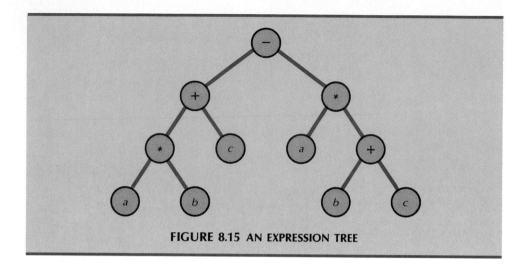

FIGURE 8.15 AN EXPRESSION TREE

the family; for example,

offspring (parent, child)

marry (wife, husband)

Write a *boolean* function, *cousin*, that is *true* if its two arguments are pointers to cousins.

8.13 Write an interactive coordinate geometry program. The user of the program should be able to write simple commands to create figures of various shapes to which names may be given. For example, you might write

A = point 0 0
B = point 2 3
L = line A B

8.14 Jobs arrive in the input queue of a computer system at a mean rate of λ and are serviced at a mean rate of μ. Write a simulation program to investigate the average queue length as a function of λ and μ. Modify the system so that there are two queues, one for high-priority jobs that arrive at a rate of λ_H and another for low-priority jobs that arrive at a rate of λ_L. No jobs are interrupted during processing but a low-priority job is started only if there are no jobs in the high-priority queue. Investigate the queue lengths for various values of λ_H and λ_L.

Note for Exercises 8.11 and 8.14. If events occur at a mean rate R, the time between any two consecutive events is a random variable

$$t = \frac{-\ln(x)}{R}$$

where x is uniformly distributed between 0 and 1.

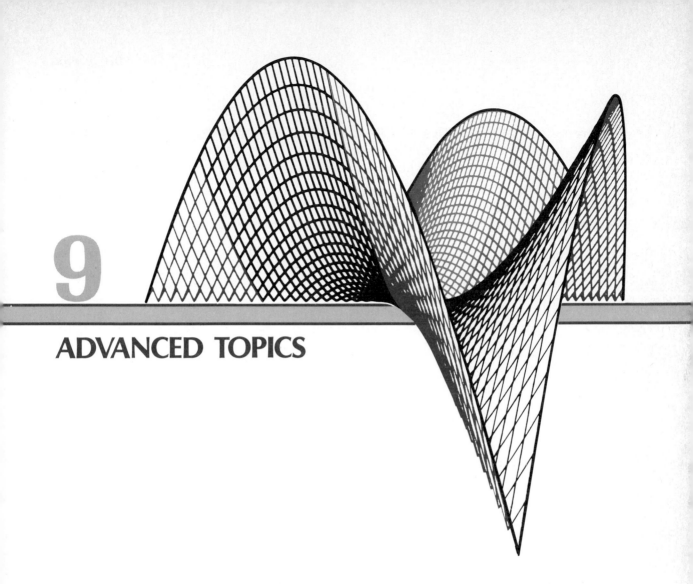

9

ADVANCED TOPICS

This is the last chapter in which we describe features of Pascal. Many programs, even complicated ones, can be written without the constructions presented in this chapter. You should be accustomed to using the simple features of Pascal before you attempt to use the new constructions.

9.1   THE goto STATEMENT

The **goto** statement is the only Pascal statement we have not used previously in this book. This is no accident: programs can be written without it. Some implementations of Pascal do not even recognize the **goto** statement.

The **goto** statement permits direct transfer of control from one part of the program to another, with certain restrictions we will describe. One common use of **goto** is to exit from a loop. The following loop is taken from Program *tableprocessor* which appears in Chapter 7.

```
oldtran := false;
index := 0;
while (index < size) and not oldtran do
  begin
    index := index + 1;
    if age (procdate) - age (table [index].invoicedate) > maxage
      then oldtran := true
  end;
if oldtran
  then
    for index := 1 to size do
      printrec (table [index])
```
(9.1)

Examination of the **while** loop reveals that it is actually a **for** loop in disguise. We could write

```
oldtran := false;
for index := 1 to size do
  if age (procdate) - age (table [index].invoicedate) > maxage
    then oldtran := true;
if oldtran
  then
    for index := 1 to size do
      printrec (table [index])
```
(9.2)

If there is no entry in the table that satisfies the condition, these program fragments are equivalent. If there are entries that satisfy the condition, fragment (9.1) will terminate as soon as one of them has been found but fragment (9.2) will examine the entire table. The **while** construction was used solely so that we could terminate the loop in the middle of the table. Moreover, we had to introduce a spurious variable, *oldtran*, in order to trip the **while** statement. We can achieve the same effect in a different way.

```
for index := 1 to size do
  if age (procdate) - age (table [index].invoicedate) > maxage
    then goto 1;
goto 2;
1 :
  for index := 1 to size do
    printrec (table [index]);
2 :
```
(9.3)

If there is an invoice older than *maxage*, the statement **goto** 1 transfers control to the statement following the label 1. If there is no such invoice, the first **for** loop terminates normally. The statement **goto** 2 bypasses the second **for** loop and transfers control to the statement following the label 2.

We now have three ways of checking for old invoices: the **while** loop (9.1), the **for** loop (9.2), and the **for** loop with exit (9.3). It is evident from this example that Pascal does not provide a simple solution to this problem. Of the three solutions presented here, the first, using a **while** loop and a state variable, is perhaps the best. The **for** loop (9.2) is misleading to the reader because it suggests that the entire table must be scanned. The **for** loop with exit (9.3) is hard to understand because of the discontinuous flow of control. Although this example illustrates the effect of the **goto** statement, it does not justify use of the **goto** statement.

The **goto** statement may also be used to solve the problem we encountered in Chapter 4: how does a function, which may be called from anywhere in the program, signal an error in a useful way? One solution is to assign a label, such as 99, at the end of the main program, to which any function detecting an error can jump. We could then write the function *squareroot* of Chapter 4 in this way:

```
function squareroot (value : real) : real;
   const
     epsilon = 1E-6;
   var
     root : real;
   begin
     if value < 0
       then
         begin
           writeln ('Squareroot argument = ', value);
           goto 99
         end
     else if value = 0
       then
         ....
```

At the end of the main program, we write

```
   ...
   99 : writeln ('Execution terminated.')
end.
```

The use of the **goto** statement in this example is somewhat more convincing than it was in the previous example because this problem is not easily solved without **goto**. An alternative solution is to define a special value that *square-root* will return if its argument is illegal. In this case, the special value could be, for example, -1.0. This approach complicates the code in which *square-root* is used because the value returned by *squareroot* must be checked at every call.

There are some important restrictions on the use of the **goto** statement. A **goto** statement can be used to jump within a level, or from an inner level to an outer level, but it cannot be used to jump from an outer level to an inner level. In particular, although you can jump out of a procedure, you cannot jump into one. Here are some correct uses of the **goto** statement.

```
label 2;
....
   procedure jumpabout;
      label 1;
      begin
         ....
         goto 1;
         ....
         goto 2;
         ....
         1 : S₁
      end;
   begin
      ....
      if p
         then goto 2;
      ....
      2 : S₂
   end.
```

Here are some incorrect uses of the **goto** statement.

```
goto 3;
....
if p
   then S₁
   else 3 : S₂
....
while p do
```

```
begin
   S₃;
   4 : S₄
end;
....
goto 4;
....
   procedure donut;
      label 5;
      begin
         ....
         5 : S₅;
         ....
      end;
   begin
      ....
      goto 5;
      ....
```

LABEL DECLARATION SYNTAX

The label used in a **goto** statement must be declared. The *label declaration section* is placed before the other declaration sections in a block. Figure 9.1 shows the syntax of the label declaration section. A label may precede any statement. The Standard limits the length of a label to four digits.

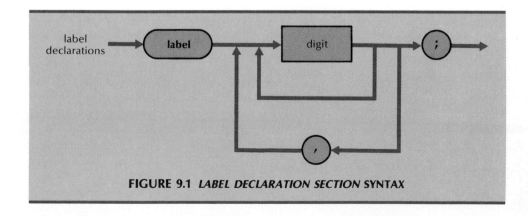

FIGURE 9.1 *LABEL DECLARATION SECTION* SYNTAX

The semicolon after *writeln* in the following example is required to separate the statement, *writeln*, from the label, 99.

```
begin
    . . . .
    goto 99;
    . . . .
    writeln;
    99 :
end
```

9.2   PROCEDURES AND FUNCTIONS AS PARAMETERS

We have seen that a procedure or a function may invoke another. Indeed, it would be hard to write nontrivial programs if this were not so. We sometimes encounter circumstances in which we wish to write a procedure or a function that will invoke another procedure or function whose effect is not determined until the program is executed. For example, we might want a function, *integrate*, such that when we called

$$integrate \ (f, \ a, \ b)$$

we obtained the value of

$$\int_a^b f(x) \, dx.$$

This would enable us to write statements such as

$$integrate \ (sin, \ 0, \ t)$$

It is possible to write such functions in Pascal. We will illustrate the technique by designing a function, *solve*, that estimates a solution of the equation

$$f(x) = 0$$

in which f is a function passed as a parameter to *solve*.

Any estimation process requires at least one initial approximation to the solution because the function f may have several zeros. The method we use to find the zero is the *secant method*, which requires two approximations to start it off. Figure 9.2 illustrates the concept. The approximations to the true root ξ are x_1 and x_2. The points

$$A_1 = (x_1, f(x_1))$$

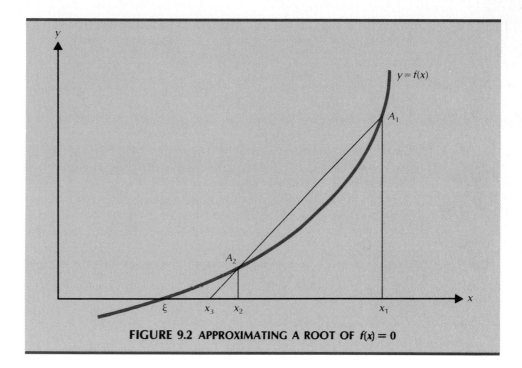

FIGURE 9.2 APPROXIMATING A ROOT OF $f(x) = 0$

and

$$A_2 = (x_2, f(x_2))$$

are on the curve

$$y = f(x).$$

We calculate a third approximation, x_3, that is the x-*coordinate* of the point of intersection of the line $A_1 A_2$ and the abscissa. If (x, y) is a point on $A_1 A_2$, we have

$$\frac{y - y_2}{x - x_2} = \frac{y_2 - y_1}{x_2 - x_1}$$

in which we have written y_1 for $f(x_1)$ and y_2 for $f(x_2)$. We know that the point $(x_3, 0)$ is on this line and therefore that

$$x_3 = x_2 - y_2 \cdot \frac{x_2 - x_1}{y_2 - y_1}.$$

From this we can derive the recurrence relation

$$x_{n+2} = x_{n+1} - f(x_{n+1}) \cdot \frac{x_{n+1} - x_n}{f(x_{n+1}) - f(x_n)}.$$

This provides a new approximation, x_{n+2}, in terms of two preceding approximations, x_n and x_{n+1}, provided that

$$f(x_{n+1}) \neq f(x_n).$$

It can be shown that $x_n \rightarrow \xi$ as $n \rightarrow \infty$ provided that the initial approximations are good enough, $f'(\xi) \neq 0$, and $f''(x)$ is continuous within the interval we are considering. The most important of these conditions is usually $f'(\xi) \neq 0$. This condition implies that we cannot use this technique to find repeated roots. We could not, for example, find the zero of the function illustrated in Fig. 9.3. A mathematical demonstration of convergence does not necessarily mean that a program based on the method will always work; rounding errors in the computation may invalidate the mathematical results. The secant method works quite well with reasonable functions.

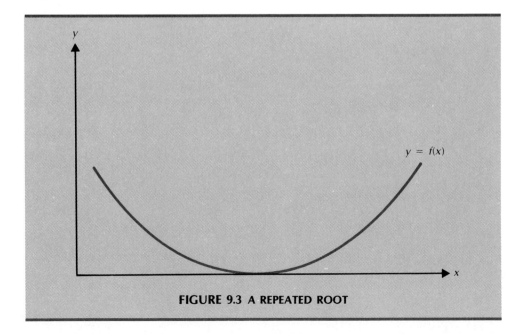

FIGURE 9.3 A REPEATED ROOT

We require a termination condition for the calculation. An iteration changes the current approximation by an amount

$$\delta = -f(x_{n+1}) \cdot \frac{x_{n+1} - x_n}{f(x_{n+1}) - f(x_n)}.$$

We terminate the calculation when

$$|\delta / x_{n+1}| < \epsilon.$$

The function *solve* requires four parameters: two approximations to the root, a value for ϵ, and the function $f(x)$. The heading of *solve* is written

```
function solve (x1, x2, epsilon : real;
                function f (x : real) : real) : real;
```

The formal parameter f has the same form as the heading of the functions that are to be passed as actual parameters when the program is executed. The name, type, and formal parameters are all specified. The name x is arbitrary; it refers to nothing else in the program and is simply a "place holder."

Program *equations* uses the function *solve* to find the smallest positive roots of the equations

$$\cos(x) \cosh(x) - 1 = 0 \qquad\qquad (9.4)$$
$$\cos(x) \cosh(x) + 1 = 0 \qquad\qquad (9.5)$$

which arise in elementary vibration theory. Figure 9.4 shows graphs of the functions

$$y = \cos(x) \cosh(x)$$
$$y = -1$$
$$y = 1$$

from which we can see that the first nonzero root ξ_1 of (9.4) satisfies

$$\pi < \xi_1 < 2\pi$$

and the first root ξ_2 of (9.5) satisfies

$$0 < \xi_2 < \pi.$$

In Program *equations* we define the functions

$$ccp = \cos(x)\ \cosh(x) + 1$$
$$ccm = \cos(x)\ \cosh(x) - 1$$

and call *solve* twice.

```pascal
{ Demonstrate functional parameters. }
program equations (input, output);
  const
    tolerance = 1E-6;
  var
    approx1, approx2 : real;

  { Find a root of f(x) = 0, given two approximations,
    x1 and x2, and a tolerance, epsilon. }
  function solve (x1, x2, epsilon : real;
                      function f (x : real) : real) : real;
    var
      x3, y1, y2, delta : real;
      solved : boolean;
    begin
      solved := false;
      y1 := f (x1);
      y2 := f (x2);
      repeat
        delta := - y2 * (x2 - x1) / (y2 - y1);
        x3 := x2 + delta;
        if abs (delta / x2) < epsilon
          then solved := true
          else
            begin
              x1 := x2;
              x2 := x3;
              y1 := y2;
              y2 := f (x2)
            end { else }
      until solved;
      solve := x3
    end; { solve }

  { A function to be passed to solve }
  function ccp (x : real) : real;
    var
      expx : real;
    begin
      expx := exp (x);
      ccp := cos (x) * (expx + 1 / expx) / 2 + 1
    end; { ccp }
```

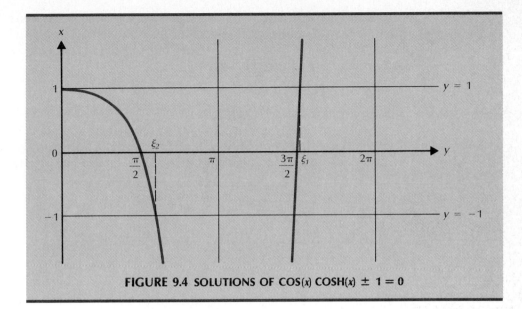

FIGURE 9.4 SOLUTIONS OF COS(x) COSH(x) ± 1 = 0

```
{ Another function to be passed to solve }
function ccm (x : real) : real;
  var
    expx : real;
  begin
    expx := exp (x);
    ccm := cos (x) * (expx + 1 / expx) / 2 - 1
  end; { ccm }
begin { equations }
  read (approx1, approx2);
  writeln (solve (approx1, approx2, tolerance, ccp));
  writeln (solve (approx1, approx2, tolerance, ccm))
end. { equations }
```

INPUT		OUTPUT
5	7	4.694092
		4.730040

Not all procedures and functions can be passed as parameters. The parameters of the procedure or the function that is passed as a parameter must be value parameters. These are headings of procedures that could *not* be passed as parameters to other procedures:

```
procedure p1 (var x, y : real);
procedure p2 (function f : real);
```

Procedures and functions that are passed as parameters may refer to non-local identifiers in the usual way. Care is necessary, however, when we use the same identifier in different scopes. Program *scopes* illustrates this.

```
program scopes (output);
  const
    num = 1;
  procedure doit (procedure p);
    const
      num = 2;
    begin
    p
    end; { doit }
  procedure print;
    begin
      writeln (num)
    end; { print }
  begin { scopes }
    doit (print)
  end. { scopes }
```

When we execute this program, it will print either 1 or 2, but it is not obvious which of these values it will print. In fact, the program prints 1 because the procedure *print* is declared in an environment in which *num* = 1. Values of non-local identifiers in a procedure are determined by the environment in which the procedure is declared, not by the environment within which it is executed. Although for brevity we have illustrated this with a constant, *num*, in Program *scopes*, the same applies for identifiers that denote types or variables.

9.3   MEMORY ALLOCATION

In Chapter 8 we saw how to use the standard procedure *new* to create a new record during execution and to set the value of a pointer pointing to it. In reality, of course, the procedure *new* does not "create" a record; it simply finds an unused area of memory of the appropriate size and sets the pointer accordingly. The area of memory reserved for dynamic variables is often called the *heap,* in contrast to the area used for static variables (global variables and local variables of procedures) which is called the *stack.*

If the program continues to call *new,* there will come a time when all the memory allocated to the heap has been consumed and the program will fail. In many cases, however, the program will be able to release dynamic variables it no longer requires. Program *buses* of Chapter 8, for example, has no further use for an event record after the event has been processed. Because the procedure *new* has no way of knowing which areas of memory are still in use, the released records cannot be reused unless they are marked explicitly by the program. There is a standard procedure, *dispose,* that releases the record to which its argument is a pointer. *New* and *dispose* are complementary.

```
new (p);
  { use record p↑ }
dispose (p)
```

The precise effect of *dispose* is not specified in the Pascal Standard, so the details of its implementation are left to the compiler writer. The simplest version of *dispose* will do nothing at all. More sophisticated versions will enable some or all of the memory to be reused. You can obtain some idea of how effective *dispose* is on your implementation by running Program *testdispose.* If this program runs to completion, either your computer has more than one million words of memory or *dispose* is returning unused records to the heap.

```
program testdispose (output);
  const
    size = 1000;
    numberofnodes = 1000;
  type
    link = ↑ node;
    node = array [1..size] of integer;
  var
    p : link;
    n : 1..numberofnodes;
  begin
    for n := 1 to numberofnodes do
      begin
        new (p);
        dispose (p)
      end { for }
  end. { testdispose }
```

It is bad programming practice to write a program to test a property of a language. You should refer instead to the specification of the language. In this case, we are testing an *implementation* property not specified in the Pascal Standard. Of course, if you have a reference manual for the implementation you are using, you should use it rather than Program *testdispose*.

If the procedure *dispose* does not enable memory to be reused, you will have to keep track of available memory yourself. The simplest way to do this is to maintain a linked list of unused records, called the *free list*. Whenever a new record is required, it is taken from the free list unless the free list is empty, in which case the procedure *new* is used. When the program finishes using a record, the record is returned to the free list. All records on the free list are variants with the tag *free*. A pointer variable is used as the base of the free list. In these declarations we show only the *free* variant:

```
type
  kind = (free, ...);
  link = ↑ cell;
  cell =
    record
      case tag : kind of
        free : (next : link);
        ....
    end;
var
  freelist : link;
....
```

We define two procedures, *create* and *release*, each with a single parameter of type *link*.

```
procedure create (var p : link);
  begin
    if freelist = nil
      then new (p)
      else
        begin
          p := freelist;
          freelist := freelist↑.next
        end
  end; { create }
```

```
              procedure release (p : link);
                begin
                  p↑.tag := free;
                  p↑.next := freelist;
                  freelist := p
                end; { release }
```

The initialization for the main program contains the statement

```
    freelist := nil
```

so that the free list is initially empty. At first, new records are obtained by the procedure *new* because *freelist* is **nil**. As soon as some records have been released by the program using the procedure *release*, they will appear on the free list and will be reused by the procedure *create*. Note that because Pascal binds a pointer to a particular type, the free list can contain records of only one type.

In general, different variants of a record will require different amounts of memory. When the procedure *new* is used to allocate space for a new record, it will allocate enough memory for the largest variant. In order to use memory efficiently, you should therefore try to make the variants approximately equal in size, although this may not be easy to do if you do not know how data structures are represented by your computer. In particular, try to avoid the situation in which one variant is much larger than all the rest.

Pascal does provide a mechanism to help you use memory efficiently. The procedure *new* may be called with more than one parameter, as in

```
    new (p, t)
```

where *t* is a constant tag field for the variant required. Values may be assigned to the variable fields of this record in the usual way, but the tag value must be set to *t* and must not be altered subsequently. A record created in this way must be disposed by calling

```
    dispose (p, t)
```

Program *circles*, which appeared in Section 6.8, used variant records. Here are the declarations for the type *figure* that we used in Program *circles*.

```
          type
            shape = (empty, point, line, circle);
            coordinate =
              record
                xcoor, ycoor : real
              end;
```

```
            figure =
              record
                case tag : shape of
                  empty : ( );
                  point : (position : coordinate);
                  line : (xcoeff, ycoeff, con : real);
                  circle : (center : coordinate; radius : real)
              end;
          var
            f, g : figure;
            coor : coordinate;
```

The call

```
    new (f)
```

will create a record large enough to hold any variant. This record may be disposed by calling

```
    dispose (f)
```

The call

```
    new (f, point)
```

will create a record large enough to hold a figure of the kind *point*. This record may not be large enough to hold a figure of the kind *line* or *circle*. It must be disposed by calling

```
    dispose (f, point)
```

We cannot change the kind of record created in this way and we cannot make assignments to entire variables. For example, we cannot write

```
    new (g);
    f↑ := g↑;
```

or

```
    f↑.tag := circle
```

We can, however, make assignments to the components of *f↑*, provided that these are consistent with the tag value with which *f↑* was created. For example, we can write

```
    f↑.position := coor
```

If the record type has nested variants, a single variant is specified uniquely by a tag value at each level. In this case the calls to *new* and *dispose* take the form

$$new \ (p, \ t1, \ t2, \ \dots \ , \ tn)$$

9.4   CONFORMANT ARRAY PARAMETERS

The actual and formal parameters of each procedure and function in a Pascal program must match in number and type. The compiler checks that a program conforms to this rule. Parameter type checking usually aids program development but there are situations in which the rules are too restrictive. A procedure that multiplies 10 by 10 matrices, for example, cannot be used to multiply 5 by 5 matrices. The Pascal Standard proposes the *conformant array schema* as a solution to this problem.

Suppose that a program contains the declarations

```
type
  shortstring = array [1..10] of char;
  longstring - array [1..50] of char;
var
  short : shortstring;
  long : longstring;
```

The following procedure prints a *shortstring*.

```
procedure print (s : shortstring);
  var
    i : 1..10;
  begin
    for i := 1 to 10 do
      write (s [i])
  end; { print }
```

We can write

```
print (short)
```

We cannot write

```
print (long)
```

because the types of the actual and formal parameters conflict. We can, however, rewrite this procedure using a conformant array parameter.

```
procedure print (s : array [first..last : integer] of char);
  var
    i : integer;
  begin
    for i := first to last do
      write (s [i])
  end; { print }
```

Using this version of *print,* we can write both

```
print (short)
```

and

```
print (long)
```

in the program. As we can see from this example, the names *first* and *last* behave like value formal parameters within the procedure body. There are no explicit actual parameters corresponding to *first* and *last,* but the compiler can provide the actual parameters by referring to the declaration of the array passed to the procedure.

We can also use conformant array parameters to describe multidimensional arrays. The following heading introduces a procedure that can process any rectangular matrix of real numbers.

```
procedure processmatrix
  (matrix : array [lo..hi : integer] of
              array [min..max : integer] of real);
```

We can abbreviate this definition in the following way.

```
procedure processmatrix
  (matrix : array [lo..hi : integer; min..max : integer] of real);
```

Unfortunately, most Pascal compilers do not support conformant array parameters. Instead, almost all compilers relax the strict type rules of Pascal for strings, and a few have ad hoc mechanisms for passing arrays of different sizes to a procedure.

CONFORMANT ARRAY PARAMETER SYNTAX

Figure 9.5 shows the syntax of a conformant array schema. A conformant array schema defines the type of a formal parameter. Figure 9.6 shows how a conformant array schema may be used in a formal parameter list.

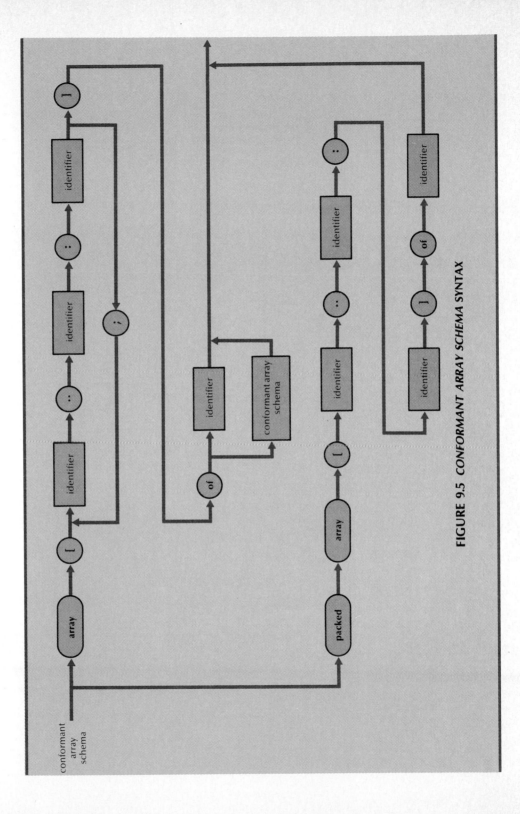

FIGURE 9.5 CONFORMANT ARRAY SCHEMA SYNTAX

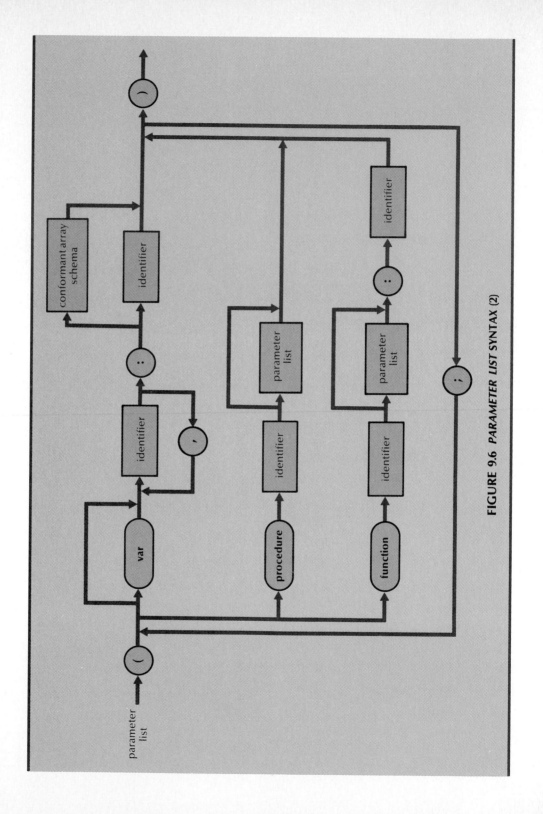

FIGURE 9.6 *PARAMETER LIST SYNTAX (2)*

9.5 EXERCISES

9.1 Write two equivalent versions of a program, one with **goto** statements and one without **goto** statements. Try to choose a problem that makes the **goto** version shorter, simpler, and faster than the version without the **goto** statements.

9.2 Write a function, *max*, such that

$$max \ (f, \ a, \ b)$$

finds the maximum value of $f(x)$ in the interval $a \leqslant x \leqslant b$ and returns the corresponding value of x.

9.3 Write a real function, *integrate*, such that

$$integrate \ (f, \ a, \ b)$$

returns an approximate value of

$$\int_a^b f(x) \ dx$$

9.4 Write a procedure, *chop*, which disposes every node of a binary tree. *Chop* has one parameter that is a pointer to the root node of the tree.

9.5 Is it possible to define a Pascal function, f, in such a way that the expression $f(f)$ can be compiled?

9.6 Using conformant array schemas, write functions that calculate

  a) the mean
  b) the standard deviation

of a vector that consists of an arbitrary number of *real* values.

9.7 Write a procedure that calculates

$$C = A \times B$$

where A, B, and C are matrices. Suppose that A, B, and C are respectively m by k, k' by n, and m' by n' matrices. The multiplication can be performed only if $k = k'$, $m = m'$, and $n = n'$.

9.8 Program *copylist*, shown below, reads a list of numbers terminated by zero. It constructs a linked list of these numbers, not including the zero, and prints this list.

  a) Suppose that the heading of function *makecell* is changed to

```
function makecell (n : integer;
                  function f : ptr) : ptr;
```

  Does this affect the behavior of the program?

  b) Suppose that the declaration of *p* in function *makecell* is made global. Does the program still work? Does it work if the change described in (a) is also made?

```pascal
{ Read a list of numbers and print it.
  The list is terminated by zero. }
program copylist (input, output);
  type
    ptr = ↑cell;
    cell = record
                data : integer;
                next : ptr
            end; { cell }
  procedure print (p : ptr);
    begin
      if p ≠ nil
        then
          begin
            write (p↑.data);
            print (p↑.next)
    end; { print }
  function makelist : ptr;
    var
      n : integer;
    function makecell (n : integer; f : ptr) : ptr;
      var
        p : ptr;
      begin
        new (p);
        p↑.data := n;
        p↑.next := f;
        makecell := p
      end; { makecell }

    begin { makelist }
      read (n);
      if n = 0
        then makelist := nil
        else makelist := makecell (n, makelist)
    end; { makelist }
  begin { copylist }
    print (makelist);
    writeln
  end. { copylist }
```

10

PROGRAM DESIGN

In the first chapter of this book we defined a computer program as a sequence of instructions. Most of the content of Chapters 2 through 9 was a description of the various forms these instructions may assume and their effects. In this chapter, the last, we discuss various aspects of the programmer's task. Our starting point is the assumption that we have a problem to solve and that we intend to write a computer program that is, in some sense, a solution to that problem. We will also assume that the problem is amenable to solution by a computer: we require output results that are a well-defined function of input data. It is not difficult to write a perfect program that fits onto a page, but it is very difficult indeed to write a program of a hundred pages and to be certain that it is entirely correct. In this chapter we consider systematic techniques for the development of large programs.

The computer does not *solve* a programming problem; that is the programmer's job. Solving the problem consists of finding an algorithm that will provide the required mapping from input to output. Writing the program consists of expressing this algorithm in a fashion accceptable to the computer. Because the computer is a machine without imagination or common sense, the algorithm must be presented to it in a precise and unambiguous manner.

It is well known that some programs do not always yield correct results. There are a number of possible reasons for this: the problem may be stated incorrectly; the algorithm chosen may not be a true solution of the problem; the program may not be an accurate implementation of the algorithm; or the program may be executed with the wrong data. We are concerned here with only two of these sources of error: the choice of an incorrect algorithm and the inaccurate implementation of an algorithm. There are two ways of ensuring that the program we produce is free of either of these errors. We can employ a system of program development that leads inevitably to correct programs, or we can devise a means of demonstrating that a completed program contains no errors.

In many environments the computer is used as a sophisticated toy. A hit-or-miss approach to programming can be tolerated in such environments because the potential consequences of a programming error are not particularly serious. Computers are being used more and more in environments where the consequences of an error may be very serious. In these environments a haphazard programming methodology is irresponsible and dangerous. A programmer whose programs occasionally fail should be compared to an accountant whose financial statements occasionally do not balance or an architect whose buildings occasionally collapse.

10.1 PROGRAM DEVELOPMENT

Modern techniques for program development are essentially formal versions of traditional methods of programming. We begin our discussion of program development by reviewing these methods. Three phases are involved in the traditional method of program construction: design, implementation, and testing. The design phase, usually carried out by an "analyst," leads to a specification in a natural language such as English. The specification is given to a "programmer" who writes a program from it. Although traditional programming techniques are shrouded in mystery, a few programmers have revealed their secrets, so we know that the techniques consist of a combination of guesses, hunches, tricks, inspiration, and some programming principles. When the programmer claims that the program is complete, it is tested, first by the programmer and then sometimes by the analyst. *Testing* consists of running the program with input data intended to exercise it thoroughly. Later, tests may be carried out with "real data", that is, by running the program in the environment in which it will eventually be used. Discrepancies between the program and the specification may be found, in which case the program is modified and tested again. Sometimes the results delivered by the program cast doubt upon the specification and the whole process must be repeated: revise the specification, modify the program, test it again, and compare the results to the revised specification.

Under carefully controlled conditions, this technique can produce working programs. Sometimes it fails altogether and the project is abandoned. In many instances, perhaps the majority, it produces a program that works correctly most of the time but that occasionally fails or gives incorrect results. If we use a program frequently, we get to know its habits and learn to live with them. If we use the same program rarely, its errors may be very disconcerting.

Many people have expressed concern about the lack of rigor in traditional programming methods, and numerous ways of improving the situation have been suggested. Most of these suggestions involve the introduction of a formal programming system. Mathematicians have spent several centuries trying to remove uncertainties from their theories and deductions, and they are familiar with both the advantages and disadvantages of formal systems. For programmers there is an additional advantage to be gained from the construction of a formal programming system. Once we have devised a set of rules for creating correct computer programs, we can express these rules in the form of a computer program and let the computer write our programs for us. The computer will never be able to do all of the work, but even if it does only some of the simple chores, we will have more time and energy to devote to more interesting and creative phases of program design.

The most important development to date in automatic program construction has been the introduction of high-level programming languages and compilers for them. As we have seen, a program is an expression of a solution in a language acceptable to the computer, and programming is the process of translating the solution into such a language. A compiler can perform a significant proportion of the translation for us. High-level languages, and compilers for them, extend the range of problems we can solve with the aid of a computer.

Another important development is the widespread use of standard functions and program libraries. It is better that one skilled programmer, or a skilled team, develop procedures to perform standard tasks, and that these procedures should be used by everybody, than that each programmer develop a personal solution. Probably most Pascal programmers who use standard functions, such as *ln* and *sqrt,* do not know how logarithms and square roots are calculated, and this is as it should be. Apart from the standard functions of a lan-

guage, there are libraries of procedures and functions. A programmer with no
more training in mathematics than high school algebra should have no difficulty
computing matrix inverses or fast Fourier transforms. These well-established
tools are not, however, the subject of this chapter. Here we describe a popular
contemporary method of program development and some elementary ideas of
program verification.

From the viewpoint of the program designer, the most important fact about
a computer program is that it is hierarchical. As we saw in Chapter 4, hierarchical structure is obtained by the use of procedures. A program will require
high-level procedures to carry out large, difficult tasks, such as "solve a set of
simultaneous equations." These high-level procedures will call procedures at
lower levels in the hierarchy, down to primitive procedures at the lowest level,
such as "read a character." The high-level procedures will express the general
and abstract features of the solution and the low-level procedures will contain
the details of the implementation. The first important decision we must take
when we design a new program is whether to start at the most abstract level
and work down, or to start at the most concrete, detailed level and work up. Following the advice of a number of distinguished authors, we advocate the former
method, top-down program development. In this kind of development, writing
the program consists of proposing a very abstract solution and then successive-
ly *refining* it until it is entirely expressed in the chosen programming language.

Procedures themselves do not refine the solution; they merely enable us to
express the refinements we have made in a convenient notation. There are
three principal refinement techniques. Appropriate mnemonics for them are:
"divide the problem," "make finite progress," and "analyze cases."

We apply the first of these by *dividing* the problem into disjoint subproblems
and then solving each subproblem in turn. We use the word "disjoint" to mean
that the parts of subproblems are independent of one another. For example,
many problems in data processing can be immediately divided into three steps.

```
read the data;
perform calculations;
print the results
```

If there are more data than can be stored in memory at one time, this schema is
unsuitable. In such a case, the following schema is more appropriate.

```
repeat
    read some data;
    perform calculations;
    print results
until no more data
```

This demonstrates the second refinement technique: make finite progress. We reason that if we have a way of making finite progress towards the solution and we apply it repeatedly, we will eventually arrive at the complete solution. The precise definition of "finite progress" is important, and we will return to it later in this chapter when we discuss program verification. In the example above, suppose that the items of data can be numbered $1, 2, \ldots, N$, and that the statement "read some data" reads at least one item. We can assert that at most N steps will be required to obtain the solution.

The third refinement technique is "analyze cases." Suppose that, in the example above, the data can be divided into four classes: *sheep, pigs, goats,* and *donkeys.* It is then natural to use a different procedure for each class of data.

```
repeat
    read an item of data;
    case class of
        sheep : process sheep;
        pig : process pig;
        goat : process goat;
        donkey : process donkey
    end;
    print results
until no more data
```

The refinement techniques are applied at each level until there is nothing more to be refined. In this example, we now have six subproblems.

```
read an item of data
process sheep
process pig
process goat
process donkey
print results
```

The next step is to refine these into still simpler problems by using any of the same three refinement techniques.

Note how naturally these methods of refinement relate to Pascal statements. The result of dividing a problem is a statement sequence or a compound statement. The iterative method, make finite progress, can be modeled by a **for, while,** or **repeat** statement. Case analysis can be modeled either by a **case** statement or, in situations in which cases are most easily distinguished by boolean expressions, by an **if** statement or a compound **if** statement. We can introduce procedures at any level we please. When procedures are used in top-down program development, the finished program retains traces of the design process and these traces contribute to the clarity of the program.

In practice, top-down development does not always proceed in the orderly manner described here. Sometimes the refinement may lead to subproblems that are not disjoint or that are insoluble. Before committing ourselves to a particular refinement, we should *look ahead* and attempt to foresee its consequences. Sometimes, despite looking ahead, we make a mistake and have to *backtrack,* undoing some of the refinements we have made. The amount of look-ahead and backtracking we need to solve a problem depends on the complexity of the problem and on our experience.

Top-down development is not the only systematic programming methodology. It does not always yield efficient solutions or provide deep insight into the nature of the problem. We have described it here because it is a method that is well documented, reliable, and safe. Section 10.5 demonstrates the application of top-down development to a typical programming problem.

10.2 TESTING

A computer program, like any other product, should be tested before it is used. One way of testing a program is to execute it once for each possible combination of input data. It is not difficult to see that in most cases this is impractical. A typical computer can represent perhaps a billion different integers. If we were to test exhaustively a program that read just one integer, we would have to execute it a billion times and verify a billion sets of results. Clearly, we have to reduce the number of tests somehow. One way to reduce it would be to make random tests. Although random tests may reveal gross errors in the program, for example, that it invariably gives the wrong answer, it is extremely unlikely that random testing will reveal singularities in the behavior of a program. For example, a program that uses values of $\tan(x)$ might give unreliable results only when $x \simeq \pi/2$. Random testing would probably not detect this.

If we were testing another product, say a car, we would consider neither exhaustive testing, which would presumably involve driving the car along every road in the country, nor random testing. Rather, we would classify the surfaces over which the car was expected to drive and devise appropriate tests: we would use roads that were smooth or bumpy, straight or curved, level or inclined, and so on. By doing this, we would be considering parts of the car that might fail and testing them to see if they did fail. We would base our tests on what we know about the internal structure of the car. In a similar way, we must study the internal structure of a program in order to construct test data for it.

Suppose we have a program that contains a statement intended to assign to z the value of max (x, y), the greater of x and y.

```
if x > y
    then z := x
    else z := y
```

A programmer designing test data for this program would observe that there are two cases, $x > y$ and $x \leqslant y$, and would ensure that the test data included values that would test both of these cases. In its general form, this method ensures that every *path* of the program is executed during testing. For example, Program *quadratic*, which we developed in Section 3.1, is shown with five sets of input data that correspond to the five paths of the program. The principle used here is that the decisions made within the program divide the set of input data into five classes, each class of input data resulting in the execution of a different path in the program. In general it is not sufficient merely to test all paths or even all combinations of paths. A predicate may be in error, as in the following example:

```
var
    x, y : integer;
    ....
    if ((x + y) div 2) = x
        then write ('x = y')
        else write ('x ≠ y')
```

Both branches of this statement can be tested using test data, $(x = 2, y = 2)$ and $(x = 3, y = 2)$, without revealing the error, although the statement fails for $(x = 2, y = 3)$. Despite these difficulties, systematic methods for finding a sufficient set of test data have been proposed.

10.3 VERIFICATION

There are many large and complex programs that sometimes fail despite apparently thorough testing. Compilers, for example, may be used hundreds of times a day to the satisfaction of most of their users and yet occasionally reject a valid program. Some operating systems run continuously for days and then unexpectedly collapse. In these cases, an unusual combination of events has led the process to a state unanticipated by the programmer. Programs as complex as these can never be tested completely. A compiler, for example, must accept any finite string of symbols, and if the string happens to conform to the language definition, the compiler must generate a semantically equivalent object program. An operating system is even more difficult to test because it must support many processes running concurrently. When an operating system fails, it is often impossible even to recreate the circumstances that led to the failure.

It is now widely believed that rather than testing programs, we should be attempting to *prove* that they function correctly. Because a proven statement is no more reliable than the assumptions underlying the proof, we must define the meaning of each construction in the language before we can prove the correctness of a program written in that language. It is feasible to do this only if we assume the existence of an ideal processor, so we cannot usually guarantee that a proven program will run correctly on an actual computer. We can, however, claim that the program is correct, even though the computer cannot execute it correctly.

A detailed study of program proving, or program *verification* as it is also called, is beyond the scope of this book. We give an introductory treatment of program verification based on an informal interpretation of the semantics of Pascal. This is by no means a futile exercise because an understanding of the techniques of program verification is an aid to clarity in programming. As we write a program, we have a mental image of the intended operation of the program. Many of the concepts used in program verification are formalized versions of these mental images.

Suppose we write the statement

$$y := 1 / x$$

in which x and y are real variables. When we write this statement, we must have reason to believe that x is nonzero. We also expect that after the statement has been executed, y will have the value $1/x$. Our account of program verification is a development of this simple concept. We associate two *boolean* expressions with each statement of the program. The first of these *boolean* expressions is called the *precondition* of the statement. It expresses what we know to be true before the statement is executed. The second *boolean* expression is called the *postcondition* of the statement. It expresses what we know to be true after the statement has been executed. We write the conditions as comments before and after the statement.

```
{ precondition }
statement
{ postcondition }
```

Suppose that at a point in the program where we know that $x > 0$, we write the statement

$$y := 1 / x$$

Because the assignment does not alter the value of x, we know that after the statement has been executed, $x > 0$ and $y = 1 / x$. We can write

$$\{ \ X > 0 \ \}$$
$$y \ := \ 1 \ / \ x$$
$$\{ \ (X > 0) \ \textbf{and} \ (Y = 1 \ / \ X) \ \}$$

We have written X and Y for the current values of the variables x and y. We will continue to use the convention of denoting current values by capital letters in the ensuing discussion. We assume that the program will be executed by an ideal processor, and we ignore the possibility that the result of an assignment may be out of range or inaccurate.

In the previous example, the statement increased our knowledge of the state of the process, but this is not always the case. In the next example, we know less about the value of x after the statement has been executed than before.

$$\{ \ X = 0 \ \}$$
$$read \ (x)$$
$$\{ \ ? \ \}$$

After the *read* statement, we know nothing at all about the value of x. It follows that the postcondition must be true for all values of x. One postcondition that is true for all values of x is the condition *true*. We can write

$$\{ \ X = 0 \ \}$$
$$read \ (x)$$
$$\{ \ true \ \}$$

Although it seems strange, *true*, in the context of program verification, is an expression of total ignorance about the state of the program.

Next, we consider a sequence of statements.

$$c \ := \ a \ + \ b;$$
$$d \ := \ c \ * \ c$$

We express our ignorance about the initial values of the variables by writing the precondition *true*. The postcondition of the first statement is clearly

$$C = A + B.$$

This is also the precondition for the second statement. From the second statement we can deduce

$$D = C * C,$$

and therefore the postcondition for the program is

$$(C = A + B) \text{ and } (D = C * C).$$

This simplifies to

$$D = (A + B)^2$$

and we can write

```
{ true }
c := a + b;
{ C = A + B }
d := c * c
{ D = (A + B)² }
```

All this may seem rather obvious. Verification becomes more interesting when we consider decisions and loops. Let us look first at the program that calculated $max(x, y)$.

```
if x > y
    then z := x
    else z := y
```

We know nothing about the initial values of the variables, so the first precondition is $true$. From our knowledge of the **if** statement, we can derive preconditions for the **then** and **else** clauses.

```
{ true }
if x > y
    then
        { X > Y }
        z := x
    else
        { not (X > Y) }
        z := y
```

The corresponding postconditions are derived from our knowledge of the effect of the assignment statements.

```
{ true }
if x > y
    then
        { X > Y }
        z := x
        { (X > Y) and (Z = X) }
    else
        { not (X > Y) }
        z := y
        { not (X > Y) and (Z = Y) }
```

To obtain the postcondition for the whole statement, we note that exactly one branch of the **if** statement is executed. Exactly one of the two postconditions must be true, and we have as the final postcondition

$$((X > Y) \text{ and } (Z = X)) \text{ or } (\text{not } (X > Y) \text{ and } (Z = Y))$$

which is clearly equivalent to

$$Z = max \ (X, \ Y).$$

The approach we have used in the previous example is not very systematic. There are other directions from which we can approach the problem. Let us take the assertion

$$\{ \ P \ \} \ S \ \{ \ Q \ \}$$

in which S may be a sequence of statements or an entire program. We do not usually need to derive the postcondition Q, as we did in the previous example, because we already know what it is. Our task is to demonstrate that S establishes Q. The next example illustrates this. We consider a simple program that finds the greatest common divisor of two positive nonzero integers.

```
{ (X > 0) and (Y > 0) }
u := x;
v := y;
while u ≠ v do
  if u > v
    then u := u - v
    else v := v - u
{ U = gcd (X, Y) }
```

The program is based on the following results of elementary number theory.

Theorem

1. For any $A > 0$, gcd $(A, A) = A$.
2. For any A and B such that $A > B > 0$, gcd $(A - B, B) =$ gcd (A, B).
3. For any A and B such that $0 < A < B$, gcd $(A, B - A) =$ gcd (A, B).

Each iteration of the **while** loop accomplishes two things. First, the absolute difference between U and V, $|U - V|$, becomes smaller. Second, by the theorem, the truth of

$$gcd \ (U, \ V) = gcd \ (X, \ Y)$$

is maintained. The loop terminates when $U = V$, or $|U - V| = 0$, and

$$gcd \ (U, \ V) = gcd \ (U, \ U) = U.$$

Every correct loop construction has two components.

- A fixed, or *invariant,* component ensures that when the loop terminates, a specific condition is satisfied.
- A changing component ensures that progress is being made and hence that the loop eventually terminates.

In the greatest common denominator program, we note that U and V are initially positive, and the smaller is always subtracted from the larger, so that they both remain positive. This suggests that the complete invariant for the loop is

$$(U > 0) \textbf{ and } (V > 0) \textbf{ and } (\gcd (U, V) = \gcd (X, Y)).$$

We start verifying the program by writing

```
{ (X > 0) and (Y > 0) }
u := x;
v := y;
while u ≠ v do
    { (U > 0) and (V > 0) and (gcd (U, V) = gcd (X, Y)) }
```

The **if** statement distinguishes the two cases, $U > V$ and $U < V$. Note that $U = V$ is excluded by the **while** condition. We have

```
if u > v
    then
        { (U > V > 0) and (gcd (U, V) = gcd (X, Y)) }
        u := u − v
    else
        { (V > U > 0) and (gcd (U, V) = gcd (X, Y)) }
```

For the case $U > V$, write $U' = U - V$. Because $U > V$, we know that $U - V > 0$, and hence $U' > 0$. Also,

$$\gcd (U', V) = \gcd (U - V, V) = \gcd (U, V) = \gcd (X, Y)$$

and therefore

$$(U' > 0) \textbf{ and } (V > 0) \textbf{ and } (\gcd (U', V) = \gcd (X, Y)).$$

If we now write U for U', which is the effect of the assignment statement, we have shown that the proposed invariant is still true after the **then** clause has been executed. Using a similar argument, we can show that the assignment

```
v := v − u
```

of the **else** clause also maintains the truth of the proposed invariant. We have therefore established two things.

- The proposed invariant is true on entry to the loop.
- If the proposed invariant is true at the beginning of an iteration, it is still true at the beginning of the next iteration.

Using the principle of mathematical induction, we can now assert that the proposed invariant remains true for as long as the **while** statement is executed. It is therefore a suitable invariant for this loop.

The **while** loop terminates when $U = V$, so the postcondition for the **while** statement is

$$(U > 0) \text{ and } (V > 0) \text{ and } (gcd(U, V) = gcd(X, Y)) \text{ and } (U = V).$$

From this we can derive

$$gcd(X, Y) = gcd(U, V) = gcd(U, U) = U$$

as required. We have demonstrated that the program will find the value of $gcd(X, Y)$ if the loop terminates.

We have not yet proved that the expression $u \neq v$ eventually becomes false. In order to prove that eventually $U = V$, we note that

$$0 < min(U, V) \leqslant max(U, V)$$

in which $min(U, V)$ is the lesser and $max(U, V)$ is the greater of U and V. During each iteration of the loop, we execute either

```
u := u - v
```

or

```
v := v - u
```

Whichever we execute, it is still true that

$$0 < min(U, V) \leqslant max(U, V)$$

but $max(U, V)$ must have diminished by at least 1 because $U \neq V$ and both are integers. Therefore, within a finite number of steps,

$$0 < min(U, V) = max(U, V)$$

and so $U = V$. It follows that the program will terminate after a finite number of steps.

We can verify a **for** loop by constructing an equivalent **while** loop. This program sums the elements of an array, a, whose index type is 1..n:

```
s := 0;
for i := 1 to n do
    s := s + a [i]
```

We write this in the equivalent form

```
s := 0;
i := 1;
while i ⩽ n do
  begin
    s := s + a [i];
    i := i + 1
  end
```

Let s_i denote

$$\sum_{k=1}^{i} a\,[k]$$

and define s_0 to be zero. On entry to the first iteration of the loop,

$$(I = 1) \textbf{ and } (S = 0).$$

Using the definition of S_0, we have

$$S = 0 = S_0 = S_{1-1} = S_{I-1}$$

so we can write the precondition for the **while** statement as

$$(I = 1) \textbf{ and } (S = S_{I-1}).$$

After the first assignment within the loop,

$$S = S_{I-1} + A\,[I] = S_I.$$

After the second statement, let the new value of I be I', so

$$I' = I + 1$$

and

$$S_I = S_{I'-1}.$$

The body of the **while** statement now looks like this.

```
begin
  { S = S_{I-1} }
  s := s + a [i];
  { S = S_I }
  i := i + 1
  { S = S_{I-1} }
end
```

Therefore $S = S_{I-1}$ is the correct loop invariant. On exit from the loop, we know that

$$I > N$$

and during the preceding iteration

$$I \leqslant N$$

and so now

$$I = N + 1$$

and

$$S = S_{I-1} = S_N$$

as required. We can now prove termination by noting that I starts at 1 and increases by 1 during each iteration. The loop therefore terminates after exactly N iterations.

We do not need any new concepts to verify procedures and functions. The preconditions for a procedure will define constraints on the values of its actual parameters. Well-written procedures check the values of their parameters and have less restrictive preconditions. The postcondition of a procedure expresses the result it is expected to produce. These conditions are inserted in the calling program wherever the procedure is invoked. If the procedure has side effects, these conditions will be much harder to write. This provides some justification for the recommendation that we should try to avoid accessing or altering global variables from procedures.

Recursive procedures and functions are more interesting. We will discuss the verification of a simple recursive function. The factorial function $f(n) = n!$ may be defined recursively.

$$0! = 1,$$
$$n! = n * (n-1)! \quad \text{for } n > 0.$$

The corresponding function for positive arguments may be written

```
function f (n : integer) : integer;
  begin
    { N ⩾ 0 }
    if n = 0
      then
        { N = 0 }
        f := 1
        { (N = 0) and (F (0) = 1) }
      else
        { N > 0 }
        f := n * f (n - 1)
        { (N > 0) and (F (N) = N * F (N - 1)) }
    { (N = 0) and (F(0) = 1) or (N > 0)
      and (F (N) = N * F (N - 1)) }
  end;
```

The proofs we require are straightforward. Note, however, that we must include a proof that the call $f(n-1)$ is valid. We know that

$$N > 0$$

and therefore that

$$N - 1 \geqslant 0.$$

Thus $n - 1$ is a permissible actual parameter for f. We have proved that

$$f(0) = 1$$

and

$$f(n) = n * f(n-1) \qquad \text{for } n > 0.$$

It follows from the definition of $n!$ that

$$f(0) = 0!$$

and

$$\text{if } f(n-1) = (n-1)!, \text{ then } f(n) = n!.$$

Using the second of these relations for $n = 1,2,3, \ldots$, we have proved informally

$$f(1) = 1!$$
$$f(2) = 2!$$
$$f(3) = 3!$$
$$\ldots$$

and hence, by the principle of induction, that

$$f(n) = n!.$$

The foregoing arguments have been based on a simple and intuitive concept of the effect of each kind of Pascal control structure. For a rigorous theory of verification we require axioms that precisely define the meaning, or *semantics*, of each control structure. These axioms define a *proof-rule* for each Pascal statement. We give an outline of these rules.

For the assignment statement,

$$v := E$$

the precondition is obtained by substituting e for V in the postcondition.

For the **if** statement we have

```
{ p }
if b
    then
        { p and b }
        S₁
        { q₁ }
    else
        { p and not b }
        S₂
        { q₂ }
{ q₁ or q₂ }
```

We must prove that executing S_1 with precondition p **and** b gives postcondition q_1 and that executing statement S_2 with precondition p **and not** b gives postcondition q_2. Because exactly one of the statements S_1 or S_2 is executed, the postcondition for the **if** statement is q_1 or q_2. The **case** statement is treated analogously, one proof being required for each case label.

Loops are verified inductively. If we have

```
{ p }
while b do
    { i }
    S
{ i and not b }
```

we have to prove that p implies i and that S maintains the truth of i. For the **repeat** statement

```
{ p }
repeat
    { i }
    S₁; S₂;...; Sₙ
until q
{ i and q }
```

We must prove that p implies i and that the statement sequence $S_1; S_2; \ldots; S_n$ preserves the truth of i. We have already seen how to construct a **while** loop from a **for** loop.

To prove termination, we look for a function, f, with the properties:

- Initially $f = f(0) > 0$.
- During each iteration, f decreases by at least 1.
- The process terminates when $f \leqslant 0$.

If such a function can be found, it is easy to prove that the loop will be executed at most $f(0)$ times. In the previous example, we could have chosen $f(N) = N - I$.

The importance of choosing a suitable function can be seen from the following example.

```
var
  term, sum : real;
begin
  term := 1;
  sum := 0;
  repeat
    term := term / 2;
    sum := sum + term
  until sum >= 1
end
```

Assuming that we have a computer with unlimited precision, a finite quantity will be added to *sum* during each iteration, and yet the termination condition will never be satisfied. On an actual computer, either *term* would eventually become zero and the program would continue to loop until the operating system intervened, or at some point the division would produce an overflow condition and this would cause the operating system to abort the program.

We have only skimmed the surface of program verification in this section. We have not considered the difficulties of verifying programs that use *real* variables, make assignments to components of arrays, or use pointers or **goto** statements. In fact, the program fragments we have verified have all been rather trivial. Verifying nontrivial programs is difficult and tedious, and large programs will probably not be verified until automatic verification techniques are available. However, there are some lessons to be learned. If you try verifying a few programs yourself, you will discover that program verification provides valuable insight into the task of program construction. If, as you write a program, you think about how you would set about proving it correct, your programming style will improve. Inserting important preconditions and postconditions as comments will make your programs easier to read. Finally, use proven algorithms rather than ad hoc devices for standard programming tasks.

10.4 DEBUGGING

When we use structured programming, top-down design, and program verification, our intention is to produce programs without errors. Consequently, "debugging" has become something less than a polite word. Unfortunately, bugs do not go away simply because we do not speak of them. The most dutiful programmer, carefully verifying each line, may still write "$-$" where "$+$" was intended, or *sqr* where *sqrt* was intended.

In this book we have frequently made suggestions for improving the readability of programs. For example, we have recommended the use of good layout, declarations for all constants, meaningful names for variables, tag values to discriminate variants, and the avoidance of side effects. If you follow these recommendations, your programs will be more readable and they will tend to have fewer bugs. Moreover, when they do fail, the bugs will be easier to find.

There are no general rules for finding bugs. Each bug is unique. Debugging requires intuition, inspiration, and experience. Here we offer a few hints for debugging, some of them general, the rest specific to Pascal.

When your program has a bug, examine *all* the evidence. The "evidence" consists of the text of the program itself, the input data that it reads, the output that it generates, and diagnostic information provided by the run-time system if the failure led to abnormal termination. You should consider anything that is not exactly as you expect it to be as an aid to finding the bug. If there is not enough evidence, you can generate more. You can rerun the program with different data, or you can insert *write* statements into it to check intermediate results and then rerun it with the same data. If you think you have identified the section of the program that contains the bug but there appears to be nothing wrong with it, look somewhere else. In particular, look at the parts of the program that were executed *before* the suspect area. If you cannot find anything wrong with the program, show it to your friends. Do not explain how you think the program should work; by doing so you may communicate your mental "set" and obscure their view of the problem. When you have found the bug, make sure that it accounts for *all* the anomalous behavior of the program. If it does not, look for more bugs.

There are a few Pascal constructions that are involved frequently in obscure errors. Check that compound **if** statements are constructed correctly. Do not be misled by incorrect layouts such as

```
if p
then
    if q
        then S₁
    else S₂
```

the effect of which is correctly expressed by the layout

```
if p
  then
    if q
      then S₁
      else S₂
```

If p is *false* or if $j > k$, the statement S will not be executed in either of the constructions

```
while p do
  S
```

or

```
for i := j to k do
  S
```

On the other hand, the body of a **repeat** statement is always executed at least once.

Check that variable formal parameters are prefixed by **var**. Omission of **var** can lead to very puzzling errors. If you are using records with variants, check that the fields you access are consistent with the tag values.

It is easy to leave out a comment terminator in a Pascal program. The compiler may not be able to detect this error, as in the following example in which the closing brace has been omitted from the first comment.

```
reset (infile);   { Previous input stream closed.
lines := 0;       { Start line count for new stream. }
```

The compiler interprets "{ Previous . . . stream. }" as a single comment and ignores the assignment statement altogether. Some compilers print relative code addresses in the left margin of the listing. If these addresses do not increase, there is a strong possibility that the compiler is processing statements as if they were comments.

The scope rules of Pascal sometimes cause problems. Suppose that in modifying an inner procedure of a large program, we introduce a new local variable but forget to declare it. Usually the compiler will issue an "undeclared variable" error message, but if there is a global variable with the same name and type, there will be no compiler diagnostic even though subtle bugs may have been introduced.

10.5 APPLICATION: A CROSS-REFERENCE GENERATOR

This section is devoted to the development of a program that uses some of the techniques described in this chapter. We use top-down development for both the algorithm and the data structures of the program. We do not attempt to prove that the program is correct. The program is a cross-reference generator.

SPECIFICATION: CROSS-REFERENCE GENERATOR

Read a source text containing up to 999 lines. Print a list consisting of one entry for each distinct word in the text. Each entry consists of the word itself followed by a list of the numbers of the lines on which it appears. A "word" is a string of consecutive uppercase letters. Letters after the twentieth letter of a word may be ignored. The words are listed in alphabetical order. If a word occurs twice in one line, the line number should be printed only once. The output must be formatted for pages of 60 lines, and no line may contain more than 80 characters.

This program is somewhat similar to Program *concordance* which we developed in Sections 6.6 and 8.5, but more information must be stored in each word entry. We first "divide the problem." The program falls naturally into two steps: construct the table of words, and then print it. The alternative construction, read a little, print a little, and repeat, is inappropriate because we must scan the entire source text before we can start printing. We will assume that there is sufficient memory available to store all the necessary information. This assumption is reasonable in view of the limit of 999 lines of text. We require a data structure into which we can insert words and from which we can later print the words in alphabetical order. A binary search tree is an appropriate choice of data structure. We can now write the first and most abstract version of the program.

```
program crossreference (input, output);
  type
    treepointer = ↑ node;
    node =
      record
        entry : entrytype;
        left, right : treepointer
      end;
  var
    wordtree : treepointer;
  begin
    wordtree := nil;
    buildtree (wordtree);
    printtree (wordtree)
  end.
```

This program is manifestly correct, so far as it goes. We cannot execute it yet because we have not yet defined *entrytype*, *buildtree*, and *printtree*.

We use two principles to refine *buildtree*. The first is repetition: during each iteration we process one word of the text. This guarantees that we finish building the tree in finite time. The second principle is "divide the problem": first get the word, then put it into the tree.

```
procedure buildtree (var tree : treepointer);
  var
    currentword : wordtype;
    currentline : counter;
  begin
    currentline := 1;
    while not eof do
      begin
        getword (currentword, currentline);
        if not eof
          then entertree (tree, currentword, currentline)
      end { while }
  end;
```

This procedure has introduced four new undefined entities: two types, *word-type* and *counter*, and two procedures, *getword* and *entertree*. We can define the new types without much difficulty.

```
const
  maxlines = 999;
  maxwordlen = 20;
type
  counter = 1..maxlines;
  wordindex = 1..maxwordlen;
  wordtype = packed array [wordindex] of char;
```

With this established, we can proceed with the refinement of *getword*. This procedure is based on similar procedures that have appeared previously in this book.

```
procedure getword (var word : wordtype; var line : counter);
  var
    currentchar : char;
    index, blankindex : 0..maxwordlen;
```

```
begin
  currentchar := blank;
  while not (eof or (currentchar in letters)) do
    getchar (currentchar, line);
  if not eof
    then
      begin
        index := 0;
        while currentchar in letters do
          begin
            if index < maxwordlen
              then
                begin
                  index := index + 1;
                  word [index] := currentchar
                end;
            if eof
              then currentchar := blank
              else getchar (currentchar, line)
          end; { while }
        for blankindex := index + 1 to maxwordlen do
          word [blankindex] := blank
      end
end;
```

The procedure *getchar*, called by *getword*, provides the next character from the input file and maintains the line counter. Procedure *getchar* is developed using case analysis. The cases to consider are end of file, end of line, and neither of these. *Getchar* inserts a blank character between lines to ensure that the program does not concatenate the first word of a line with the last word of the previous line. Both *getchar* and *getword* may return with *eof* = *true*.

```
procedure getchar (var ch : char;
                   var lin : counter);
  begin
    if eof
      then ch := blank
      else if eoln
        then
```

```
            begin
              ch := blank;
              lin := lin + 1;
              readln
            end
          else read (ch)
      end;
```

We continue with the refinement of *buildtree* by elaborating the call

entertree (tree, currentword, currentline)

In order to do this, we must first consider in more detail the refinement of *entry-type*, the type we are using for entries in the word tree. An entry must be able to store a word and some line numbers. Looking ahead to the printing phase, we see that we have to print the line numbers in ascending sequence. This, however, is exactly the order in which the program will encounter them. The structure should therefore permit first-in/first-out access, and a queue is suitable. As we saw in Chapter 8, a queue can be implemented as a list with a pointer to its head and another pointer to its tail. We can therefore write

```
      type
        entrytype =
          record
            wordvalue : wordtype;
            firstinqueue, lastinqueue : queuepointer
          end;
```

The queue items each contain a line number and a pointer to the next item in the queue.

```
      type
        queuepointer = ↑ queueitem;
        queueitem =
          record
            linenumber : counter;
            nextinqueue : queuepointer
          end;
```

At this point it is convenient to summarize the constants and types we have introduced.

```
const
  maxlines = 999;
  maxwordlen = 20;
type
  counter = 1..maxlines;
  wordindex = 1..maxwordlen;
  wordtype = packed array [wordindex] of char;
  queuepointer = ↑ queueitem;
  queueitem =
    record
      linenumber : counter;
      nextinqueue : queuepointer
    end; { queueitem }
  entrytype =
    record
      wordvalue : wordtype;
      firstinqueue, lastinqueue : queuepointer
    end; { entrytype }
  treepointer = ↑ node;
  node =
    record
      entry : entrytype;
      left, right : treepointer
    end; { node }
```

The procedure *entertree* is derived by case analysis. On entry, its first parameter points to the tree or one of its subtrees. If this pointer is **nil**, we create a new entry and set the pointer to it. Otherwise, we compare the word stored in the node to the word we have just read. If they are equal, we have only to add the current line number to the list, unless it is there already, in which case *lastinqueue* must point to it. Otherwise, the words are not equal, and we search either the left or the right subtree of this node by calling *entertree* recursively. This is the conventional algorithm for binary tree insertion.

```
procedure entertree (var subtree : treepointer;
                         word : wordtype;
                         line : counter);
```

```
begin
  if subtree = nil
    then create a new entry
  else if word = subtree↑.entry.wordvalue
    then append line number to list
  else if word < subtree↑.entry.wordvalue
    then entertree (subtree↑.left, word, line)
  else entertree (subtree↑.right, word, line)
end;
```

The actions "create a new entry" and "append line number to list" are developed using standard algorithms.

```
{ Create a new entry. }
begin
  new (subtree);
  with subtree↑ do
    begin
      left := nil;
      right := nil;
      with entry do
        begin
          wordvalue := word;
          new (firstinqueue);
          lastinqueue := firstinqueue;
          with firstinqueue↑ do
            begin
              linenumber := line;
              nextinqueue := nil
            end { with firstinqueue↑ }
        end { with entry }
    end { with subtree↑ }
end

{ Append a list item. }
with subtree↑, entry do
  if lastinqueue↑.linenumber ≠ line
    then
      begin
        new (nextitem);
        with nextitem↑ do
```

```
          begin
              linenumber := line;
              nextinqueue := nil;
          end; { with nextitem↑ }
          lastinqueue↑.nextinqueue := nextitem;
          lastinqueue := nextitem
      end
  else { Word is on same line. }
```

This completes the development of the input phase, and we turn to the refinement of *printtree* (*wordtree*). Since we will be printing entries from a binary search tree, we can anticipate that we will use binary tree traversal to print the entries and subtrees of a node. It is useful to look ahead a little and consider how the output will be arranged. The paging can be controlled by a procedure, *printline*, which keeps track of the current position on the page. We decide at this stage how many line numbers will be printed on a line. The word may occupy up to 20 positions. Because the maximum line length is 80 characters, there will be 60 print positions for line numbers. The largest line number is 999, which has three digits. If we leave five print positions for each number, there will be at least two blanks between each pair of numbers. It follows that we can print 12 numbers on a line. The program can perform these calculations itself, and it is better if it does so. We define these constants and subrange types.

```
          const
              maxlinelen = 80;
              maxonpage = 60;
              numbergap = 2;
              radix = 10;
          type
              pageindex = 1..maxonpage;
              lineindex = 1..maxlinelen;
```

This is the first version of procedure *printtree*:

```
      procedure printtree (tree : treepointer);
          var
              pageposition : pageindex;
              numberwidth, maxonline : lineindex;
```

```
begin
  numberwidth := trunc (ln (maxlines) / ln (radix))
                         + 1 + numbergap;
  maxonline := (maxlinelen - maxwordlen) div numberwidth;
  pageposition := maxonpage;
  printentry (tree, pageposition)
end;
```

We do not pass *numberwidth* and *maxonline* as parameters to *printentry*. Their values are constant, and it is sufficient to ensure that *printentry* is within their scope.

The procedure *printentry* performs an inorder traversal of the word-tree, using the schema

```
process nodes in the left subtree;
process the current node;
process nodes in the right subtree
```

Processing a node consists of first printing the word in it and then traversing the list of items containing the line numbers. The procedure *printline* controls the paging, and the constant *entrygap* determines the number of blank lines between successive words.

```
{ Cross-reference Generator

Author:          Peter Grogono
Written:         24 September 1977
Last Modified:   22 February 1983

Purpose

   Generate a cross-reference listing from a text-file.

Specification

   The program reads a text-file from file ''input'' and
   writes a cross-reference listing to the file ''output.''
   The cross-reference listing contains one entry for each
   distinct word in the source text. A word is a string of
   letters. An entry displays the word and the number of
   each line on which it occurred. For restrictions, see
   the constant declaration section. }
```

program *crossreference*
```
  ( { read text from } input,
    { write listing to } output);
```

```
const
  maxlines = 999;    { Longest document permitted }
  maxwordlen = 20;   { Longest word read without truncation }
  maxlinelen = 80;   { Length of output line }
  maxonpage = 60;    { Size of output page }
  headingsize = 3;   { Number of lines for heading }
  entrygap = 1;      { Number of blank lines between entries }
  numbergap = 2;     { Number of blanks between line numbers }
  radix = 10;        { Assume decimal numbers }
  blank = ' '; cha = 'A'; chz = 'Z';
  heading = 'Cross-reference Listing';
type
  counter = 1..maxlines;
  wordindex = 1..maxwordlen;
  pageindex = 1..maxonpage;
  lineindex = 1..maxlinelen;
  wordtype = packed array [wordindex] of char;
  queuepointer = ↑ queueitem;
  queueitem =
    record
      linenumber : counter;
      nextinqueue : queuepointer
    end; { queueitem }
  entrytype =
    record
      wordvalue : wordtype;
      firstinqueue, lastinqueue : queuepointer
    end; { entrytype }
  treepointer = ↑ node;
  node =
    record
      entry : entrytype;
      left, right : treepointer
    end; { node }
var
  wordtree : treepointer;
  letters : set of char;
```

```
{ Read the text and construct a tree
  containing the cross-reference data. }
procedure buildtree (var tree : treepointer);
  var
    currentword : wordtype;
    currentline : counter;

  { Read one word from the text. }
  procedure getword (var word : wordtype;
                     var line : counter);

    var
      currentchar : char;
      index, blankindex : 0..maxwordlen;

    { Read one character from the text. }
    procedure getchar (var ch : char;
                       var lin : counter);
      begin { getchar }
        if eof
          then ch := blank
          else if eoln
            then
              begin
                ch := blank;
                lin := lin + 1;
                readln
              end { then }
          else read (ch)
      end; { getchar }

    begin { getword }
      currentchar := blank;
      while not (eof or (currentchar in letters)) do
        getchar (currentchar, line);
      if not eof
        then
          begin
            index := 0;
            while currentchar in letters do
              begin
                if index < maxwordlen
                  then
```

```
                      begin
                        index := index + 1;
                        word [index] := currentchar
                      end; { then }
                  if eof
                    then currentchar := blank
                    else getchar (currentchar, line)
                end; { while }
              for blankindex := index + 1 to maxwordlen do
                word [blankindex] := blank
            end { then }
        end; { getword }
  { Put the current word into the cross-reference tree. }
  procedure entertree (var subtree : treepointer;
                           word : wordtype;
                           line : counter);
    var
      nextitem : queuepointer;
    begin { entertree }
      if subtree = nil
        then
          begin { Create a new entry. }
            new (subtree);
            with subtree↑ do
              begin
                left := nil;
                right := nil;
                with entry do
                  begin
                    wordvalue := word;
                    new (firstinqueue);
                    lastinqueue := firstinqueue;
                    with firstinqueue↑ do
                      begin
                        linenumber := line;
                        nextinqueue := nil
                      end { with firstinqueue↑ }
                  end { with entry }
              end { with subtree↑ }
          end { then }
```

```pascal
        else { Append a list item. }
          with subtree↑, entry do
            if word = wordvalue
              then
                begin
                  if lastinqueue↑.linenumber ≠ line
                    then
                      begin
                        new (nextitem);
                        with nextitem↑ do
                          begin
                            linenumber := line;
                            nextinqueue := nil
                          end; { with nextitem↑ }
                        lastinqueue↑.nextinqueue := nextitem;
                        lastinqueue := nextitem
                      end { then }
                end { then }
              else if word < wordvalue
                then entertree (left, word, line)
                else entertree (right, word, line)
  end; { entertree }

begin { buildtree }
  currentline := 1;
  while not eof do
    begin
      getword (currentword, currentline);
      if not eof
        then entertree (tree, currentword, currentline)
    end { while }
end; { buildtree }
{ Print the tree constructed by buildtree. }
procedure printtree (tree : treepointer);
  var
    pageposition : pageindex;
    numberwidth, maxonline : lineindex;

  { Print the entry for one symbol. }
  procedure printentry (subtree : treepointer;
                        var position : pageindex);
    var
      index : wordindex;
      itemcount : 0..maxlinelen;
      itemptr : queuepointer;
```

```
      { Print one line of the cross-reference listing. }
      procedure printline (var currentposition : pageindex;
                                newlines : pageindex);
        var
          linecounter : pageindex;
        begin { printline }
          if currentposition + newlines < maxonpage
            then
              begin
                for linecounter := 1 to newlines do
                  writeln;
                currentposition := currentposition + newlines
              end { then }
            else
              begin
                page (output);
                writeln (heading);
                for linecounter := 1 to headingsize   1 do
                  writeln;
                currentposition := headingsize + 1
              end { else }
        end; { printline }

      begin { printentry }
        if subtree ≠ nil
          then
            with subtree↑ do
              begin
                printentry (left, position);
                printline (position, entrygap + 1);
                with entry do
                  begin
                    for index := 1 to maxwordlen do
                      write (wordvalue [index]);
                    itemptr := firstinqueue;
                    while itemptr ≠ nil do
                      begin
                        itemcount := itemcount + 1;
                        if itemcount > maxonline
                          then
                            begin
                              printline (position, 1);
                              write (blank:maxwordlen);
                              itemcount := 1
                            end; { then }
```

```
                              write (itemptr↑.linenumber:numberwidth);
                              itemptr := itemptr↑.nextinqueue
                         end { while }
                    end; { then, with entry }
                  printentry (right, position)
               end { with subtree↑ }
         end; { printentry }
      begin { printtree }
        numberwidth := trunc (ln (maxlines) / ln (radix))
                         + 1 + numbergap;
        maxonline := (maxlinelen - maxwordlen) div numberwidth;
        pageposition := maxonpage;
        printentry (tree, pageposition)
      end; { printtree }
   begin { crossreference }
     letters := [cha..chz];
     wordtree := nil;
     buildtree (wordtree);
     printtree (wordtree)
   end. { crossreference }
```

10.6   AN APPRAISAL OF PASCAL

The languages we use have a profound effect on the way we think. While it may
be true that our inspirations are not the result of linguistic mental processes,
most of our conscious thoughts are linguistic in nature. Although we can translate from one language to another, the flavor of the message is often lost in the
translation. The same is true of programming languages: we tend to think of
solutions of programming problems in our favorite programming language. A
problem will seem easy to us if it is simple to program the solution in that language. Professional programmers should be familiar with several programming
languages so that when they are confronted with a problem they will select the
most appropriate language for its solution at an early stage.

In this book we have been concerned exclusively with Pascal. The example
programs have been selected to perform calculations for which Pascal is appropriate, and problems for which Pascal is inappropriate have not been considered. We now consider Pascal in a more objective way, looking first at its
strengths and then at its weaknesses.

An important feature of Pascal is its sparseness. There are few basic constructions, but because these can be combined in many ways the language is

powerful. In particular, both algorithms and data structures can be constructed hierarchically.

The sparse nature of Pascal is its most important asset, and it benefits the language in at least four ways. First, Pascal is relatively simple to compile and Pascal programs run efficiently on most computers. Second, well-written Pascal programs are easy to read and understand. Third, the recursive nature of Pascal structures permits top-down development techniques to be applied in a natural and simple way. Fourth, with a few exceptions, Pascal control structures are easy to verify because their semantics are simple.

On the other hand, Pascal is not too sparse. There are several languages with fewer constructions than Pascal, and although these languages are capable of expressing any algorithm that can be expressed in Pascal, the resulting programs may be very obscure. In Pascal, a compromise has been achieved. There is enough variety to express most basic algorithms concisely but not so much that the language is baroque.

The quest in Pascal for efficiency has led to a lack of portability. A program is *portable* if it can be run with few changes on different kinds of computers. The designer of a programming language specifies standards that must be respected in any implementation of the language. These standards should be sufficient to make programs written in the language portable. We will illustrate the connection between standards and efficiency with a simple example. It is reasonable for a language designer to require that *real* arithmetic be provided because most computers have either hardware or a standard software package for performing *real* calculations. It would be unreasonable, however, for a language designer to insist that the results of *real* calculations be accurate to exactly ten places of decimals because this would give rise to serious inefficiency on almost all computers. In the case of Pascal, some of the standards are too lenient. The fact that Pascal does not specify a representation for characters, for example, makes it very difficult to write programs that are completely independent of the character set of a particular computer. The most useful data structure we have for writing such programs is **set of** *char,* but this type is illegal in many Pascal implementations.

There are three criticisms frequently directed at Pascal. The first is that the file handling capabilities of Pascal are inadequate. Although Pascal provides automatic conversion facilities for text files, these cannot be used in production programs because no provision is made for error conditions. Although Pascal is the best language we have for teaching programming, the important techniques of random access cannot be taught with it. The second criticism refers to Pascal arrays: the size of an array is determined at compile-time. It is very difficult to write useful programs for numerical analysis or string manipulation in Pascal because there are no dynamic arrays. The conformant array schema is a solution to this problem, but only a few compilers support it. The third objection is that there is no loop construction with an exit. There are many situations in which we want to jump out of a loop from its middle. We can do this in Pascal only by introducing state variables or by using **goto** statements. The scope rules inherited by Pascal from Algol are inadequate for large programs. This deficiency is remedied in some recent languages, including Pascal's successor, Modula 2.

The drawbacks of Pascal are minor when they are considered in the perspective of Pascal's advantages over other contemporary languages. Pascal has a secure place in the handful of programming languages that have achieved widespread implementation and that have won worldwide popularity. Pascal notation is used in a large proportion of the papers published in programming literature. Pascal is being used increasingly at both academic and industrial computer installations. There is a new generation of languages in which a debt to Pascal is acknowledged. Each year Pascal is chosen as the first computer language to teach at an increasing number of schools. Pascal is already fifteen years old, and it is possible that the language in its present form may not be used for many more years. There is no doubt, however, that its concepts will be used by programming language designers for many years to come.

10.7 EXERCISES

10.1 If you know a high-level language other than Pascal, write a comparison of the two languages. Consider, among other factors
   a) constant, type, and variable declarations;
   b) the scope of variables;
   c) dynamic data structures;
   d) input and output.
   Write programs in Pascal and in the other language you know and compare
   e) ease of coding;
   f) ease of debugging;
   g) ease of verification;
   h) compilation and execution times;
   i) memory used by the object programs.

10.2 Select a Pascal program, either from this book or elsewhere, and prove that it is correct.

10.3 The procedure below performs a binary search of the ordered array *v*. Find an invariant for the **repeat** loop.

```
type
   vector = array [min..max] of real;
procedure binarysearch (v : vector;
                            key : real;
                        var found : boolean;
                        var mid : integer);
   var
      lo, hi : integer;
   begin
      { v [min] ⩽ key ⩽ v [max] and v is ordered }
      lo := min;
      hi := max;
      repeat
         mid := (lo + hi) div 2;
         if key > v [mid]
            then lo := mid + 1
            else hi := mid − 1
      until (v [mid] = key) or (lo > hi);
      found := lo ⩽ hi
   end; { binarysearch }
```

10.4 Program *crossreference* fails if it is given a file containing more than 999 lines. This problem highlights a weakness of many programming languages, including Pascal: it is difficult to recover gracefully from an error detected at a low level of the program. One solution is to pass the error up to the top level through each intervening procedure, and another is to return directly to the top level using a **goto** statement. Implement both of these solutions in Program *crossreference* and compare them.

10.5 Program *crossreference* can be used to provide a cross-reference listing for Pascal programs. To perform this function usefully, the program should read identifiers rather than words, should not reference reserved words, and should ignore comments. Modify it to do this.

10.6 Write a nonrecursive program that lists the operations necessary to move the Tower of Hanoi (Section 4.4). Describe the development of your program in detail.

10.7 Write a program that accepts as input a syntactically correct Pascal program in any format and generates a listing of the same program with the layout conventions described in Appendix D.

10.8 Develop Program *calculator* of Chapter 4 into a useful software tool. Some examples of the facilities you could add to it are
   a) function evaluation (e.g., *sin*, *cos*, *sqrt*, *exp*, *ln*);
   b) radix conversion (enable calculations to be performed in binary, octal, etc.);

    c) control of output format;

    d) complex number calculations.

Do *not* "patch up" the original program. Write a complete specification for your calculator and use top-down development techniques to implement it.

10.10 The problem of making change (see Exercise 3.6) is more interesting if the number of coins available is limited. Suppose, for example, that you have one quarter and four dimes and that you must pay forty cents. The simple algorithm fails because it uses the larger denominations first. Write a program that makes change, if possible, for a specified amount from a specified number of coins.

REMARKS, RESOURCES, AND REFERENCES

The computer programming language Pascal is named after the French philosopher, mathematician, physicist, and inventor Blaise Pascal (1623–1662). Blaise Pascal designed and constructed the first machine capable of mechanically performing the four fundamental operations of arithmetic. The machine was constructed in 1642 and Pascal received a patent for it in 1649.

Pascal was the first language to embody in a coherent way the concepts of structured programming defined in the late sixties by Edsger Dijkstra and C. A. R. Hoare. For this reason it is a landmark in the history of programming languages. Pascal was developed by Niklaus Wirth at Eidgenossische Technische Hochschule (ETH) in Zurich. It was based on the language ALGOL 60 and is both more powerful and easier to use than that language. Pascal is now widely accepted both as a useful language that can be efficiently implemented and as an excellent teaching tool.

Pascal is to a large extent the work of one man, not of a committee. Pascal compromises between simplicity and expressive power, efficiency and portability, conciseness and redundancy. Its success is testimony to the skill with which the conflicting goals of language design were resolved.

There are two reasons for programming in a high-level language, such as Pascal, rather than in a low-level assembly language. First, it is easier to write programs in a high-level language. Second, and more important, it is easier to read and understand a program written in a high-level language. Professional programmers spend much of their time revising programs written by themselves or others. If these programs are not clear and easy to understand, attempts at revision will eventually ruin them. It is therefore as important to learn how to read and modify programs as it is to learn how to write them.

If you have read this book and want to do more than merely write Pascal programs, you will want to learn more about the language, its development, and its implementation. In this section we discuss briefly some of the problems and issues of Pascal and of programming in general. We conclude with an alphabetical list of some of the significant books and papers that have been written about Pascal since Wirth [1971a] introduced it. Moffat [1980] provides a classified Pascal bibliography that is more complete than this one but refers only to works published before June 1980.

R.1   PERSPECTIVES ON PASCAL

The primary source book for Pascal is the *User Manual and Report* by Jensen and Wirth [1976]. Two other books by Wirth use Pascal notation: *Systematic Programming—An Introduction* [1973]; and *Algorithms + Data Structures = Programs* [1976b]. The concepts upon which Pascal is based were introduced in *Structured Programming*, by Dahl, Dijkstra, and Hoare [1972].

Barron [1981] edited the proceedings of a conference devoted entirely to Pascal. At the conference, held in Southampton, England, in 1977, a number of significant papers on Pascal were presented, including Ammann [1977b], and Welsh, Sneeringer, and Hoare [1977].

The gradual acceptance of Pascal by the programming community is well charted in the academic literature. Wirth introduced Pascal [1971a, 1972] and subsequently appraised it [1975]. Pascal was criticized by Habermann [1973]; Lecarme and Desjardins [1974] responded to these criticisms. Welsh, Sneeringer, and Hoare [1977] discuss the ambiguities and insecurities of Pascal. Moffat [1981a, 1981b] analyzes the concept of type in Pascal. Desjardins [1978] and Sale [1979a] discuss aspects of Pascal type-compatibility and scope rules that have been misunderstood or overlooked by implementors. Pascal has been criticized by several other authors, including Baker [1980], Cailliau [1982], Conradi [1976], Levy [1982], and Prael [1982].

Various authors have published papers comparing Pascal to other languages. Feuer and Gehani [1982] compare Pascal and C as application languages. Their conclusions are somewhat negative: they find that there are many applications for which neither language is suitable. Nutt [1978] compares Pascal and FORTRAN for introductory courses in programming. He concludes that students gain more from an introductory Pascal course than from an introductory FORTRAN course. Venema and deRivieres [1978] compare Pascal with its descendant, Euclid. Euclid is a systems implementation language designed for ease of verification. The aim of the Euclid project was to produce a language that differed from Pascal only in areas relevant to verification.

A formal system of program verification requires a firm theoretical foundation. Hoare and Wirth [1973] have contributed an axiomatic basis for a large subset of Pascal. More recently, Watt [1979] has demonstrated an extended attribute grammar for Pascal.

R.2   PERSPECTIVES ON PROGRAMMING

Programming requires not only fluency in one or more programming languages but also skill in problem solving, algorithm design, and algorithm analysis. *Programming in Pascal* is devoted almost entirely to Pascal and only mentions other important aspects of the programmer's expertise. *Problem Solving and Computer Programming*, by Grogono and Nelson [1982] uses Pascal as a vehicle for an exploration of the problem-solving aspects of programming.

The cornerstone of computer science is algorithm design and analysis. Two of the most influential books about the design and analysis of algorithms are *Fundamental Algorithms* by Knuth [1973], and *The Design and Analysis of Algorithms* by Aho, Hopcroft, and Ullman. The latter book has been revised and reissued as *Data Structures and Algorithms* [1983].

Program *circles* in Chapter 6 is based on an example given by Birtwistle et al. [1973] in their book about the programming language SIMULA. SIMULA was elegantly constructed but ahead of its time. Although it was developed during the mid-sixties, the importance of its facilities for data abstraction and coroutines was not recognized until almost ten years later.

Program *update* in Chapter 7 is based on an algorithm by Feijen. It is described by Dijkstra [1976] in a book that both demonstrates a formal approach to program development and contains some beautiful algorithms.

SOFTWARE TOOLS

We work most effectively when we have appropriate tools. Software tools are computer programs intended to help programmers develop software. Kernighan and Plauger [1976] described a useful set of software tools written in RATFOR (RATional FORtran); this book was revised and was recently reissued as *Software Tools in Pascal* [Kernighan and Plauger, 1981]. The library of tools written in Pascal for the development of Pascal programs is growing. Source program formatters have been published by Condict et al. [1978], and Hueras and Ledgard [1977, 1978].

Program measurement, which is analysis of the run-time behavior of programs, is an important topic that we have not discussed. Techniques for analyzing Pascal programs have been described by Matwin and Missala [1976], Mickel [1978], and Yuval [1975]. Miner [1978] presents a program that compares text files and reports the differences between them.

Kruseman Aretz [1982] has written a program that draws syntax diagrams from the grammar of a programming language. The syntax diagrams in this book are adapted from diagrams produced by this program from the Pascal Standard.

PROGRAMMING STYLE

The Elements of Programming Style, by Kernighan and Plauger [1974], is a valuable introduction to the concepts of programming style, but it does not discuss Pascal. Atkinson [1978, 1979] and Marca [1981] discuss aspects of Pascal programming style.

Papers on structured programming that are of interest to Pascal programmers have been published by Cichelli [1976], Lecarme [1974], Ledgard [1973], and Wirth [1971b, 1974].

R.3   RESOURCES

THE PASCAL STANDARD

The effort to standardized Pascal began in 1975 when A. M. Addyman joined the British Standards Institute (BSI) Working Group DPS/13. The Working Group produced a "first working draft" of the Standard in April 1978. Later in the same year the International Standards Organization (ISO) and the American National Standards Institute (ANSI) entered the arena. Both accepted the BSI draft as a starting point. Various drafts of the Standard were published by Addyman et al. [1979a, 1979b], and Addyman [1980a, 1980b]. The BSI adopted the Standard in September 1981 as "BS 6192: 1982." This Standard is identical to the ISO first draft, "DIS 7185."

The term "Standard" in this book refers to the ISO second draft proposal, "DP 7185.1," distributed in North America by ANSI [1981]. It is likely that the final ISO and ANSI standards will not differ substantially from this version. The ANSI Committee on Pascal, X3J9, has refused to include conformant array parameters in the first version of the ANSI Pascal Standard. (We discuss conformant array parameters in Section 9.4.)

The Pascal Standard is based on the *Pascal Report* written by Jensen and Wirth [1976], and the language defined by the Standard differs in only a few particulars from the language described in the *Report*. The conservative approach to standardization will disappoint those who hoped that the language would be extended. It is, however, the correct approach. Large investments of time and effort have already been made in compilers that compile the language that is defined by the *Report*. In addition, the existence of a standard that defines a core language does not preclude the subsequent definition of compatible extensions.

IMPLEMENTATION

Pascal was originally implemented on the CDC 6600 computer at Eidgenossische Technische Hochschule in Zurich. During the seventies, many people became interested in Pascal and the language was implemented on many other machines.

The first Pascal compiler was developed by stepwise refinement. The development of the compiler has been described by Ammann [1973, 1977a, 1977b], and by Wirth [1971c]. Ammann [1973] defines six major refinement steps of which only the last two, address assignment and code generation, are machine-dependent. It is necessary to repeat only these steps to create a compiler for another machine. The *P-compiler*, which generates intermediate code for an abstract stack machine, was constructed in this way by Nori et al. [1976]. The code generated by the P-compiler is called *P-code*. UCSD Pascal, a widely used version of Pascal for microcomputers, uses the P-compiler and a P-code interpreter. Bates and Cailliau [1977] and Berry [1978] have described their experiences with the Pascal P-compiler. Aspects of P-code are discussed by Nelson [1979], Perkins and Sites [1979], and Sites [1979].

Most Pascal compilers place static variables on a run-time stack and dynamic variables on a run-time heap. Marlin [1979] has shown that an implementation using only a heap is feasible. Shapiro et al. [1981] have described a system called PASES, a complete environment for the development of Pascal programs. Kranc [1982] is one of several authors who have proposed separate compilation facilities for Pascal. Bishop [1981] speculates on the feasibility of a Pascal machine.

Other Pascal implementations have been described by Bron and deVries [1976], DEC PDP-11; Desjardins [1976], Xerox Sigma 6; Grosse-Lindemann and Nagel [1976], DEC 10; Hansen et al. [1979], TI 980, TI 990, IBM S/370; Rudmik and Lee [1979], DEC PDP-11; Thibault and Manuel [1973], CII Iris 80; and Welsh and Quinn [1972], ICL 1900. Chung and Yuen [1978] showed that Pascal can be implemented on a microcomputer using BASIC as a starting point. Several microcomputer implementations of Pascal are now available.

PASCAL VALIDATION SUITE

The Pascal Validation Suite consists of several hundred small Pascal programs. Each program tests one feature of a Pascal language processor for correctness. There is no known Pascal compiler that passes all of the tests, although some compilers score considerably higher than others. The Pascal Validation Suite is described by Sale [1979b]. Version 2.2 was published by Wichmann and Sale [1979]. Wichmann [1983] describes Version 3. Dixon [1982] describes a Pascal compiler-testing facility based on the Pascal Validation Suite and other software.

EXTENSIONS AND VARIATIONS

Many authors have proposed extensions to Pascal. Some of the more interesting papers are by Iglewski et al. [1978], Kittlitz [1976], Leblanc [1978, 1979], Sale [1981], and Tennent [1983]. The specific issue of incorporating dynamic arrays into Pascal has been debated by Condict [1977], Conradi [1976], Kittlitz [1977], McLennan [1975], Pokrovsky [1976], and Wirth [1976a].

Pascal has been widely criticized for its input and output features, particularly as they relate to interactive programming. Many authors have proposed extensions to Pascal I/O, including Bron and Dijkstra [1976], Bykat [1982], Cichelli [1980b], Clark [1979], Kaye [1980], Rowland [1981], and Wallace [1979].

Several groups have implemented languages that have a Pascal core and features for concurrent programming or data abstraction. Brinch Hansen [1975, 1976] introduced Concurrent Pascal. Welsh and McKeag [1980] published a compiler and a simple operating system written in Pascal-Plus. Campbell and Kolstad [1980a, 1980b] describe PATH Pascal.

Wirth [1981] has implemented an interpretive subset, Pascal-S, for use as a teaching tool, and Cichelli [1980a] has developed Pascal-I, an interactive version of Pascal-S.

GYPSY [Ambler et al., 1977], MESA [Geschke et al., 1977], Euclid [Lampson et al., 1977], CLU [Liskov et al., 1977], and TELOS [Travis et al., 1977] are recent programming languages whose design has been influenced by Pascal. Wirth [1982] has designed and implemented Modula-2, a successor to Pascal that incorporates data abstraction facilities that aid modular programming.

PASCAL NEWS

Pascal News is the official publication of the Pascal User's Group and is sent to all members of the group. It contains a wealth of information about Pascal in the form of letters, reviews, articles, implementation notes, and complete programs. Back issues and current copies of *Pascal News* are available from

Pascal News
c/o Charles J. Gaffney
2903 Huntingdon Road
Cleveland, Ohio 44120
U.S.A.

R.4 REFERENCES

Addyman, A. M., et al. [1979a]. The BSI/ISO Working Draft of Standard Pascal. *Pascal News*, 14, January 1979, 4–50.

Addyman, A. M., et al. [1979b]. A Draft Description of Pascal. *SOFTWARE—Practice & Experience*, 9, 5, May 1979, 381–424.

Addyman, A. M. [1980a]. A Draft Proposal for Pascal. *SIGPLAN Notices*, 15, 4, April 1980, 1–66.

Addyman, A. M. [1980b]. Pascal Standardization. *SIGPLAN Notices*, 15, 4, April 1980, 67–69.

Aho, A. V., Hopcroft, J. E., and Ullman, J. D. [1983]. *Data Structures and Algorithms*. Addison-Wesley, 1983.

Ambler, A. L., Good, D. I., Browne, J. C., Burger, W. F., Cohen, R. M., Hoch, C. G., and Wells, R. E. [1977]. GYPSY: A Language for Specification and Implementation of Verifiable Programs. *SIGPLAN Notices*, 12, 3, March 1977, 1–10.

Amman, U. [1973]. The Method of Structured Programming Applied to the Development of a Compiler. In *Proceedings ACM International Computing Symposium, Davos, 1973*. Ed. Gunther et al. North Holland Publishing, 1974.

Amman, U. [1977a]. On Code Generation in a Pascal Compiler. *SOFTWARE—Practice & Experience*, 7, 1977, 391–423.

Amman, U. [1977b]. The Zurich Implementation. In *Pascal—The Language and Its Implementation*. Ed. D. W. Barron. Wiley, 1981.

ANSI [1981]. DP 7185.1 Specification for the Computer Programming Language Pascal: Second Draft. *Pascal News*, 20, December 1980, 1–83.

Atkinson, L. V. [1978]. Know the State You Are In. *Pascal News*, 13, December 1978, 66–69.

Atkinson, L. V. [1979]. Pascal Scalars as State Indicators. *SOFTWARE—Practice & Experience*, 9, 6, June 1979, 427–432.

Baker, H. G. [1980]. A Source of Redundant Identifiers in Pascal Programs. *SIGPLAN Notices*, 15, 2, February 1980, 14–16.

Barron, D. W. (ed.) [1981]. *Pascal—The Language and Its Implementation*. Wiley, 1981.

Bates, D., and Cailliau, R. [1977]. Experience with Pascal Compilers on Minicomputers. *SIGPLAN Notices*, 12, 11, November 1977, 10–22.

Berry, R. E. [1978]. Experience with the Pascal P-Compiler. *SOFTWARE—Practice & Experience*, 8, 5, 1978, 617–628.

Bishop, J. M. [1981]. A Pascal Machine? In *Pascal—The Language and Its Implementation*. Ed. D. W. Barron. Wiley, 1981.

Birtwistle, G. M., Dahl, O-J., Myrhaug, B., and Nygaard, K. [1973]. *SIMULA Begin*. Auerbach, 1973.

Brinch Hansen, P. [1975]. The Programming Language Concurrent Pascal. *IEEE Transactions on Software Engineering*, SE-1, 2, June 1975, 199–207.

Brinch Hansen, P. [1976]. The SOLO Operating System. *SOFTWARE—Practice & Experience*, 6, 1976, 139–205.

Bron, C., and deVries, W. [1976]. A Pascal Compiler for the PDP11. *SOFTWARE—Practice & Experience*, 6, 1976, 109–116.

Bron, C., and Dijkstra, E. J. [1979]. A Discipline for the Programming of Interactive I/O in Pascal. *SIGPLAN Notices*, 14, 12, December 1979, 59–61.

Bykat, A. [1982]. An Extension to Pascal Input-Output Procedures. *SIGPLAN Notices*, 17, 1, January 1982, 40–41.

Cailliau, R. [1982]. How to Avoid Getting SCHLONKED by Pascal. *SIGPLAN Notices*, 17, 12, December 1982, 31–40.

Campbell, R. H., and Kolstad, R. B. [1980a]. An Overview of PATH Pascal's Design. *SIGPLAN Notices*, 15, 9, September 1980, 13–14.

Campbell, R. H., and Kolstad, R. B. [1980b]. PATH Pascal User Manual. *SIGPLAN Notices*, 15, 9, September 1980, 15–24.

Chung, K-M., and Yuen, H. [1978]. A "Tiny" Pascal Compiler. Parts 1, 2, 3. *BYTE*, 3, 9, 10, 11, 1978.

Cichelli, R. J. [1976]. Design Data Structures by Step-Wise Refinement. *Pascal News*, 5, September 1976, 7–13.

Cichelli, R. J. [1980a]. Pascal-I–Interactive, Conversational Pascal-S. *SIGPLAN Notices*, 15, 1, January 1980, 34–44.

Cichelli, R. J. [1980b]. Fixing Pascal's I/O. *SIGPLAN Notices*, 15, 5, May 1980, 19.

Clark, R. G. [1979]. Interactive Input in Pascal. *SIGPLAN Notices*, 14, 2, February 1979, 9–13.

Condict, M. N. [1977]. The Pascal Dynamic Array Controversy and a Method for Enforcing Global Assertions. *SIGPLAN Notices*, 12, 11, November 1977, 23–27.

Condict, M. N., Marcus, R. L., and Mickel, A. [1978]. Pascal Program Formatter. *Pascal News*, 13, December 1978, 45–58.

Conradi, R. [1976]. Further Critical Comments on Pascal, Particularly as a Systems Programming Language. *SIGPLAN Notices*, *11*, 11, November 1976, 8–25.

Dahl, O-J., Dijkstra, E. W., and Hoare, C. A. R. [1972]. *Structured Programming*. Academic Press, 1972.

Desjardins, P. [1976]. A Pascal Compiler for the Xerox Sigma 6. *SIGPLAN Notices*, *8*, 6, June 1976, 34–36.

Desjardins, P. [1978]. Type Compatibility Checking in Pascal Compilers. *Pascal News*, 11, February 1978, 33–34.

Dijkstra, E. W. [1976]. *A Discipline of Programming*. Prentice-Hall, 1976.

Dixon, D. F. [1982]. A Pascal Compiler Testing Facility. *SIGPLAN Notices*, *17*, January 1982, 23–26.

Feuer, A. R., and Gehani, N. H. [1982]. A Comparison of the Programming Languages C and Pascal. *ACM Computing Surveys*, *14*, 1, March 1982, 73–92.

Geschke, M., Morris, J. H., and Satterthwaite, E. H. [1977]. Early Experience with MESA. *COMM ACM*, *20*, 8, August 1977, 540–552.

Grogono, P. D., and Nelson, S. H. [1982]. *Problem Solving and Computer Programming*. Addison-Wesley, 1982.

Grosse-Lindemann, C. O., and Nagel, H. H. [1976]. Postlude to a Pascal Compiler for the DEC System 10. *SOFTWARE—Practice & Experience*, 6, 1, 1976, 29–42.

Habermann, A. N. [1973]. Critical Comments on the Programming Language Pascal. *Acta Informatica*, *3*, 1, 1973, 45–57.

Hansen, G. J., Shoults, G. A., and Cointment, J. D. [1979]. Construction of a Portable, Multi-Pass Compiler for Extended Pascal. *SIGPLAN Notices*, 14, 8, August 1979, 117–126.

Hartmann, A. C. [1977]. *A Concurrent Pascal Compiler for Minicomputers*. Springer-Verlag, 1977.

Hoare, C. A. R., and Wirth, N. [1973]. An Axiomatic Definition of Pascal. *Acta Informatica*, *3*, 1973, 335–355.

Hueras, J., and Ledgard, H. F. [1977]. An Automatic Formatting Program for Pascal. *SIGPLAN Notices*, *12*, 7, July 1977, 83–84.

Hueras, J., and Ledgard, H. F. [1978]. Pascal Prettyprinting Program. *Pascal News*, 13, December 1978, 34–45.

Iglewski, M., Madey, J., and Matwin, S. [1978]. A Contribution to an Improvement of Pascal. *SIGPLAN Notices*, *13*, 1, January 1978, 45–58.

Jensen, K., and Wirth, N. [1976]. *Pascal User Manual and Report*. (2nd ed.) Springer-Verlag, 1976.

Kaye, D. R. [1980]. Interactive Pascal Input. *SIGPLAN Notices*, *15*, 1, January 1980, 66–68.

Kernighan, B. W., and Plauger, P. J. [1974]. *The Elements of Programming Style*. McGraw-Hill, 1974.

Kernighan, B. W., and Plauger, P. J. [1976]. *Software Tools*. Addison-Wesley, 1976.

Kernighan, B. W., and Plauger, P. J. [1981]. *Software Tools in Pascal*. Addison-Wesley, 1981.

Kittlitz, E. N. [1976]. Block Statements and Synonyms in Pascal. *SIGPLAN Notices*, *11*, 10, October 1976, 32–35.

Kittlitz, E. N. [1977]. Another Proposal for Variable Size Arrays in Pascal. *SIGPLAN Notices*, *12*, 1, January 1977, 82–86.

Knuth, D. E. [1973]. *The Art of Computer Programming*, Vol. 1: *Fundamental Algorithms*. (2nd ed.) Addison-Wesley, 1973.

Kranc, M. E. [1982]. A Separate Compilation Facility for Pascal. *SIGPLAN Notices*, *17*, 5, May 1982, 38–46.

Kruseman Aretz, F. E. J. [1982]. Syntax Diagrams for ISO Pascal Standard. *SIGPLAN Notices*, *17*, 10, October 1982, 73–78.

Lampson, B. W. [1977]. Report on the Programming Language Euclid. *SIGPLAN Notices*. *12*, 2, February 1977, 1–77.

LeBlanc, R. J. [1978]. Extensions to Pascal for Separate Compilation. *SIGPLAN Notices*, *13*, 9, September 1978, 30–33.

LeBlanc, R. J., and Fischer, C. N. [1979]. On Implementing Separate Compilation in Block-structured Languages. *SIGPLAN Notices*, *14*, 8, August 1979, 139–143.

Lecarme, O. [1974]. Structured Programming, Programming Teaching, and the Language Pascal. *SIGPLAN Notices*, *9*, 7, July 1974, 15–21.

Lecarme, O., and Desjardins, P. [1974]. Reply to a Paper by A. N. Habermann on the Programming Language Pascal. *SIGPLAN Notices*, *9*, 10, October 1974, 21.

Ledgard, H. F. [1973]. The Case for Structured Programming. *BIT*, *13*, 1973, 45–57.

Levy, E. B. [1982]. The Case Against Pascal as a Teaching Tool. *SIGPLAN Notices*, *17*, 11, November 1982, 39–41.

Liskov, B., Snyder, A., Atkinson, R., and Schaffert, C. [1977]. Abstraction Mechanisms in CLU. *COMM ACM*, *20*, 8, August 1977, 564–576.

MacLennan, B. J. [1975]. A Note on Dynamic Arrays in Pascal. *SIGPLAN Notices*, *10*, 9, September 1975, 39–40.

Marca, D. [1981]. Some Pascal Style Guidelines. *SIGPLAN Notices*, *16*, 4, April 1981, 70–80.

Marlin, C. D. [1979]. A Heap-based Implementation of the Programming Language Pascal. *SOFTWARE–Practice & Experience*, *9*, 2, February 1979, 101–120.

Matwin, S., and Missala, M. [1976]. A Simple Machine Independent Tool for Obtaining Rough Measurements of Pascal Programs. *SIGPLAN Notices*, *11*, 8, August 1976, 42–45.

Mickel, A. [1978]. Augment and Analyze. *Pascal News*, 12, June 1978, 23–32.

Miner, J. F. [1978]. Compare Two Text Files. *Pascal News*, 12, June 1978, 20–23.

Moffat, D. V. [1980]. A Categorized Pascal Bibliography (June 1980). *SIGPLAN Notices*, *15*, 10, October 1980, 63–75.

Moffat, D. V. [1981a]. Enumerations in Pascal, Ada, and Beyond. *SIGPLAN Notices*, *16*, 2, February 1981, 77–82.

Moffat, D. V. [1981b]. A Model for Pascal-like Typing. *SIGPLAN Notices*, *16*, 7, July 1981, 66–74.

Nelson, P. A. [1979]. A Comparison of Pascal Intermediate Languages. *SIGPLAN Notices*, 14, 8, August 1979, 208–213.

Nori, K. V., Ammann, U., Jensen, K., Nageli, H. H., and Jacobi, C. [1976]. *The Pascal P-Compiler: Implementation Notes.* (Rev. ed.) Instituts für Informatik, ETH, Zurich, July 1976.

Nutt, G. J. [1978]. A Comparison of Pascal and FORTRAN as Introductory Programming Languages. *SIGPLAN Notices*, 13, 2, February 1978, 57–62.

Perkins, D. R., and Sites, R. L. [1979]. Machine Independent Pascal Code Optimization. *SIGPLAN Notices*, 14, 8, August 1979, 201–207.

Pokrovsky, S. [1976]. Formal Types and Their Application to Dynamic Arrays in Pascal. *SIGPLAN Notices*, 11, 10, October 1976, 36–42.

Prael C. E. [1982]. Pascal for Operating Software? A Critical Examination. *SIGPLAN Notices*, 17, 3, March 1982, 53–57.

Rowland, D. A. [1981]. An Extension to Pascal READ and WRITE Procedures. *SIGPLAN Notices*, 16, 9, September 1981, 81–82.

Rudmik, A., and Lee, E. S. [1979]. Compiler Design for Efficient Code Generation and Program Optimization. *SIGPLAN Notices*, 14, 8, August 1979, 127–138.

Sale, A. H. J. [1979a]. SCOPE and PASCAL. *SIGPLAN Notices*, 14, 9, September 1979, 61–63.

Sale, A. H. J. [1979b]. The Pascal Validation Suite—Aims and Methods. *Pascal News*, 16, October 1979, 5–9.

Sale, A. H. J. [1981]. Proposal for Extension to Pascal: Addition of Repeat and Until as Identifiers. *SIGPLAN Notices*, 16, 4, April 1981, 98–103.

Shapiro, E., Collins, G., Johnson, L., Ruttenburg, J. [1981]. PASES: a Programming Environment for Pascal. *SIGPLAN Notices*, 16, 8, August 1981, 50–57.

Sites, R. L. [1979]. Machine Independent Register Allocation. *SIGPLAN Notices*, 14, 8, August 1979, 221–225.

Tennent, R. D. [1983]. Three Proposals for Extending Pascal. *Pascal News*, 24, January 1983, 32–39.

Thibault, D., and Manuel, P. [1973]. Implementation of a Pascal Compiler for the CII Iris 80 Computer. *SIGPLAN Notices*, 8, 6, June 1973, 89–90.

Travis, L., Honda, M., LeBlanc, R., and Zeigler, S. [1977]. Design Rationale for TELOS, a Pascal Based AI Language. *SIGPLAN Notices*, 12, 8, August 1977, 67–76.

Venema, T., and de Rivieres, J. [1978]. Euclid and Pascal. *SIGPLAN Notices*, 13, 3, March 1978, 57–69.

Wallace, B. [1979]. More on Interactive Input in Pascal. *SIGPLAN Notices*, 14, 9, September 1979, 76.

Watt, D. A. [1979]. An Extended Attribute Grammar for Pascal. *SIGPLAN Notices*, 14, 2, February 1979, 60–74.

Welsh, J., and McKeag, M. [1980]. *Structured System Programming.* Prentice-Hall, 1980.

Welsh, J., and Quinn, C. [1972]. A Pascal Compiler for the ICL 1900 Series Computer. *SOFTWARE—Practice & Experience*, 2, 1972, 72–77.

Welsh, J., Sneeringer, W. J., and Hoare, C. A. R. [1977]. Ambiguities and Insecurities in Pascal. *SOFTWARE—Practice & Experience*, 7, 1977, 685–696.

Wichmann, B. A. [1983]. Status Report on Version 3.0 of the Pascal Test Suite. *Pascal News*, 24, January 1983, 20–22.

Wichmann, B. A., and Sale, A. H. J. [1979]. The Pascal Validation Suite Version 2.2. *Pascal News*, 16, October 1979, 10–141.

Wirth, N. [1971a]. The Programming Language Pascal. *Acta Informatica*, *1*, 1971, 35–64.

Wirth, N. [1971b]. Program Development by Stepwise Refinement. *COMM. ACM*, *14*, 4, April 1971, 221–227.

Wirth, N. [1971c]. Design of a Pascal Compiler. *SOFTWARE—Practice & Experience*, *1*, 1971, 309–333.

Wirth, N. [1972]. The Programming Language Pascal and Its Design Criteria. In *Infotech State of the Art Report No. 7: High Level Languages*. Infotech, 1972.

Wirth, N. [1973]. *Systematic Programming—An Introduction*. Prentice-Hall, 1973.

Wirth, N. [1974]. On the Composition of Well-Structured Programs. *ACM Computing Surveys*, *6*, 4, December 1974, 247–259.

Wirth, N. [1975]. An Assessment of the Programming Language Pascal. *IEEE Transactions on Software Engineering*, *SE-1*, 2, June 1975, 192–198.

Wirth, N. [1976a]. Comments on a Note on Dynamic Arrays in Pascal. *SIGPLAN Notices*, *11*, 1, January 1976, 37–38.

Wirth, N. [1976b]. *Algorithms + Data Structures = Programs*. Prentice-Hall, 1976.

Wirth, N. [1981]. Pascal-S: A Subset and its Implementation. In *Pascal—The Language and Its Implementation*. (ed.) D. W. Barron. Wiley, 1981.

Wirth, N. [1982]. *Programming in Modula-2*. Springer-Verlag, 1982.

Yuval, G. [1975]. Gathering Run Time Statistics Without Black Magic. *SOFTWARE—Practice & Experience*, 5, 1975, 105–108.

APPENDIXES

APPENDIX A   THE VOCABULARY OF PASCAL

Pascal programs consist of letters, digits, and other characters. In the Pascal programs in this book we have used both uppercase and lowercase letters. Some computers do not have facilities for reading and printing lowercase characters. If your installation does permit the use of lowercase letters, be sure you know how they are processed by the Pascal compiler.

A.1   RESERVED WORDS

Reserved words in Pascal are treated as indivisible symbols. They cannot be used for anything other than the purpose for which they are defined in the language. Because reserved words and punctuation symbols guide the syntax analyzer of a compiler, using a reserved word inappropriately may cause curious error messages.

and	**downto**	**if**	**or**	**then**
array	**else**	**in**	**packed**	**to**
begin	**end**	**label**	**procedure**	**type**
case	**file**	**mod**	**program**	**until**
const	**for**	**nil**	**record**	**var**
div	**function**	**not**	**repeat**	**while**
do	**goto**	**of**	**set**	**with**

A.2   IDENTIFIERS

Identifiers are names chosen by the programmer to denote constants, types, variables, procedures, and functions. An identifier consists of letters and digits. The first character of an identifier must be a letter. All compilers treat as distinct two identifiers that differ in their first eight characters. Standard identifiers are recognized by the compiler even though they are not defined in the program. A standard identifier may be redefined either locally or globally within a program.

Standard Constants

false
true
maxint

Standard Types

integer	*char*
boolean	*text*
real	

Standard Files

input
output

Standard Functions

abs	*ord*
arctan	*pred*
chr	*round*
cos	*sin*
eof	*sqr*
eoln	*sqrt*
exp	*succ*
ln	*trunc*
odd	

Standard Procedures

get	*put*	*rewrite*
new	*read*	*unpack*
pack	*readln*	*write*
page	*reset*	*writeln*

A.3   OTHER SYMBOLS

The remaining Pascal symbols are listed below. The first column contains the standard symbol. The second column, if present, contains a synonym that may be used if the standard symbol is not available. The third column contains a brief, not necessarily complete, description of the function of the symbol. These symbols and synonyms are not universally accepted, and therefore room has been left for you to write in the symbols used at your installation.

Standard Symbol	Synonym	Function
+		plus
−		minus
*		multiply
/		divide
<		is less than
≤	< =	is less than or equal to
=		is equal to
≠	< >	is not equal to
≥	> =	is greater than or equal to
>		is greater than
∧	**and**	boolean conjunction
∨	**or**	boolean inclusive disjunction
¬	**not**	boolean negation
:=		becomes
,		separates items in a list
;		separates statements
:		separates variable name and type
'		delimits character and string literals
.		decimal point, record selector, and program terminator
..		subrange specifier
↑	@	file and pointer variable indicator
(		start parameter list or nested expression
)		end parameter list or nested expression
[	(.	start subscript list or set expression
]	.)	end subscript list or set expression
{	(*	start a comment
}	*)	end a comment

APPENDIX B   PASCAL SYNTAX DIAGRAMS

This appendix consists of a complete set of syntax diagrams for Standard Pascal. They are derived from machine-drawn diagrams published by F. E. J. Kruseman Aretz.

Some of the syntax diagrams in the text are simplified versions. The versions that appear in this appendix are complete.

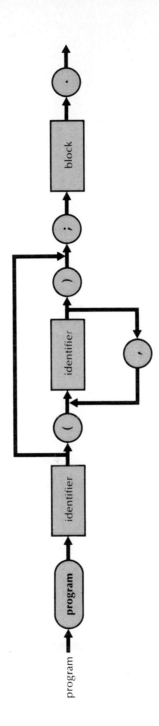

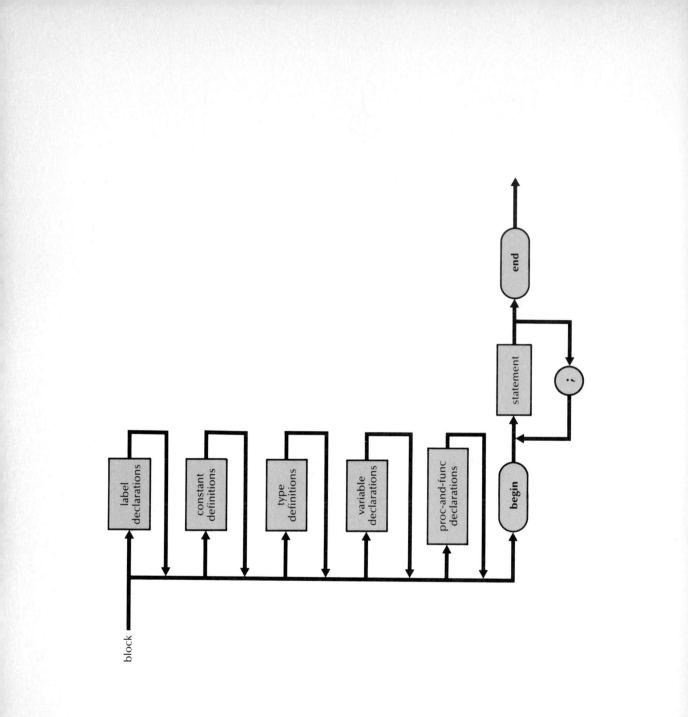

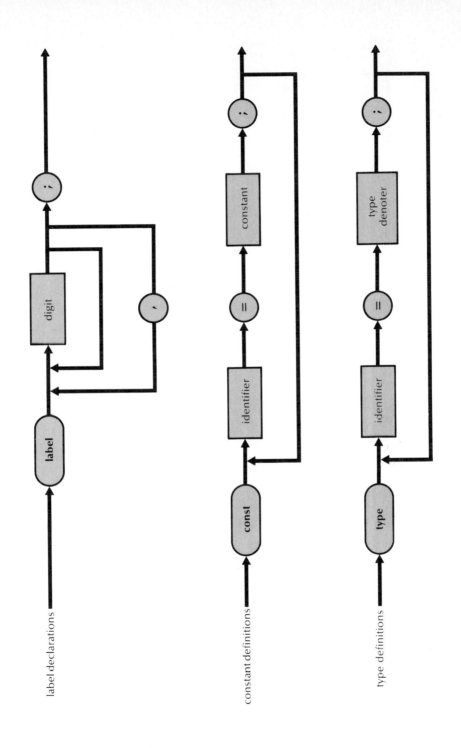

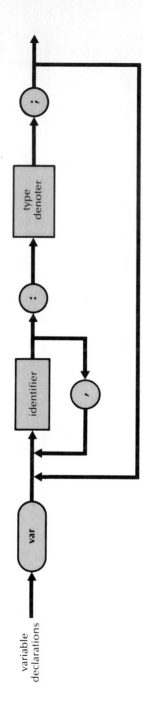

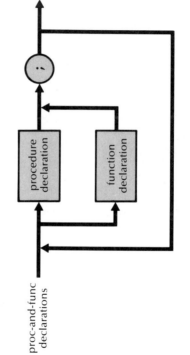

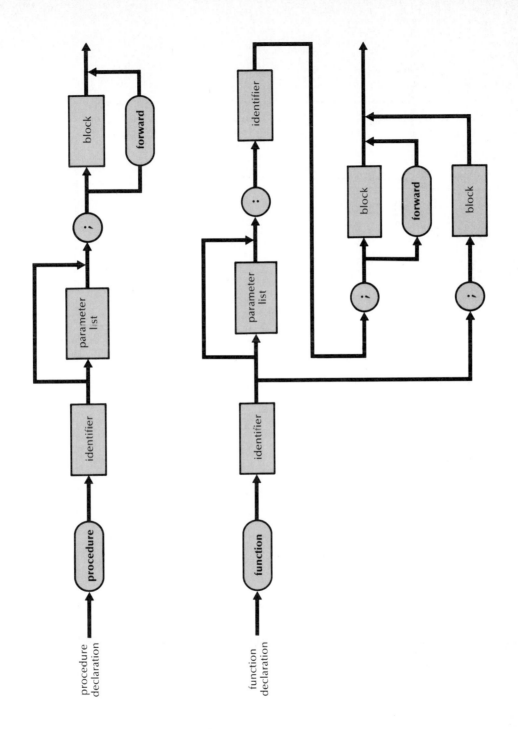

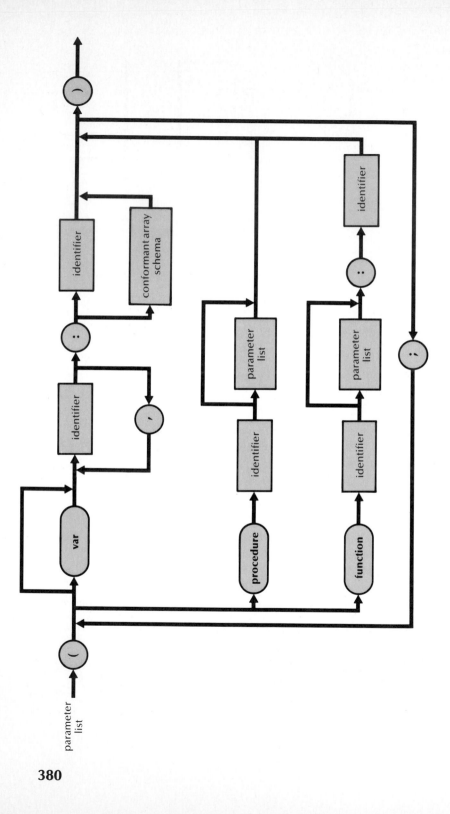

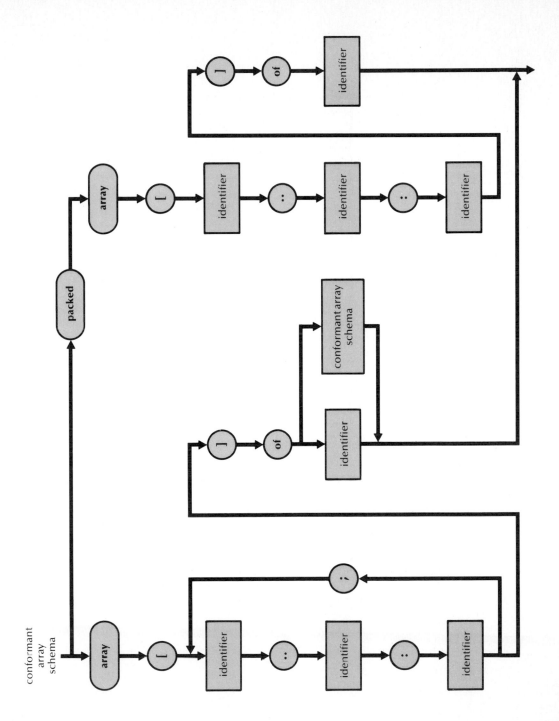

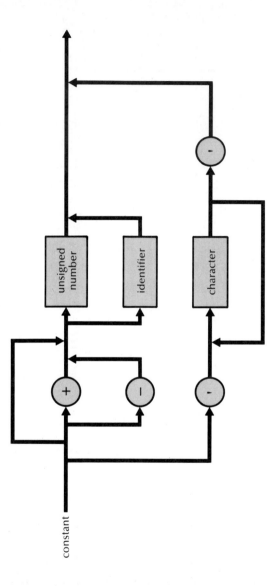

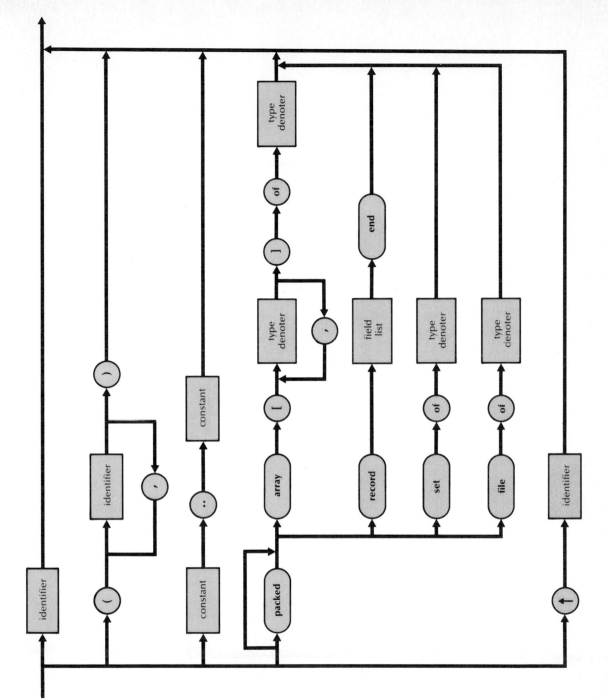

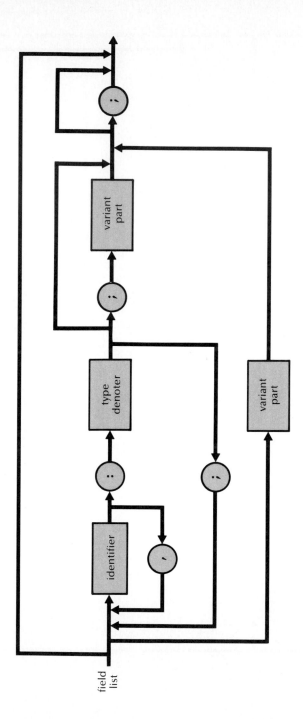

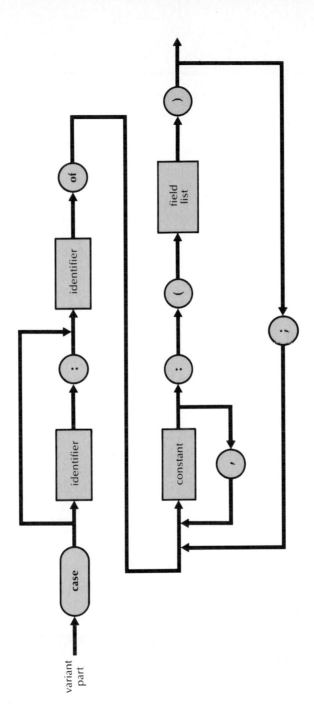

385

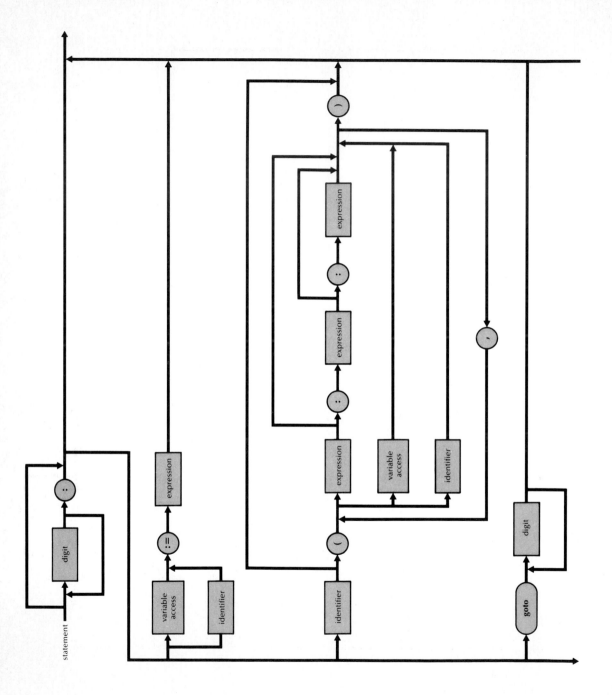

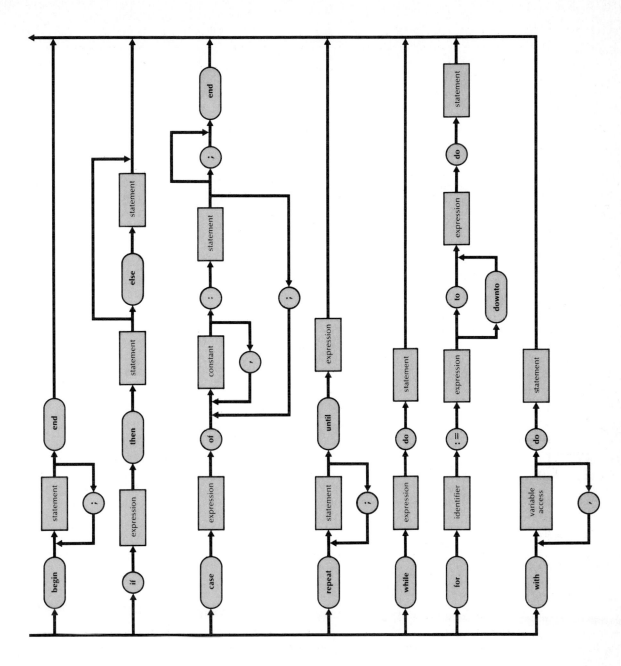

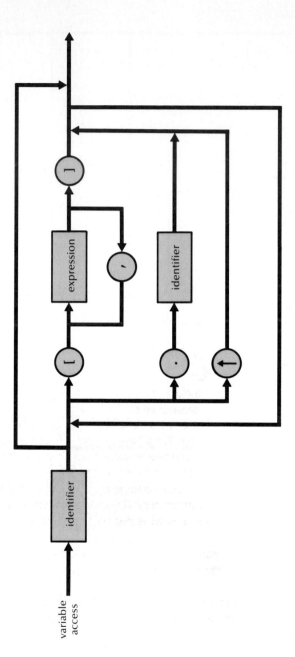

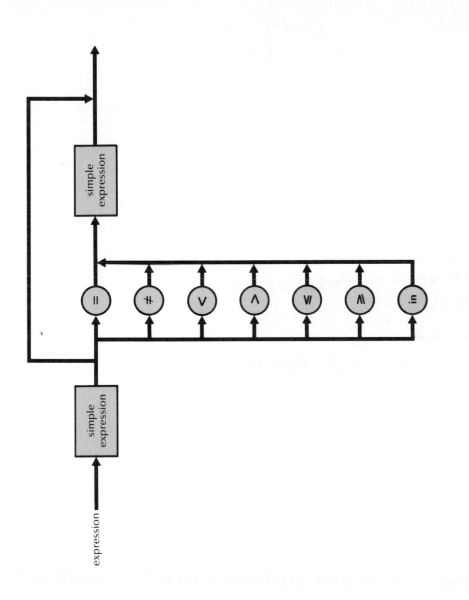

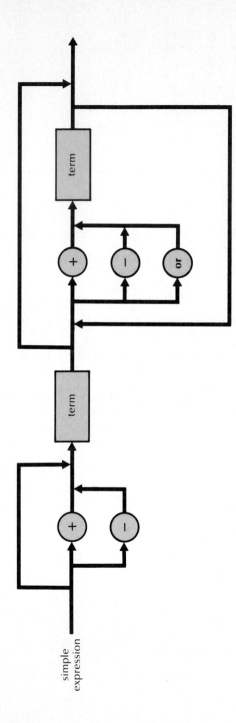

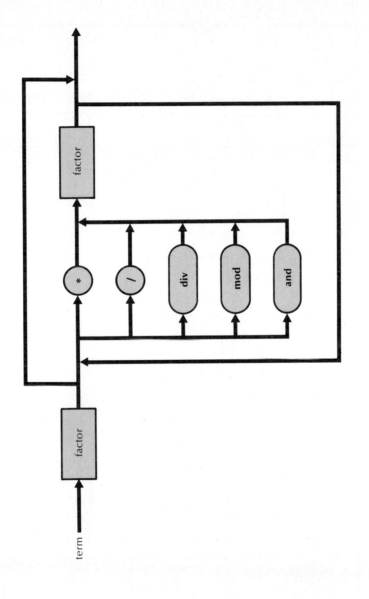

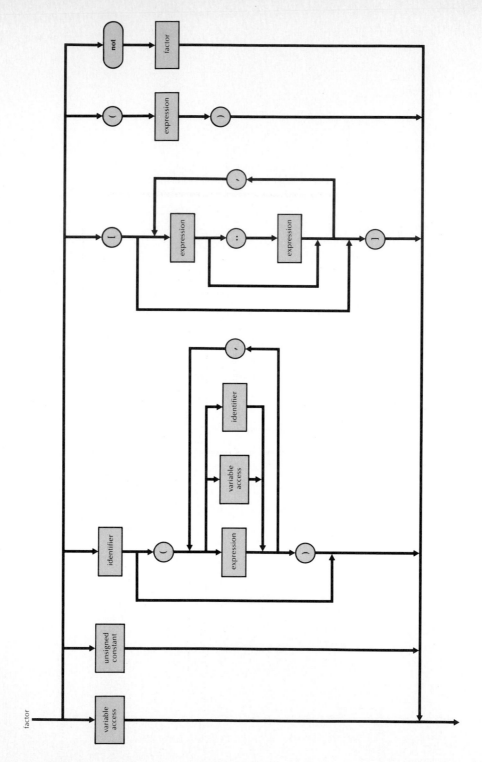

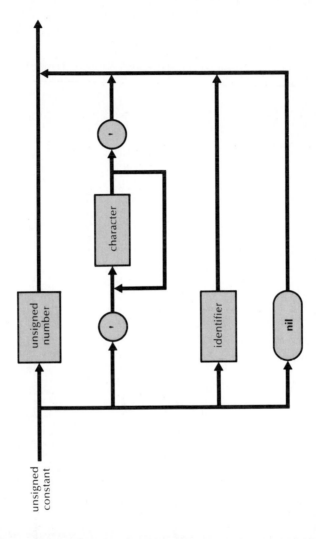

unsigned
constant

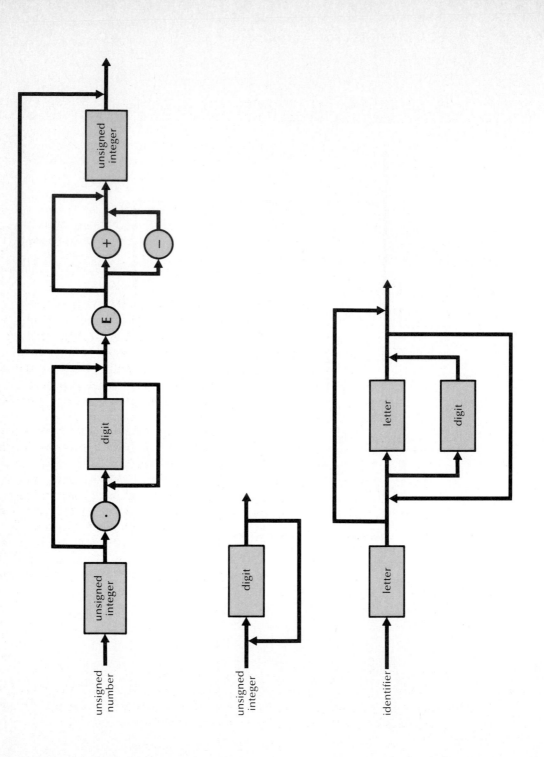

APPENDIX C PASCAL PORTABILITY AND IMPLEMENTATION

The task of a language designer is to specify the precise meaning of each language feature. The task of a language implementor is to construct a system, based on a compiler or interpreter, that processes programs according to the designer's intent.

If a language is to achieve widespread use, implementations for a variety of computer systems must exist. If we write a program for one system, we will usually have to expend some effort if we want it to run correctly on another system. A program that can be moved easily from one system to another is called a *portable* program. If a language has features that encourage the writing of portable programs, we call it a *portable language*.

In principle, it would be possible to design and implement a fully portable language. Any program written in such a language would run without change and would produce the same results on any system. However, a fully portable language would be restrictive or inefficient. The designer of a practical language must leave some features of the language undefined so that the implementor has enough freedom to construct an efficient language-processor for a particular computer. Lack of portability is the inevitable consequence of this freedom.

There is another reason for lack of portability. An implementor usually does not implement the language according to the design. If the language is lacking in features that are widely considered to be useful, the implementor will add them to the language. For example, many implementors have added string-processing capabilities to Pascal. If, on the other hand, the language is very rich, features that the implementor cannot be bothered with or cannot understand are left out. This has happened to languages such as PL/I, Algol-68, and Ada.

It is possible to write Pascal programs that are both efficient and portable. You cannot do this, however, without some knowledge of implementation techniques and practices. In this appendix, we discuss differences between various implementations of Pascal.

C.1 IDENTIFIERS

The Pascal Standard does not require both uppercase and lowercase letters. Most Pascal compilers accept but do not distinguish between uppercase and lowercase letters in reserved words and identifiers. Thus

firstentry and *FirstEntry*

denote the same object. Some compilers allow identifiers with embedded underscores, such as

> `Balance_Due`

Most compilers, but not all, treat the underscore as a significant character. These compilers distinguish between the identifiers

> `Last_Entry` and `LastEntry`

Some early Pascal compilers use only the first eight characters when they compare identifiers. This is all that was required by the *Pascal Report*. To these compilers, the identifiers

> `nextchar` and `nextcharpos`

are equivalent. The Pascal Standard requires the compiler to use all the characters of an identifier in the comparison. Some recent compilers respect this.

There are several standard identifiers that a Pascal implementor is obliged to provide. These are listed in Appendix A. In addition to these, most implementors provide additional standard identifiers. These additional identifiers are implementation-dependent and should not be used in portable programs.

C.2 STANDARD TYPES

INTEGER

Integer arithmetic is exact. Pascal implementations differ only in the number of integers they can represent. The implementation provides a standard identifier, *maxint*, whose value is that of the largest integer that can be represented. The set of representable integers is

> $-maxint, \ldots, -2, -1, 0, 1, 2, \ldots, maxint.$

Some implementations provide another identifier, *minint*, whose value is that of the smallest integer that can be represented. Usually

> $minint = -maxint - 1.$

For example, if *maxint* = 32767, *minint* would be −32768. *Minint* is not defined in the Pascal Standard, and you should not use it if you want to write portable programs.

REAL

The range and precision of floating-point quantities vary widely between machines. There is no equivalent of *maxint* for *real* values. Programs that use *real* arithmetic are usually not portable, whether they are written in Pascal or in another language.

If you want portability in a program that uses an iterative method to obtain a *real* result, you should define symbolic constants for convergence criteria. The following statement, for example, is unacceptable.

```
repeat
    ....
until abs (error) < 1E-6
```

The literal 1E-6 should be replaced by a constant.

```
const
    epsilon = 1E-6;  { Tolerance for 7-digit arithmetic }
....
repeat
    ....
until abs (error) < epsilon
```

Fieldwidth and precision parameters in calls to *write* and *writeln* are another aid to portability. Include them whenever you are writing the values of reals.

BOOLEAN

The Standard specifies that *boolean* is implicitly defined by the enumerated type definition

```
type
    boolean = (false, true);
```

Consequently, *ord* (*false*) = 0, and *ord* (*true*) = 1.

CHAR

Pascal inherits the character set used by the underlying hardware. The most widely used character set is probably ASCII, which conforms to an ISO Standard. There are 128 characters in the full ASCII character set, of which 95 are "graphic" and 33 are "control." The graphic characters are the visible characters and the space character. Control characters are intended to have an effect on a receiving device. *Carriage-return*, *line-feed*, *tab*, and *bell* are control characters.

The Pascal Standard does not mention control characters, but the functions *chr* and *ord* can sometimes be used to process control characters. A few implementations provide additional features for handling control characters.

An ASCII character requires seven bits of storage. Many modern computers use 8-bit bytes as their units of storage. Some Pascal implementations use a byte to represent a character and thus provide an extended set of 256 characters.

The Standard requires the following properties, and it is safe to assume that a character set has them.

$$\text{'a'} < \text{'b'} < \ldots < \text{'z'}$$
$$\text{'A'} < \text{'B'} < \ldots < \text{'Z'}$$
$$ord\,(\text{'1'}) = ord\,(\text{'0'}) + 1$$
$$ord\,(\text{'2'}) = ord\,(\text{'0'}) + 2$$
$$\ldots\,.$$
$$ord\,(\text{'9'}) = ord\,(\text{'0'}) + 9$$

Do not assume that

$$succ\,(\text{'a'}) = \text{'b'}$$
$$succ\,(\text{'b'}) = \text{'c'}$$
$$\ldots\,.$$
$$succ\,(\text{'y'}) = \text{'z'}$$

The only subranges of characters that are completely portable are subranges of digits, for example,

```
type
    decimaldigits = '0'..'9';
    octaldigits = '0'..'7';
```

Subranges of letters are not fully portable. The subranges

$$\text{'a'..'z'} \qquad \text{and} \qquad \text{'A'..'Z'}$$

both include characters that are not digits in the EBCDIC code used by IBM machines.

C.3   OTHER TYPES

SETS

Sets are a useful feature of Pascal, but they have been implemented in so many different ways that they are a hindrance to portability. It should be possible to define a set of any reasonable size. Some compilers allow us to do so, but many do not. The type

```
set of char
```

is useful and would seem to be a minimal requirement, but many compilers, including the original Pascal compiler written at ETH in Zurich, do not allow it.

There is a genuine problem for the implementor of Pascal sets. A compiler should be able to allocate a string of 41 (or more) bits for a variable declared by

```
var
    years : set of 1960..2000;
```

When the type of a set cannot be determined from the program text, as in a statement that begins

```
if result in [3,5,7..19,163]
    then ....
```

it is difficult for the compiler to generate sensible code.

POINTERS

All compilers support pointer types and the standard procedure *new*. The effect of *dispose* varies, however, and some implementations do not support it at all.

Some implementations provide two procedures, *mark* and *release*, for heap control. These procedures are used in pairs.

```
mark (ptr);
....
new (a); .... ; new (b);                                          (C.1)
....
release (ptr)
```

The identifiers *ptr*, *a*, and *b* are pointers. The execution of *release* (*ptr*) releases the space that has been allocated to the heap since the last call to *mark* (*ptr*). After the call *release* (*ptr*) in (C.1), the variables *a*↑ and *b*↑ are no longer accessible to the program. The procedures *new*, *mark*, and *release*, without *dispose*, enable us to use the heap as an auxiliary stack.

STRINGS

Most implementors have decided that the type-compatibility rules of Pascal are too strict for string-handling. The solutions adopted include both the relaxation of the rules for arrays of characters and the introduction of a new standard type, *string*. The variety of these solutions contributes significantly to the lack of portability of Pascal programs.

RECORDS

In the interests of portability, you should avoid the use of variant records that do not have tag fields.

C.4   EXPRESSIONS

The value of the expression

$$P \text{ and } Q$$

is *false* if P is false, whatever the value of Q. Some compilers generate code that does not evaluate Q if P evaluates to *false*. This makes it possible to write statements such as

$$\textbf{if } (p \neq \textbf{nil}) \textbf{ and } (p\uparrow.data = \text{'A'})$$
$$\textbf{then } \dots . \qquad\qquad (\text{C.2})$$

You should not use statements like (C.2) in portable programs. Some implementations will evaluate

$$p\uparrow.data = \text{'A'}$$

when p is **nil**, and this evaluation will cause a run-time error. The safe way to write this statement is

$$\textbf{if } p \neq \textbf{nil}$$
$$\textbf{then}$$
$$\qquad \textbf{if } p\uparrow.data = \text{'A'}$$
$$\qquad\qquad \textbf{then } \dots .$$

C.5   STATEMENTS

Most Pascal statements have such simple semantics that an implementor has few choices. The two exceptions are the **case** statement and the **goto** statement. Suppose that a program contains this statement.

```
case switch of
    1 : S₁;
    2 : S₂;                                            (C.3)
    3 : S₃
end
```

This statement is semantically equivalent to the following **if** statement.

```
if switch = 1
    then S₁
else if switch = 2
    then S₂                                           (C.4)
else if switch = 3
    then S₃
else error
```

If *switch* does not have one of the values 1, 2, or 3, the procedure *error* is called and the program terminates. Many implementions do not detect the error and proceed to the next statement. Some implementations allow

otherwise *statement*

before the final **end** of the **case** statement so that programmers can provide an appropriate default action.

Although statement (C.4) is equivalent to statement (C.3), it should not be used as a model for the compiler because it is inefficient. If there are many case labels, the form (C.4) requires numerous tests. It is better to use the value of *switch* as an index into an array, each component of which contains the address of the code for the corresponding action. An array used in this way is often called a *jump table* by assembly language programmers.

The jump table wastes space if the case labels are sparsely distributed over a wide range. For example, if the case labels are 1, 2, and 100, the compiler will construct a table with 100 entries, 97 of which contain the address of the error procedure.

The **goto** statement is implemented in many different ways. Some compilers forbid it altogether. Others allow **goto** statements provided that the statement and the label to which it refers are in the same procedure.

C.6   INPUT AND OUTPUT

Input and output are difficult areas for language designers. In some cases the problems are inherently difficult. In other cases there are good solutions, but it may be difficult to find a single solution that can be applied to all computer systems.

A full implementation of Pascal must provide the procedures *get* and *put*. *Read* and *write* are defined using *get* and *put*, as we saw in Chapter 7. Interactive programs that use these versions of *read* and *write* do not work properly because of the "lookahead" features of these procedures. For this reason, although most implementations provide a reasonable way of writing interactive programs, it is not easy to write a portable interactive program.

Pascal treats files as "formal parameters" of a program. When a program is run, the operating system is expected to pass files to it as "actual parameters." Although this concept is derived from CDC systems, it is a useful abstraction. There are many operating systems that do not provide such a convenient association between the "logical files" processed by the program and the "physical files" maintained by the system. Pascal programs running under these systems must perform the associations themselves. In practice, this task is usually left to the programmer.

In Pascal, a file may be a component of an array or of a record. This can be useful. For example, Wirth gives an external sorting program based on an array of work files. Most implementations, however, do not allow this construction. The type

$$\text{file of file of } T$$

is not usually implemented.

Pascal does not support random-access files. Some implementations provide random-access features, but these are usually dependent on a particular operating system and are not portable.

C.7   COMPILER DIRECTIVES

A *compiler directive* is an instruction to the compiler. Some compiler directives affect the compiled program and some do not. A compiler directive that tells the compiler to include range-checking code in the program clearly has an effect on the compiled program. On the other hand, a compiler directive that tells the compiler to generate a listing of the source program has no effect on the compiled program.

Although most implementations provide a number of compiler directives, there has been no attempt at standardization. A compiler directive written at one installation may be illegal, or have no effect or a different effect, at another installation.

Pascal compiler directives are placed inside comments. The first character of the comment must be "$". Each compiler directive consists of a letter followed by a parameter. Parameters are separated by commas. Here is a typical compiler directive group.

$$\{ \ \texttt{\$A-,ISTRLIB,S+} \ \}$$

This tells the compiler to turn switch "A" off, include the file "STRLIB", and turn switch "S" on.

APPENDIX D PROGRAMMING CONVENTIONS

Syntactic and semantic rules determine whether or not a program can be compiled. A compilable program, however, is not necessarily a readable program. Readability is of great importance in a program, and in order to encourage it, programming conventions are often defined. Such conventions cover the aspects of programming that are irrelevant to the compiler. These include choice of identifiers, use of uppercase or lowercase letters, organization of comments, and layout.

Many organizations establish programming conventions and insist that programmers use them. From time to time, individuals publish their own conventions in the hope that others will follow their example. However many sets of conventions are available and however much we recommend them, there are no definitive conventions for programming.

The programming conventions described in this appendix are designed to help you write readable programs. They are recommended, but you may choose to adopt other conventions or no conventions at all. If you do decide to use these conventions, you will produce programs that are readable by other people in your organization and in the general programming community. You can be sure that any Pascal programmer anywhere will find your programs readable. More importantly, you will probably make fewer mistakes when you are writing programs.

D.1 PROGRAM DESCRIPTION

A program should start with a comment that includes at least the following information.

- a brief title for the program
- the name of the programmer or chief programmer

- a description of what the program does
- a description of the input required by the program and the output it produces

If the program employs complicated algorithms that require lengthy explanation, give references to your own documentation or to the book or journal in which you found the algorithm, for example:

The symbol table is a balanced binary tree. See "Algorithm A" in *The Art of Computer Programming*, Volume 3: *Sorting and Searching*; D. E. Knuth, page 455.

Introduce each procedure in the program with a brief description in a consistent format. Procedure documentation should describe what the procedure does, how it does it, and the role of each parameter. When the program is being written by only one person, the author's name need not appear before each procedure. If the program is being written by a team, the name of the author of the procedure should be given.

D.2   COMMENTS

Use comments to clarify potentially obscure sections of the program. Do not clutter up the program with unnecessary comments and, above all, do not write comments that contain nothing that is not obvious from the program. Do not, for example, write

```
num := num + 1 { increment num }
```

Organize comments neatly. When comments occupy several lines, each line should start in the same column, even if there are no program statements to the left of the comment, for example:

```
var
  sum1, sum2,      { sums of samples }
  sumsq1, sumsq2,  { sums of squared samples }
  sumprod          { sums of products }
    : real;
```

D.3   DECLARATIONS

Choose descriptive names for constants, types, variables, procedures, and functions.

CONSTANTS

Constants should have global scope. It is easier to locate a constant definition if there is one constant declaration section at the beginning of the program than if constants are declared in every procedure. The program should not contain literals other than 0 and 1 outside the constant declaration section. Literal strings, however, may be used in *write* statements.

TYPES

In most cases, types should also have global scope, but if a type is used in only one procedure, it may be declared as a local type for that procedure.

PROCEDURES AND FUNCTIONS

Procedures and functions may be declared locally, but this does not necessarily make the program more readable. Some compilers limit the number of levels to which procedures can be nested.

A procedure should access only its parameters and its local variables. If a nonlocal variable must be accessed by a procedure, provide suitable comments. Functions should not access nonlocal variables at all.

D.4 PROGRAM LAYOUT

Leave one blank line before a label, a constant, a type, or a variable declaration section. Leave two or more blank lines before the beginning of the main program and before a procedure or a function declaration. Use blank lines to divide complicated sections of the program into chunks small enough to be assimilated easily by the reader. Leave one blank on each side of algebraic operators, one blank on each side of ' = ' and ':' in declarations, and one blank on each side of the operator ' : = ' in assignment statements.

The reserved word **program** is always written in the left margin. In this book we have indented the reserved words **const**, **type**, **var**, **procedure**, and **function** according to the nesting level, but it is also acceptable to write them in the left margin, provided that the result is not confusing. Procedure nesting should, however, be indicated by indentation.

In the following layouts, $S_1, S_2, \ldots, S_n$ are statements, possibly compound statements; b is a *boolean* expression; i is a scalar variable; and $expr_1$ and $expr_2$ are scalar expressions.

LAYOUT FOR A COMPOUND STATEMENT

```
begin
  S₁ ;
  S₂ ;
  ...
  Sₙ
end
```

LAYOUT FOR THE if STATEMENT

```
if  b
  then  S₁
  else  S₂
```

If S_1 and S_2 are compound statements, use

```
if  b
  then
    S₁
  else
    S₂
```

LAYOUT FOR THE repeat STATEMENT

```
repeat
  S₁ ;
  S₂ ;
  ...
  Sₙ
until  b
```

LAYOUT FOR THE while STATEMENT

```
while  b do
  S
```

LAYOUT FOR THE for STATEMENT

```
for  i := expr₁ to expr₂ do
  S
```

LAYOUT FOR THE case STATEMENT

The case selector is c, and $a_1, a_2, \ldots, a_n$ are case labels.

```
case c of
    a₁ : S₁;
    a₂ : S₂;
    ...
    aₙ : Sₙ
end { case }
```

LAYOUT FOR THE with STATEMENT

v is a record identifier.

```
with v do
    S
```

When the statement controlled by a **then**, **else**, **while**, **for**, or **with** clause is compound, annotate the final **end**.

```
while b do
    begin
        S₁;
        S₂;
        ...
        Sₙ
    end { while }
```

D.5   PORTABILITY

A program is *portable* if it can be run without alteration on systems other than the one for which it was written. Whenever you write a program, consider the possibility that it will one day be run at another installation. If there is a chance that it will, write it as much as possible in a machine-independent way. Unfortunately, Pascal has not been defined in a way that makes it easy to write portable programs.

Appendix C contains a complete discussion of the issues relating to portability of Pascal programs.

D.6 AUTOMATIC FORMATTING

Many computer installations have a program that will automatically format a Pascal program. This is relatively easy to do in Pascal because the nesting level, and hence the required indentation, can be determined from the reserved words in the program. Whether or not you use a formatting program is largely a matter of taste. Programmers who write programs with good, intelligible layouts should never be compelled to use a formatting program. However, if you feel that counting blanks is something the computer can do better than you can, you will prefer to use a formatting program. Sometimes the compiler itself will provide a formatted listing, and you will have no choice in the matter.

There are two good reasons for using a formatting program, even if you are justifiably proud of your own layouts. First, formatted programs are consistent, and if a group of programmers all use the same formatting program, they will find each other's programs easy to read. Second, although it is not difficult to enter a new program neatly, it can be extremely tedious to preserve correct layout when you are revising a program.

In the long term, automatic formatters will probably be replaced by editing programs that format the text as it is entered or revised. If you are lucky enough to have access to one of these editors, use it as much as possible.

INDEX